POCKET
ENCYCLOPEDIA

HERBS

Contributing editor
Lesley Bremness

Dorling Kindersley
London • New York • Munich • Melbourne • Delhi

DK

A Dorling Kindersley Book

www.dk.com

First published in Great Britain in 1990
by Dorling Kindersley Limited,
80 Strand, London WC2R ORL

Designed and edited by Swallow Books,
260 Pentonville Road, London N1 9JY

British Library Cataloguing in Publication Data

DK pocket encyclopedia, herbs
1. Herbs
I. Bremness, Lesley
641.3'57

ISBN 0-86318-436-7

Printed and bound by South China Printing Company in Hong Kong

POCKET
ENCYCLOPEDIA

HERBS

CONTENTS

Introduction 6

INTRODUCTION

Herbs are plants to serve and delight us, offering us an ever increasing rapport with nature. Our changing understanding of the word "herb" reflects our changing relationship with the plant kingdom. There was a time when all plants were important to humankind; they were considered the children of the Earth Mother, each marked by divinity and worthy of respect. With industrialization, the rise of science and technology, our involvement with nature diminished. This change has led to a more limited concept of the term "herb" and even today, many people consider herbs to be only a dozen or so seasoning plants.

Many cultures have always held a wide view of plants. Herbs were not divided into compartments as they are in many Western minds today. To the Chinese, for example, the chrysanthemum is useful, beautiful and virtuous. Chrysanthemums were first grown for their medicinal properties and were a valued ingredient of the Taoist elixir. They were also believed to be full of magic juices and perhaps that reason contributed to their beauty.

Early writings
Early plant knowledge was passed on verbally. As both the body of knowledge and populations grew it became more important to record accurately the accumulated information on herbs for safe identification and dosage. Many of the earliest writings are about herbs which were important in ceremony, magic and medicine. Babylonian clay tablets from 3000 BC illustrate medical treatments and later they record herbal imports.

A seventeenth-century knot garden
This features contemporary plants, miniature box hedges and ornamental topiary.

During the next 1,000 years, parallel cultures in China, Assyria, Egypt and India developed a written record of mainly medicinal herbs. Early Western records of herbs describe a mixture of medicinal and magical usage of plants; and Egyptian writings dating from 1550 BC contain medical prescriptions and notes on the aromatic and cosmetic uses of herbs.

Herbs and cookery

The use of herbs in cooking features as far back as the first century cook book written by the Roman epicure, Apicius, which shows fascinating and adventurous combinations of herb flavours. Some of these are echoed in the modern recipes for soups and salads, fish and meat dishes, and desserts and drinks that you will find in this book.

For centuries herbs were a staple of daily life. In England in 1699 John Evelyn wrote *Acetaria: A Discourse of Sallets*, which listed 73 salad herbs, giving details of the part of each herb used and how it was best prepared. This broad usage continued for centuries, and even 200 years ago, the word vegetable was not commonly used – we spoke of pot herbs (for bulk in the cooking pot), salet (salad) herbs, sweet herbs (flavourings) and simples (medicinal herbs from which "compounds" were made).

Herbs as garden plants

As communities became more secure and gardening developed for pleasure, books included the aesthetic appeal of herbs as garden plants.

In his essay *Of Gardens*, Francis Bacon includes many herbs in his sketch of an ideal garden. His famous opening is often quoted: "God Almighty first planted a garden. And indeed, it is the purest of human pleasures. It is the greatest refreshment to the spirits of man." He advocates alleys of scented herbs "to have the pleasure when you walk or tread."

A country kitchen garden
The combination of herbs and vegetables is both attractive and useful.

The age of herbals

Herbals, books that provided plant descriptions and details of their medical uses, became increasingly popular in the sixteenth century. At that time three famous herbals were printed in Germany one of which, Leonhart Fuch's *De Historia Stirpium* of 1542, has charming naturalistic illustrations of herbs drawn from direct observation rather than copied from old woodcuts as in most previous herbals. His text, however, was based mostly on the writings of Dioscorides who wrote *De Materia Medica* in 512 AD.

In such books, many scholars made a valiant attempt to eliminate unscientific attitudes, but the common people – including the best known English herbalist Nicholas Culpeper – held deep beliefs about the significance of plants: plants were deemed to serve humanity, each with a purpose for our benefit.

Up to the seventeenth century, herbals had contained botany and medicine but as science emerged, plants were classified, dissected and demystified and botany and medicine went their separate ways.

In 1931, an Englishwoman, Mrs M. Grieve, decided to change this situation and wrote *A Modern Herbal* which drew together both scientific and traditional information.

The lure of herbs today

Recently, there has been a tremendous surge of interest in herbs. Research on medicinal and cosmetic uses and new ideas for decorative and scented applications are continually adding to the large body of herbal knowledge and skills. The object of this book is again to combine traditional with scientific knowledge and present the many innovative ways herbs can be used to enhance life in the home and at work.

Formal and informal
A mixture of the formal and informal usually suits a herb garden. This one has paved areas, lawn, knot garden beds, species beds and informal, cottage-style borders.

CHAPTER ONE

THE A–Z OF HERBS

Inspired by the herbals of John Gerard and Nicholas Culpeper, which were published over 300 years ago, the following pages form a contemporary guide to many of the most useful and easy-to-grow herbs. Herbs are listed alphabetically by their botanical names. Any that have been reclassified recently include the alternative (in brackets). The family name is supplied in italic after the common name. Each herb has been photographed and described in detail for easy identification. Botanical terms have been kept to a minimum throughout; those that are used are explained in the glossary on p. 232. There is also a wealth of practical information suggesting uses for each herb. To follow up these ideas consult the later chapters and the index.

Note: Read pp. 176–187 before making any medicinal preparations. If you are uncertain of a plant, do not use it. Consult a qualified practitioner whenever you have any doubts.

A colourful border
These flowering herbs are growing in the National Trust's herb garden at Acorn Bank in Cumbria. Acorn Bank is well planted with an enormous variety of traditional medicinal herbs.

Achillea millefolium

Yarrow/Milfoil *Compositae*

This unassuming plant conceals great powers. One small leaf will speed decomposition of a wheelbarrow full of raw compost; yarrow's root secretions will activate the disease resistance of nearby plants; and it intensifies the medicinal actions of other herbs. Yarrow is also a potent healer. The name *Achillea* may stem from the battle of Troy, when Achilles healed many of his warriors after being instructed in yarrow's ability to staunch the flow of blood.

Yarrow stems were used by the Druids to divine the weather, while in China they were used to foretell the future with the assistance of the *I Ching* (the Book of Changes or Yarrow Stalk Oracle).

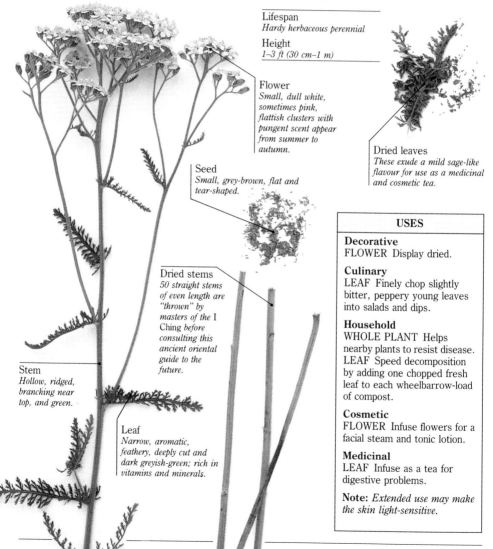

Lifespan
Hardy herbaceous perennial

Height
1–3 ft (30 cm–1 m)

Flower
Small, dull white, sometimes pink, flattish clusters with pungent scent appear from summer to autumn.

Seed
Small, grey-brown, flat and tear-shaped.

Dried leaves
These exude a mild sage-like flavour for use as a medicinal and cosmetic tea.

Dried stems
50 straight stems of even length are "thrown" by masters of the I Ching before consulting this ancient oriental guide to the future.

Stem
Hollow, ridged, branching near top, and green.

Leaf
Narrow, aromatic, feathery, deeply cut and dark greyish-green; rich in vitamins and minerals.

USES

Decorative
FLOWER Display dried.

Culinary
LEAF Finely chop slightly bitter, peppery young leaves into salads and dips.

Household
WHOLE PLANT Helps nearby plants to resist disease.
LEAF Speed decomposition by adding one chopped fresh leaf to each wheelbarrow-load of compost.

Cosmetic
FLOWER Infuse flowers for a facial steam and tonic lotion.

Medicinal
LEAF Infuse as a tea for digestive problems.

Note: *Extended use may make the skin light-sensitive.*

Alchemilla vulgaris

Lady's mantle/Dewcup *Rosaceae*

From "little magical one", the Arab *alkemelych* (alchemy), comes *Alchemilla*, so-called because of this herb's healing reputation and the dew that collects in each enfolding leaf. The crystal drops of dew have long inspired poets and alchemists and were part of many mystic potions. So powerful a herb was acquired by the Christian Church, which named it "Our Lady's mantle". Its protective role was reflected in its nickname, "a woman's best friend", as it may regulate periods, ease the menopause and clear inflammations of the female organs. One German herbalist claims prolonged use of lady's mantle tea could cut gynaecological operations by one-third. *A. vulgaris* is an aggregate name for about 21 subspecies which seem to have similar medicinal properties.

Dried leaves
These make a cosmetic astringent and staunch bleeding.

Flower
Loose clusters of small greenish-yellow flowers appear in summer.

Lifespan
Hardy herbaceous perennial

Height
6–20 in (15–50 cm)

USES

Culinary
LEAF Tear young leaves, with their mildly bitter taste, into small pieces and toss in herb salads.

Cosmetic
LEAF Infuse dried leaves as an astringent and as a facial steam for acne. Apply infusion in a cold compress for inflamed eyes and as a tonic to reduce large pores and acne. Use in creams to soften dry skin.

Medicinal
WHOLE PLANT (Green parts only) Infuse and use as a mouth rinse after tooth extraction and for diarrhoea. LEAF Decoct for a compress for healing wounds and reducing inflammation.

Leaf
Soft, blue-green and almost circular with seven to 11 rounded, toothed lobes joined by deep folds.

Stem
Hairy, slightly flattened, ridged, branching and green; usually bends outwards as flowers develop.

A. alpina
Alpine lady's mantle
Small, yellow-green clusters borne in late summer and silver-edged leaves with white, silky undersides.
Ht: 6 in (15 cm).

Young plant
A mass of fibrous roots develop into a short, dark rhizome; leaf stalks emerge directly from base.

Allium species

Alliums *Liliaceae*

One of the most popular and widespread culinary flavourings is the onion family. The value of these alliums is reflected in the Latin *unio*, "one large pearl", and the Chinese name "jewel among vegetables". Alliums also have marvellous health-giving properties. The stronger the smell, the more effective their healing powers. Pyramid builders and Roman soldiers on long marches were fed on a daily ration of garlic, whose power even extended to protection from black magic, as vampire films continue to remind us. Today, garlic is a major flavouring in many cuisines.

Chives were recorded 4,000 years ago in China and appreciated there by the traveller Marco Polo. He reported their culinary virtues to the West, where they rapidly became indispensable. Chinese chives have a garlic flavour, and the Chinese grow several forms: one for its leaves; one, 'Tenderpole', for its long-stemmed flower buds – good stir fried or as a garnish; and one to blanch (using clay pots or straw "tents" to produce yellow, sweetly flavoured bundles). These blanched chives are featured in a popular meal available on trains and street stalls in China: little finger-length pieces are served with rice and slivers of pork, often in prepacked containers with chopsticks.

Another important allium species in China and Japan is the Welsh onion (Welsh meaning "foreign"), which provides a continuous supply of onions and leaves throughout the year.

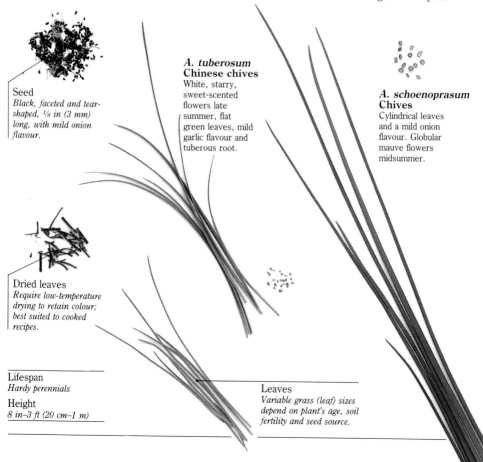

Seed
Black, faceted and tear-shaped, ⅛ in (3 mm) long, with mild onion flavour.

**A. tuberosum
Chinese chives**
White, starry, sweet-scented flowers late summer, flat green leaves, mild garlic flavour and tuberous root.

**A. schoenoprasum
Chives**
Cylindrical leaves and a mild onion flavour. Globular mauve flowers midsummer.

Dried leaves
Require low-temperature drying to retain colour; best suited to cooked recipes.

Lifespan
Hardy perennials

Height
8 in–3 ft (20 cm–1 m)

Leaves
Variable grass (leaf) sizes depend on plant's age, soil fertility and seed source.

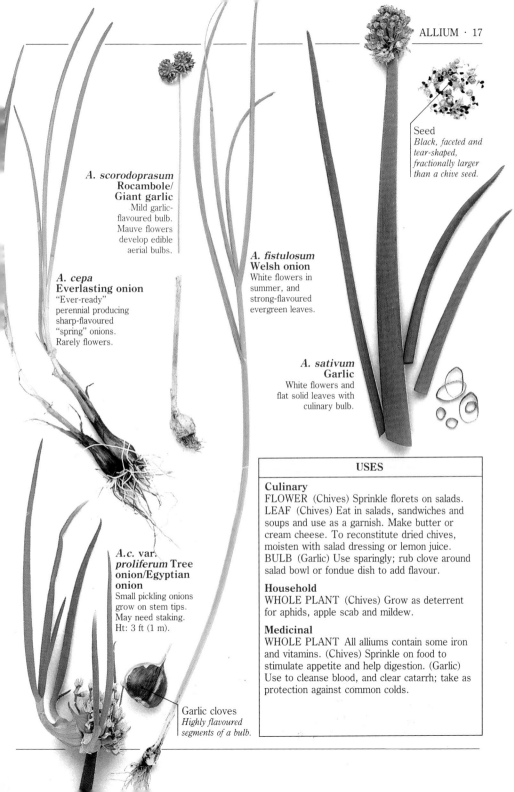

A. scorodoprasum
Rocambole/
Giant garlic
Mild garlic-
flavoured bulb.
Mauve flowers
develop edible
aerial bulbs.

A. cepa
Everlasting onion
"Ever-ready"
perennial producing
sharp-flavoured
"spring" onions.
Rarely flowers.

A. fistulosum
Welsh onion
White flowers in
summer, and
strong-flavoured
evergreen leaves.

A. sativum
Garlic
White flowers and
flat solid leaves with
culinary bulb.

Seed
*Black, faceted and
tear-shaped,
fractionally larger
than a chive seed.*

A.c. var.
proliferum Tree
onion/Egyptian
onion
Small pickling onions
grow on stem tips.
May need staking.
Ht: 3 ft (1 m).

Garlic cloves
*Highly flavoured
segments of a bulb.*

USES

Culinary
FLOWER (Chives) Sprinkle florets on salads.
LEAF (Chives) Eat in salads, sandwiches and
soups and use as a garnish. Make butter or
cream cheese. To reconstitute dried chives,
moisten with salad dressing or lemon juice.
BULB (Garlic) Use sparingly; rub clove around
salad bowl or fondue dish to add flavour.

Household
WHOLE PLANT (Chives) Grow as deterrent
for aphids, apple scab and mildew.

Medicinal
WHOLE PLANT All alliums contain some iron
and vitamins. (Chives) Sprinkle on food to
stimulate appetite and help digestion. (Garlic)
Use to cleanse blood, and clear catarrh; take as
protection against common colds.

Aloe vera (A. barbadensis)

Aloe vera *Liliaceae*

One of Cleopatra's secret beauty ingredients was reputed to be aloe vera, and it is still chosen by contemporary cosmetic firms for face and hand creams, suntan lotions and shampoos. Aloe vera has also attracted the interest of many governments for its ability to heal radiation burns, and the US government is said to be stockpiling the herb for use in the event of a nuclear disaster. It is the fresh sap from this remarkable herb that can heal skin and soothe burns.

A beautiful violet dye is produced from aloe plants native to the island of Socotra in the Indian Ocean, and it was thought to be the desire for this product that motivated Alexander the Great to conquer this island in the fourth century BC.

Leaf
Long, very fleshy, tapering, pointed, pale green blades, often with spiny teeth along margins.

Split leaves
Inside each leaf is a clear gelatinous sap, which has an immediate soothing effect on burns and forms a clear protective seal, allowing healing to take place rapidly.

Lifespan
Tender evergreen perennial

Height
12 in (30 cm)

Plant base
Stemless base, which eventually produces a flowering stem, with spikes of narrow, trumpet-shaped, yellow or orange flowers, and offshoots for propagation.

Root
Strong, light brown and fibrous.

USES

Cosmetic
LEAF Use the leaf sap to make a soothing and healing moisturizing cream, especially good for dry skin.

Medicinal
LEAF Crush sap from fresh leaves or slice them and apply as a poultice for chapped skin, dermatitis and eczema. For small burns, break off a leaf segment and apply its sap to the burn.

Note: *Always seek immediate medical attention for serious burns.*

Aloysia triphylla (Lippia citriodora)

Lemon verbena *Verbenaceae*

Lemon verbena's immediate attraction lies in its leaves, which have a clean, sharp, lemony fragrance. There is remarkably little history and legend attached to this plant, which is a native of South America. Lemon verbena was, however, brought to Europe in the seventeenth century by the Spanish, who grew it for its perfume oil. Although it is not hardy, a straw-covered pruned plant with deep roots should survive some frost. New growth can appear very late, so never discard a plant until late summer.

USES
Culinary
LEAF Infuse as herb tea. Finely chop young leaves for drinks, and fruit puddings.
Aromatic
LEAF Use in potpourri and herb pillows.
Note: *Long-term use may cause irritation.*

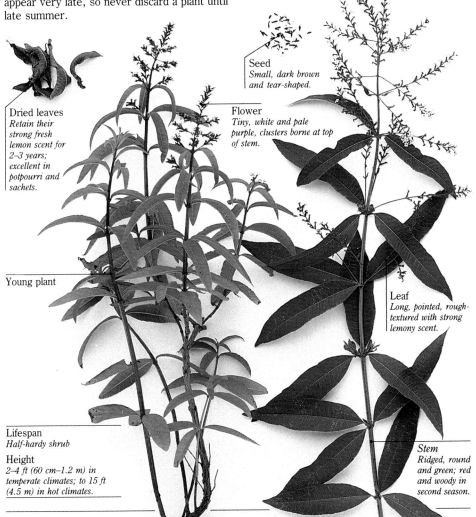

Dried leaves
Retain their strong fresh lemon scent for 2–3 years; excellent in potpourri and sachets.

Seed
Small, dark brown and tear-shaped.

Flower
Tiny, white and pale purple, clusters borne at top of stem.

Young plant

Leaf
Long, pointed, rough-textured with strong lemony scent.

Lifespan
Half-hardy shrub

Height
2–4 ft (60 cm–1.2 m) in temperate climates; to 15 ft (4.5 m) in hot climates.

Stem
Ridged, round and green; red and woody in second season.

Althaea officinalis

Marsh mallow *Malvaceae*

This is indeed the original source of the confectionery of this name. Marsh mallow's powdered root contains a mucilage that thickens in water and was heated with sugar to create a soothing sweet paste. However, today's spongy cubes share only sugar in common with the original recipe.

Marsh mallow is one of over 1,000 species in the *Malvaceae* family, all of which contain a healing mucilage. Introduced from China, marsh mallows were eaten by the Egyptians and Syrians, and mentioned by Pythagoras, Plato and Virgil. The plant was enjoyed by the Romans in barley soup and in a stuffing for suckling pig, while classical herbalists praised its gentle laxative properties.

Lifespan
Hardy herbaceous perennial

Height
6 ft (2 m)

Dried leaves
These contain mucilage and can be infused and drunk for internal inflammation or used externally as an eye compress.

Leaf
Large, velvety, toothed, tear-shaped and grey-green, containing mucilage.

Flower
Pink or white blooms, 1½ in (4 cm) across, with purple stamens, borne in late summer to early autumn.

Seed
Light brown and disc-shaped, slotted upright in a ring called a "cheese".

Dried root
Contains a highly valued thickening and softening mucilage.

Root
Thick, long, yellow-brown and tapering, with white fibrous flesh. To release mucilage, steep second- or subsequent-year roots in cold water for 8 hours.

Stem
Velvety, round and light green.

USES
Decorative
LEAF Add to posies.
Culinary
SEED Eat fresh "cheeses" alone or sprinkled like nuts onto salads.
FLOWER Toss on salads.
LEAF Mix young leaves into salads. Add to oil and vinegar. Steam as a vegetable.
Cosmetic
LEAF AND ROOT Boil leaves or use the liquid from steeped root, warmed or cold, as a soothing mucilage for dry hands, sunburn and dry hair.
Medicinal
ROOT Infuse as a tea for coughs and insomnia.

Anethum graveolens

Dill *Umbelliferae*

"Woe unto you, scribes and Pharisees, hypocrites! for ye pay tithe of mint and dill and cumin, and have omitted the weightier matters of the law" (*Matthew* 23 v. 23). This biblical reference shows that herbs had a high and sufficiently stable value to be used as tax payment. Well before that, the ancient Egyptians had recorded dill as a soothing medicine, and the Greeks knew "dill stayeth the hickets" (hiccups). During the Middle Ages, it was one of St John's Eve herbs to be prized as protection against witchcraft. Magicians used dill in their spells, while lesser mortals infused it in wine to enhance passion. Early settlers took dill to North America, where it became known as "meetin' seed", because children were given dill seed to chew during long sermons.

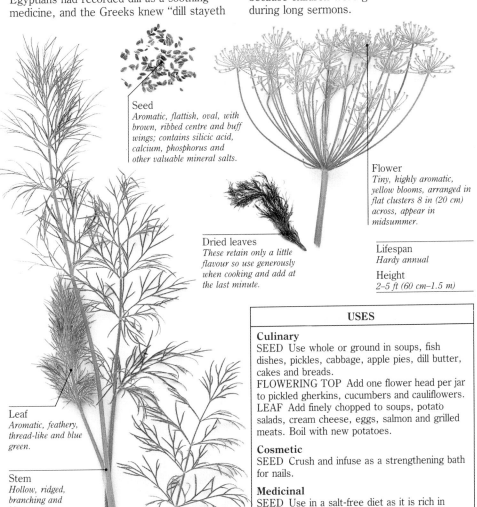

Seed
Aromatic, flattish, oval, with brown, ribbed centre and buff wings; contains silicic acid, calcium, phosphorus and other valuable mineral salts.

Flower
Tiny, highly aromatic, yellow blooms, arranged in flat clusters 8 in (20 cm) across, appear in midsummer.

Dried leaves
These retain only a little flavour so use generously when cooking and add at the last minute.

Lifespan
Hardy annual

Height
2–5 ft (60 cm–1.5 m)

Leaf
Aromatic, feathery, thread-like and blue green.

Stem
Hollow, ridged, branching and blue-green; usually one main stem per plant.

USES

Culinary
SEED Use whole or ground in soups, fish dishes, pickles, cabbage, apple pies, dill butter, cakes and breads.
FLOWERING TOP Add one flower head per jar to pickled gherkins, cucumbers and cauliflowers.
LEAF Add finely chopped to soups, potato salads, cream cheese, eggs, salmon and grilled meats. Boil with new potatoes.

Cosmetic
SEED Crush and infuse as a strengthening bath for nails.

Medicinal
SEED Use in a salt-free diet as it is rich in mineral salts.

Angelica archangelica

Angelica *Umbelliferae*

An ancient and highly aromatic plant, angelica is praised in the folklore of northern European countries as a panacea for all ills. Its name is thought to derive from the fact that, in the old calendar, it usually came into bloom around the feast day of the Archangel Michael, the Great Defender, who appeared in a vision to explain its protective powers against evil.

Angelica is a moisture-loving native of damp meadows and river banks. Its large leaves have a tropical appearance and can give the garden a lush atmosphere.

Lifespan
Three-year hardy herbaceous "biennial" (extendable to four years if emerging flower spikes are removed)

Height
3–8 ft (1–2.5 m)

Leaf
Large, glossy, divided and bright green.

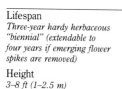

Seed
Buff, ¼ in (6 mm) long, produced in profusion, ripening late summer of third year.

Stem
Thick, hollow and ridged.

Dried root
Angelica root has the longest-lasting aroma of any part of the plant.

Crystallized stem
Choose fresh, young, green stems of pencil thickness for crystallizing.

Dried leaves
These are indispensable for herb teas.

Root
Thick, ridged, aromatic taproot, usually with two or three major side roots.

USES
Decorative FLOWER Display dried seed heads.
Culinary LEAF Stew with fruits to reduce sugar needed. STEM Crystallize for decoration.
Aromatic LEAF Use in potpourri.
Medicinal LEAF Make tea from fresh or dried leaves as a tonic for colds and to reduce flatulence.

Anthriscus cerefolium

Chervil *Umbelliferae*

In the past, the modest chervil has often been overlooked. It now enjoys increasing popularity as people discover its special delicate parsley-like flavour with a hint of myrrh. It is one of the traditional *fines herbes*, indispensable in French cuisine, and is a fresh green asset to any meal.

A graceful clump of chervil plants will retain more flavour in its feathery foliage if grown in light shade. When viewed in a herb garden by bright moonlight, the delicate clusters of tiny white flowers are like fairy dust, during spring and late summer.

Flower
Tiny white clusters borne from late summer, or in late spring from overwintered seedlings.

Seed
Dark, narrow ¼ in (6 mm) long, enclosed five in a case until ripe.

Stem
Slender, hollow, slightly ridged and branching.

Leaf
Lacy, fern-like and light green, with a pale magenta blush in late summer.

Dried leaves
Drying chervil reduces its flavour; if possible, aim for a continuous fresh supply.

USES

Culinary
LEAF Use generously in salads, soups, sauces, vegetables, chicken, white fish and egg dishes. Add chervil freshly chopped near the end of cooking to avoid flavour loss. In small quantities, it can also enhance the flavour of other herbs.
STEM Chop and use raw in salads. Cook in soups and casseroles.

Cosmetic
LEAF Use in an infusion or face mask to cleanse skin and maintain suppleness.

Medicinal
LEAF Eat raw for additional vitamin C, carotene, iron and magnesium. Infuse in tea to stimulate digestion.

Lifespan
Hardy annual

Height
10–15 in (25–38 cm)

Apium graveolens

Smallage/Wild celery *Umbelliferae*

Smallage was used to crown the victors of the
Greek Nemean games, held in honour of Zeus.
The son of the Nemean king was subsequently
killed by a snake concealed in smallage, and so
it was then carried as a funeral wreath. The
Greeks also used this herb medicinally, and
the Romans exploited its culinary properties:
stems were puréed with pepper, lovage,
oregano, onion and wine; leaves were
used with dates and pine kernels as a
stuffing for suckling pig. Much later, in the
nineteenth century, the American Shakers
grew smallage for their favourite remedies
and use in other medicinal compounds.

Seed
*Tiny, brown, oval
and aromatic.*

Dried leaves
*These have a slightly stronger
aromatic flavour than
cultivated celery and are
useful in soups, stocks,
stuffings and stews.*

Flower
*Small, greenish-cream
clusters produced in
late summer of second year.*

Stem
*Faceted, ridged,
branching and green;
flowering stem grows
in second season.*

Leaf
*Fan of aromatic,
loosely toothed,
shiny light green
leaflets, forming
upright rosette in
first year; darker
green on rising
stem in second
season.*

USES

Culinary
SEED Grind as an ingredient of celery salt. Add
to soups, curries, casseroles and pickles. Use as
a salt-substitute in a salt-free diet.
LEAF Chop small amounts into salads, cream
cheese, poultry stuffings, and use as a garnish.
Add a handful of finely chopped leaves to milk for
poaching fish and shellfish. Stir into thick
vegetable soups and stews during last 3 minutes
of cooking.

Medicinal
SEED Decoct as a sedative to calm nerves and
ease flatulence.
LEAF Rich in vitamins, mineral salts and other
active ingredients of nutritive value. Infuse as a
tonic and appetizer and to ease indigestion.

Lifespan
Hardy biennial

Height
1–3 ft (30 cm–1 m)

Armoracia rusticana

Horseradish *Cruciferae*

Now considered a flavouring herb, horseradish was originally cultivated for medicinal use. Horseradish sauce has become strongly associated with roast beef. Its sharp pungency frequently has a dramatic effect and has been known to clear sinuses in one breath – the volatile flavouring oil is released by grating the root. The oil evaporates rapidly, so horseradish is not successful in cooked dishes.

Dried leaves
These yield a yellow dye with a chrome mordant; may be used to dress skin wounds.

Root
Long, invasive and yellow with hot, pungent-tasting, white flesh. Fresh root contains calcium, sodium, magnesium and vitamin C, and has antibiotic qualities that are useful for preserving food and protecting the intestinal tract.

Leaf
Large, elliptical, pointed, scallop-edged and bright green, with pungent aroma when bruised.

Stem
Thick, deeply ridged and round.

Lifespan
Hardy perennial

Height
2–3 ft (60 cm–1 m)

USES

Culinary
LEAF Add young leaves to salads.
ROOT Make horseradish sauce to accompany roast beef, smoked or oily fish. Grate into coleslaw, dips and mayonnaise.

Household
WHOLE PLANT Grow near potatoes for more disease-resistant tubers.

Medicinal
ROOT Include grated root in everyday diet to stimulate digestion.

Note: *Avoid continuous large doses when pregnant or suffering from kidney problems.*

Artemisia species

Artemisias *Compositae*

Artemisia was the sister and wife of King Mausolus and ruled after his death in 353 BC. She was also a botanist and researcher, and this genus of 200 plants was named for her.

The medicinal values of artemisias were discovered by people living in semi-arid and temperate regions where the plants are found. In the ancient Greek text of Dioscorides, wormwood is mentioned for its internal worm-expelling property. The Chinese still use a leaf of wormwood rolled up in the nostril to stop nosebleeds. Many artemisias are also visually appealing. Their silver leaves are stunning when reflected in moonlight, and they also enhance any dried herb arrangement.

Mugwort (the species *A. vulgaris*), though less aromatic and less attractive than other artemisias, features in the magical lore of Europe, Asia and China. In the pre-Christian "Lay of the Nine Herbs", the first incantation for protection is to mugwort, who is called the "mother of herbs":

Have in mind, Mugwort, what you made known,
What you laid down, at the great denouncing.
Una your name is, oldest of herbs,
Of might against thirty, and against three,
Of might against venom and the onflying,
Of might against the vile She
who fares through the land.

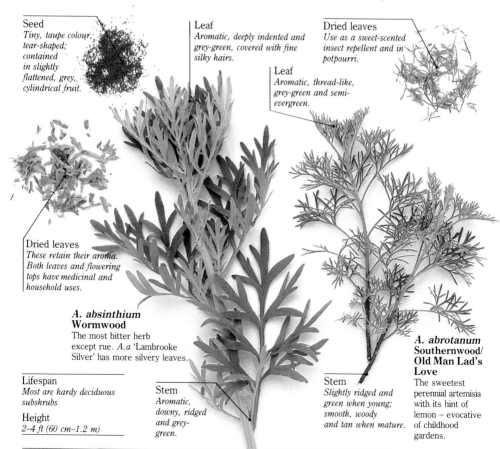

Seed
Tiny, taupe colour, tear-shaped; contained in slightly flattened, grey, cylindrical fruit.

Leaf
Aromatic, deeply indented and grey-green, covered with fine silky hairs.

Dried leaves
Use as a sweet-scented insect repellent and in potpourri.

Leaf
Aromatic, thread-like, grey-green and semi-evergreen.

Dried leaves
These retain their aroma. Both leaves and flowering tops have medicinal and household uses.

A. absinthium
Wormwood
The most bitter herb except rue. *A.a* 'Lambrooke Silver' has more silvery leaves.

A. abrotanum
Southernwood/
Old Man Lad's
Love
The sweetest perennial artemisia with its hint of lemon – evocative of childhood gardens.

Lifespan
Most are hardy deciduous subshrubs

Height
2–4 ft (60 cm–1.2 m)

Stem
Aromatic, downy, ridged and grey-green.

Stem
Slightly ridged and green when young; smooth, woody and tan when mature.

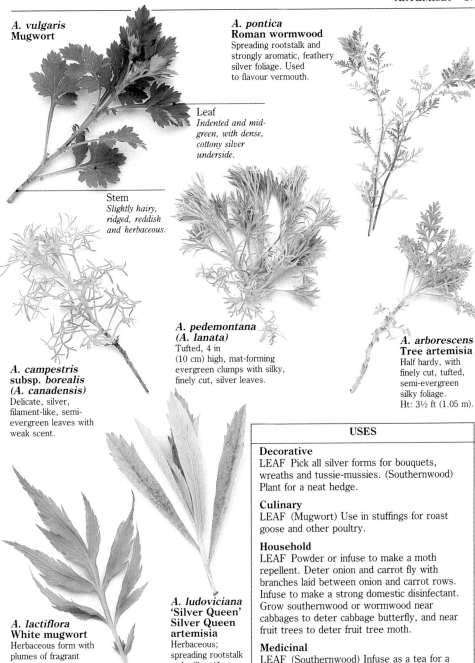

A. vulgaris
Mugwort

A. pontica
Roman wormwood
Spreading rootstalk and
strongly aromatic, feathery
silver foliage. Used
to flavour vermouth.

Leaf
Indented and mid-
green, with dense,
cottony silver
underside.

Stem
Slightly hairy,
ridged, reddish
and herbaceous.

A. pedemontana
(A. lanata)
Tufted, 4 in
(10 cm) high, mat-forming
evergreen clumps with silky,
finely cut, silver leaves.

A. arborescens
Tree artemisia
Half hardy, with
finely cut, tufted,
semi-evergreen
silky foliage.
Ht: 3½ ft (1.05 m).

A. campestris
subsp. borealis
(A. canadensis)
Delicate, silver,
filament-like, semi-
evergreen leaves with
weak scent.

A. lactiflora
White mugwort
Herbaceous form with
plumes of fragrant
cream flowers in late
summer and deeply cut
mid-green leaves, 6 in
(15 cm) long. Ht: 5 ft (1.5 m).

A. ludoviciana
'Silver Queen'
Silver Queen
artemisia
Herbaceous;
spreading rootstalk
and willow-like,
very silvery leaves.

USES

Decorative
LEAF Pick all silver forms for bouquets,
wreaths and tussie-mussies. (Southernwood)
Plant for a neat hedge.

Culinary
LEAF (Mugwort) Use in stuffings for roast
goose and other poultry.

Household
LEAF Powder or infuse to make a moth
repellent. Deter onion and carrot fly with
branches laid between onion and carrot rows.
Infuse to make a strong domestic disinfectant.
Grow southernwood or wormwood near
cabbages to deter cabbage butterfly, and near
fruit trees to deter fruit tree moth.

Medicinal
LEAF (Southernwood) Infuse as a tea for a
general tonic.

Artemisia dracunculus

Tarragon *Compositae*

Tarragon derives from the French *estragon* and the Latin *dracunculus*, a little dragon. The dragon connection may have come from tarragon's fiery tang or from its serpent-like roots. "Dragon" herbs were believed to cure the bites of venomous creatures, but tarragon's primary use today is culinary. It will also sweeten the breath, act as a soporific, and, if chewed before taking medicine, dull the taste, according to a thirteenth-century Arabian botanist, Ibn al Baithar. Two varieties of tarragon are available: French, which has the refined flavour indispensable to classic French cuisine but needs winter protection when growing; and Russian, which survives both colder and hotter climates but has a coarser flavour. French tarragon should be divided and replanted every third year. The flavour of Russian tarragon improves the longer it grows in one place.

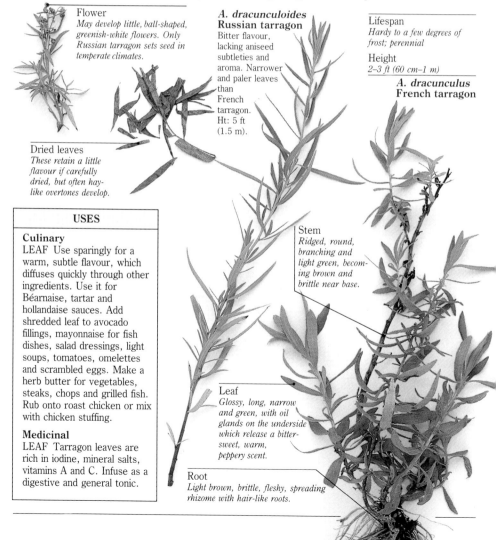

Flower
May develop little, ball-shaped, greenish-white flowers. Only Russian tarragon sets seed in temperate climates.

Dried leaves
These retain a little flavour if carefully dried, but often hay-like overtones develop.

A. dracunculoides
Russian tarragon
Bitter flavour, lacking aniseed subtleties and aroma. Narrower and paler leaves than French tarragon. Ht: 5 ft (1.5 m).

Lifespan
Hardy to a few degrees of frost; perennial

Height
2–3 ft (60 cm–1 m)

A. dracunculus
French tarragon

Stem
Ridged, round, branching and light green, becoming brown and brittle near base.

Leaf
Glossy, long, narrow and green, with oil glands on the underside which release a bitter-sweet, warm, peppery scent.

Root
Light brown, brittle, fleshy, spreading rhizome with hair-like roots.

USES

Culinary
LEAF Use sparingly for a warm, subtle flavour, which diffuses quickly through other ingredients. Use it for Béarnaise, tartar and hollandaise sauces. Add shredded leaf to avocado fillings, mayonnaise for fish dishes, salad dressings, light soups, tomatoes, omelettes and scrambled eggs. Make a herb butter for vegetables, steaks, chops and grilled fish. Rub onto roast chicken or mix with chicken stuffing.

Medicinal
LEAF Tarragon leaves are rich in iodine, mineral salts, vitamins A and C. Infuse as a digestive and general tonic.

Borago officinalis

Borage *Boraginaceae*

The common thread running through historical descriptions of borage is its ability to make men and women glad and merry, to comfort the heart, dispel melancholy and give courage. The Celtic name *borrach* meant courage and the translation of its melodic Welsh name *Llawenlys* is herb of gladness.

The flowers are a beautiful pure blue often chosen by Old Masters to paint the Madonna's robe. For courage, flowers were floated in the stirrup-cups given to Crusaders at their departure. The noble qualities of borage may derive from its high content of calcium, potassium and mineral salts, and research suggests borage works on the adrenal gland, where courage begins.

Flower
Sky blue (sometimes pink, rarely white), five-petalled stars with prominent black stamen tips nod downward in clusters.

Leaf
Dark grey-green, oval-pointed, textured, covered with prickly white hairs. Cucumber-scented juice when crushed.

Seed
Largish, brown-black, tri-sided and lozenge-shaped; often viable for up to eight years.

Stem
Sturdy, hollow, round, branching, with prickly white hairs. Cucumber-scented juice.

USES

Decorative
FLOWER Add to summer arrangements.

Culinary
FLOWER Sprinkle in salads and as a garnish; crystallize for cake decorations.
YOUNG LEAF Add to cold drinks. Chop finely in salads, soft cheese, and sandwiches.

Household
WHOLE PLANT Plant near strawberries as they stimulate each other's growth.

Medicinal
LEAF Use in a salt-free diet as borage is rich in mineral salts.

Flower heads
Pick off by grasping the black stamen tips and gently separating the flower from its green back.

Lifespan
Hardy annual

Height
1–2 ft 6 in (30–75 cm)

Brassica species

Mustard *Cruciferae*

Known since prehistoric times, mustard's uses have always been manifold: the writer Pliny, in the first century AD, listed 40 remedies with mustard as chief ingredient. The Romans also named this herb: from *mustus*, the new wine they mixed with the seed, and *ardens* for fiery. They served mustard with every imaginable dish. Its leaves are so fast growing that it was said you could grow the salad for dinner while the meat was roasting. Belief in its aphrodisiac powers ensured mustard's inclusion in love potions. Black mustard seed has the strongest flavour, brown is easier to harvest, and white mustard seed is the most preservative.

Lifespan
Hardy annual

Height
1–8 ft (30 cm–2.4 m)

Seed (Brown mustard)
Small, mid- to dark brown, bitter-tasting spheres in upright, smooth pods. Flavour is released only when ground and mixed with a liquid.

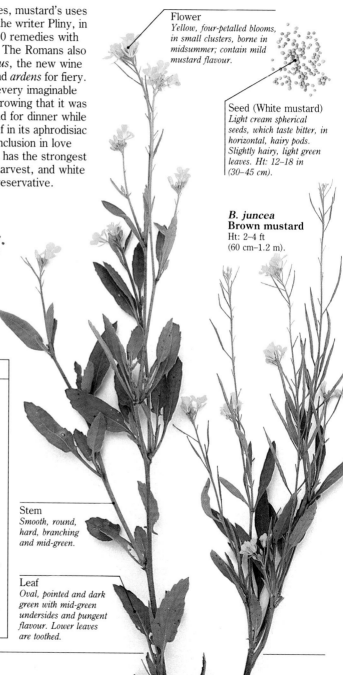

Flower
Yellow, four-petalled blooms, in small clusters, borne in midsummer; contain mild mustard flavour.

Seed (White mustard)
Light cream spherical seeds, which taste bitter, in horizontal, hairy pods. Slightly hairy, light green leaves. Ht: 12–18 in (30–45 cm).

B. juncea
Brown mustard
Ht: 2–4 ft
(60 cm–1.2 m).

Stem
Smooth, round, hard, branching and mid-green.

Leaf
Oval, pointed and dark green with mid-green undersides and pungent flavour. Lower leaves are toothed.

USES

Culinary
SEED (Black or brown mustard) Make into mustard sauce: add ground seed or powder to cold water; leave paste for 10 minutes before use. (White mustard) Use in pickles, as a strong preservative, and in mayonnaise as an emulsifier.
FLOWER Toss into salads.
LEAF Mix tender young leaves into salads.

Medicinal
SEED Use powdered to make a poultice to relieve pain and inflammation in rheumatism, arthritis and chilblains.

Note: *Mustard seed can irritate tender skins.*

Calendula officinalis

Calendula/Marigold *Compositae*

One of the most versatile herbs, calendula is popular as a cheerful cottage garden flower; for its use in cosmetic and culinary recipes; as a dye plant and for its many healing properties.

As this hardy annual seems to be in flower continuously, it attracted a botanic name which reflects the belief that it was always in bloom on the first day of each month (Latin: *calends*).

The regular supply of petals and young leaves contributed to its frequent use. Ancient Egyptians valued it as a rejuvenating herb. Hindus used it to decorate temple altars and Persians and Greeks garnished and flavoured food with its golden petals.

It is a soothing antiseptic and an excellent skin healer.

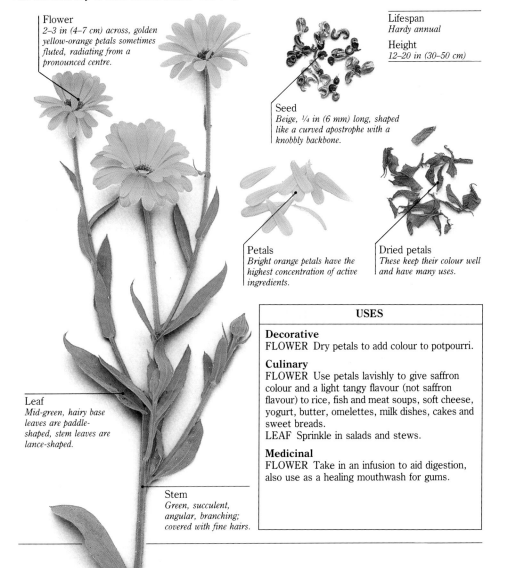

Flower
2–3 in (4–7 cm) across, golden yellow-orange petals sometimes fluted, radiating from a pronounced centre.

Lifespan
Hardy annual

Height
12–20 in (30–50 cm)

Seed
Beige, ¼ in (6 mm) long, shaped like a curved apostrophe with a knobbly backbone.

Petals
Bright orange petals have the highest concentration of active ingredients.

Dried petals
These keep their colour well and have many uses.

Leaf
Mid-green, hairy base leaves are paddle-shaped, stem leaves are lance-shaped.

Stem
Green, succulent, angular, branching; covered with fine hairs.

USES

Decorative
FLOWER Dry petals to add colour to potpourri.

Culinary
FLOWER Use petals lavishly to give saffron colour and a light tangy flavour (not saffron flavour) to rice, fish and meat soups, soft cheese, yogurt, butter, omelettes, milk dishes, cakes and sweet breads.
LEAF Sprinkle in salads and stews.

Medicinal
FLOWER Take in an infusion to aid digestion, also use as a healing mouthwash for gums.

Carum carvi

Caraway *Umbelliferae*

Definitely a herb with a pedigree, caraway has been found in the remains of Stone Age meals, Egyptian tombs, and ancient caravan stops along the Silk Road. The Arabic word for the seed, *karawya*, gives us the present name. In Shakespeare's *Henry IV*, Falstaff is offered a "pippin (apple) and dish of caraways", this being a traditional finish to an Elizabethan feast. Caraway has always been popular in Germany, and when Queen Victoria married Prince Albert, Britain renewed its interest in his favourite seed.

Such an ancient herb is not without its magical properties. Caraway was believed to be able to prevent departures, so it was used in love potions.

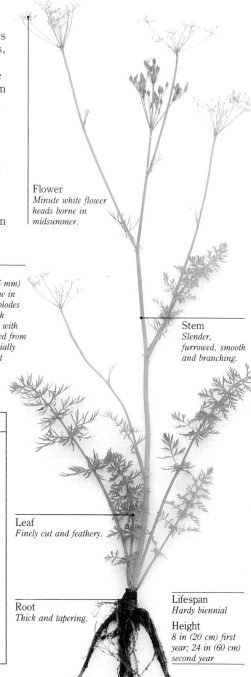

Flower
Minute white flower heads borne in midsummer.

Seed
Two aromatic, ¼ in (6 mm) long, narrow seeds grow in each capsule, which explodes when ripe. Each is dark brown, crescent shaped with pale ridges. Darkest seed from northern Europe, especially Holland, said to be best quality.

Stem
Slender, furrowed, smooth and branching.

Leaf
Finely cut and feathery.

Root
Thick and tapering.

Lifespan
Hardy biennial

Height
8 in (20 cm) first year; 24 in (60 cm) second year

USES

Culinary
SEED Sprinkle over rich meats, pork, goose and Hungarian beef stew to aid digestion. Add to cabbage water to reduce cooking smells. Use to flavour soups, breads, cakes, biscuits, apple pie, baked apples and cheese. Serve in a dish of mixed seeds at the end of an Indian meal.
LEAF Chop young leaves into salads and soups.
ROOTS Cook as a root vegetable.

Medicinal
SEED Chew raw or infused seed to aid digestion, promote appetite, sweeten the breath and relieve flatulence.

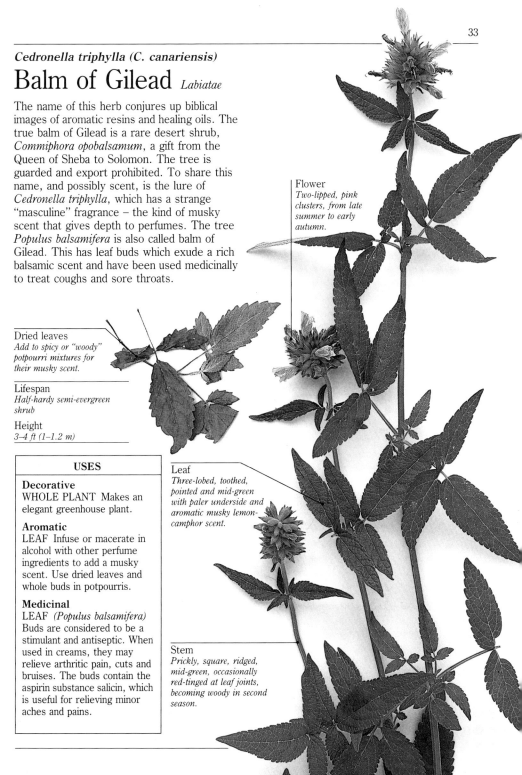

Cedronella triphylla (C. canariensis)

Balm of Gilead *Labiatae*

The name of this herb conjures up biblical images of aromatic resins and healing oils. The true balm of Gilead is a rare desert shrub, *Commiphora opobalsamum*, a gift from the Queen of Sheba to Solomon. The tree is guarded and export prohibited. To share this name, and possibly scent, is the lure of *Cedronella triphylla*, which has a strange "masculine" fragrance – the kind of musky scent that gives depth to perfumes. The tree *Populus balsamifera* is also called balm of Gilead. This has leaf buds which exude a rich balsamic scent and have been used medicinally to treat coughs and sore throats.

Flower
Two-lipped, pink clusters, from late summer to early autumn.

Dried leaves
Add to spicy or "woody" potpourri mixtures for their musky scent.

Lifespan
Half-hardy semi-evergreen shrub

Height
3–4 ft (1–1.2 m)

USES
Decorative WHOLE PLANT Makes an elegant greenhouse plant.
Aromatic LEAF Infuse or macerate in alcohol with other perfume ingredients to add a musky scent. Use dried leaves and whole buds in potpourris.
Medicinal LEAF *(Populus balsamifera)* Buds are considered to be a stimulant and antiseptic. When used in creams, they may relieve arthritic pain, cuts and bruises. The buds contain the aspirin substance salicin, which is useful for relieving minor aches and pains.

Leaf
Three-lobed, toothed, pointed and mid-green with paler underside and aromatic musky lemon-camphor scent.

Stem
Prickly, square, ridged, mid-green, occasionally red-tinged at leaf joints, becoming woody in second season.

Chamaemelum nobile (Anthemis nobilis)

Perennial chamomile *Compositae*

The Egyptians dedicated chamomile to the sun and worshipped it above all other herbs for its healing properties, while Greek physicians prescribed it for fevers and female disorders. Chamomile has inspired a proverb about energy in adversity, "like a chamomile bed, the more it is trodden the more it will spread".

Chamomile is also valued for its sweet apple-scented leaves. In a popular gardening book of 1638, William Lawson wrote of the "large walks, broad and long, like the Temple groves in Thessaly, raised with gravel and sand, having seats and banks of Camomile – all this delights the mind and brings healthy to the body". The relaxing aroma was also inhaled as snuff or smoked to relieve asthma and cure insomnia. At beauty salons, chamomile tea is often served to relax facial muscles.

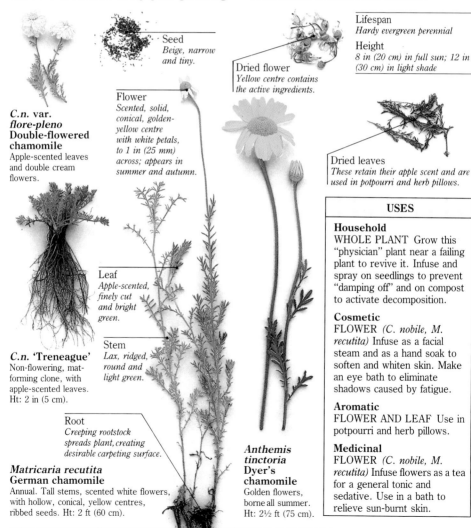

Seed
Beige, narrow and tiny.

Dried flower
Yellow centre contains the active ingredients.

Lifespan
Hardy evergreen perennial

Height
8 in (20 cm) in full sun; 12 in (30 cm) in light shade

C.n. var. flore-pleno Double-flowered chamomile
Apple-scented leaves and double cream flowers.

Flower
Scented, solid, conical, golden-yellow centre with white petals, to 1 in (25 mm) across; appears in summer and autumn.

Dried leaves
These retain their apple scent and are used in potpourri and herb pillows.

Leaf
Apple-scented, finely cut and bright green.

Stem
Lax, ridged, round and light green.

C.n. 'Treneague'
Non-flowering, mat-forming clone, with apple-scented leaves. Ht: 2 in (5 cm).

Root
Creeping rootstock spreads plant, creating desirable carpeting surface.

Matricaria recutita German chamomile
Annual. Tall stems, scented white flowers, with hollow, conical, yellow centres, ribbed seeds. Ht: 2 ft (60 cm).

Anthemis tinctoria Dyer's chamomile
Golden flowers, borne all summer. Ht: 2½ ft (75 cm).

USES

Household
WHOLE PLANT Grow this "physician" plant near a failing plant to revive it. Infuse and spray on seedlings to prevent "damping off" and on compost to activate decomposition.

Cosmetic
FLOWER *(C. nobile, M. recutita)* Infuse as a facial steam and as a hand soak to soften and whiten skin. Make an eye bath to eliminate shadows caused by fatigue.

Aromatic
FLOWER AND LEAF Use in potpourri and herb pillows.

Medicinal
FLOWER *(C. nobile, M. recutita)* Infuse flowers as a tea for a general tonic and sedative. Use in a bath to relieve sun-burnt skin.

Chenopodium bonus-henricus
Good King Henry *Chenopodiaceae*

Good King Henry has been a popular herb from Neolithic times until the last century. Its curious name is not taken from any English king but comes from Germany, where it distinguishes the plant from the poisonous mercury, known as "bad Henry".

Both Good King Henry and fat hen (*C. album*) have nutritious leaves. The seeds of fat hen, which are rich in fat and albumen, were a food supplement for primitive man, and fat hen was found in the stomach of preserved Iron Age Tollund Man. American wormseed (*C. ambrosioides*) is sometimes used to expel worms, but only under strict medical supervision as large doses are poisonous.

Variegated leaves
Such forms occasionally appear among seedlings.

Flower
Tiny greenish-yellow flowers borne in early summer on 2 in (5 cm) spikes where leaf joins stem.

Leaf
Arrow-shaped and dark green with white mealy undersides.

Stem
Tall, slender, ridged and green.

Seed
Tan coloured, rough, round and knobbly.

USES

Culinary
FLOWER Steam spikes and toss in butter like broccoli.
LEAF Eat young leaves raw in salads, cooked in stuffings, casseroles, and soups, and puréed in savoury pies.
SHOOT On rich soil, cut shoots of pencil thickness and 5 in (13 cm) tall; boil, peel and eat as asparagus.

Household
WHOLE PLANT Use to fatten poultry.

Medicinal
LEAF Eat raw or cooked as a source of iron, vitamins and minerals. A poultice and ointment cleanses and heals skin sores.

Lifespan
Hardy perennial

Height
2 ft (60 cm)

Chrysanthemum balsamita (Tanacetum balsamita)

Alecost/Costmary *Compositae*

According to Gerard, the sixteenth-century herbalist, alecost was "cherished for its sweete flowers and leaves". Its balsamic leaves and flowering tops were also important in brewing to help clear and preserve ale and to impart an astringent minty bitterness. Alecost was taken by settlers to America, where the Puritans carried a leaf in their bibles as a fragrant bookmark and to allay appetites during long sermons, giving alecost the nickname "bible leaf". The word "cost" derives from *kostos*, the Greek for a spicy oriental herb, so alecost means a spicy herb for ale, and costmary is Mary's (or women's) spicy herb, as it was used to ease childbirth.

Lifespan
Hardy herbaceous perennial

Height
2–3 ft 6 in (60 cm–1.05 m)

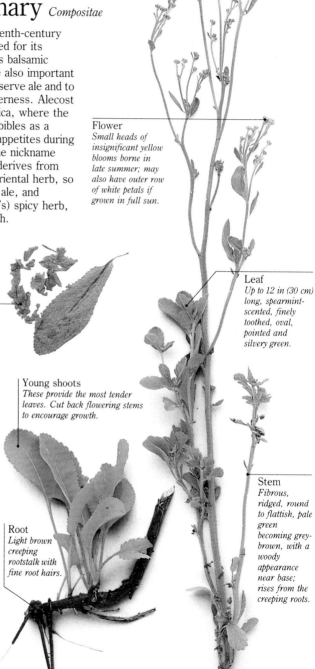

Flower
Small heads of insignificant yellow blooms borne in late summer; may also have outer row of white petals if grown in full sun.

Dried leaves
These retain a refreshing balsamic, minty lemon scent and are excellent in teas and potpourri.

Leaf
Up to 12 in (30 cm) long, spearmint-scented, finely toothed, oval, pointed and silvery green.

Young shoots
These provide the most tender leaves. Cut back flowering stems to encourage growth.

Root
Light brown creeping rootstalk with fine root hairs.

Stem
Fibrous, ridged, round to flattish, pale green becoming grey-brown, with a woody appearance near base; rises from the creeping roots.

USES

Culinary
LEAF Use in small amounts as it has a sharp tang. Add finely chopped leaves to carrot soup, salads, game, poultry stuffing and fruit cakes. Try with melted butter on peas and new potatoes. Use to clear, flavour and preserve beer.

Cosmetic
LEAF Infuse as a scented rinse water for hair or skin.

Aromatic
LEAF Use in potpourri and herb bags to intensify the scents of other herbs.

Medicinal
LEAF Infuse as a tonic tea to relieve colds, catarrh and upset stomachs.

Chrysanthemum cinerariifolium (Pyrethrum cinerariifolium)

Pyrethrum *Compositae*

Although to some the name pyrethrum includes all the single-flowered chrysanthemums, it is in fact only the flowers of *C. cinerariifolium* that contain a natural insecticide, also called pyrethrum. Because it is non-toxic to mammals and non-accumulative, pyrethrum is also used to kill pests living on the skin of man and animals. Another advantage is suggested by the traveller Chang Yee: "It is a strange coincidence that the leaves can be used for wiping the fingers after eating crabs, to wipe away the smell. Crabs, chrysanthemums, wine and the moon are the four autumn joys of our scholars, artists and poets." Garland chrysanthemum or "chop suey greens" *(C. coronarium)* is popular in oriental cuisine.

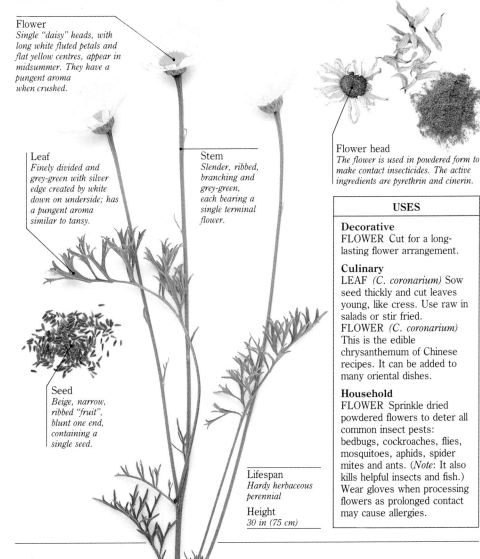

Flower
Single "daisy" heads, with long white fluted petals and flat yellow centres, appear in midsummer. They have a pungent aroma when crushed.

Leaf
Finely divided and grey-green with silver edge created by white down on underside; has a pungent aroma similar to tansy.

Stem
Slender, ribbed, branching and grey-green, each bearing a single terminal flower.

Seed
Beige, narrow, ribbed "fruit", blunt one end, containing a single seed.

Flower head
The flower is used in powdered form to make contact insecticides. The active ingredients are pyrethrin and cinerin.

Lifespan
Hardy herbaceous perennial

Height
30 in (75 cm)

USES
Decorative FLOWER Cut for a long-lasting flower arrangement.
Culinary LEAF *(C. coronarium)* Sow seed thickly and cut leaves young, like cress. Use raw in salads or stir fried. FLOWER *(C. coronarium)* This is the edible chrysanthemum of Chinese recipes. It can be added to many oriental dishes.
Household FLOWER Sprinkle dried powdered flowers to deter all common insect pests: bedbugs, cockroaches, flies, mosquitoes, aphids, spider mites and ants. (*Note*: It also kills helpful insects and fish.) Wear gloves when processing flowers as prolonged contact may cause allergies.

Cichorium intybus

Chicory/Succory *Compositae*

According to folk tales, the flowers of chicory are a beautiful clear blue because they are the transformed eyes of a lass weeping for her lover's ship, which was lost never to return. These delicate blue flowers can be changed to bright red by the acid of ants: place a flower in an ant hill and watch the colour show.

Chicory is often grown in floral clocks for the regular opening of its flowers and their closing five hours later. These opening times relate to latitude, but the leaves always align with north.

Lifespan
Hardy perennial

Height
3–5 ft (1–1.5 m)

Chicons
These are blanched heads produced by forcing roots in warmth and darkness.

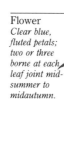

Flower
Clear blue, fluted petals; two or three borne at each leaf joint mid-summer to midautumn.

Stem
Hollow, furrowed, green with small hairs; bitter milky juice inside.

Leaf
Mid-green with hairy underside; coarsely toothed at the base; smaller arrow-shaped leaves further up the stem.

Dried petals
Attractive in potpourri.

Root
Long taproot, occasionally branching; bitter milky fluid inside.

USES

Culinary
FLOWER Use in salads; pickle buds.
LEAF Seedlings can be cut and eaten fresh.
ROOT When young, boil and serve with a sauce. Use as a coffee substitute: dig up thick, cultivated roots, wash, slice, dry slowly in gentle heat; roast and grind.
CHICON Toss in salads; braise in butter and eat as a vegetable dish.

Medicinal
LEAF A poultice soothes inflammation.
ROOT Infuse dried root to make a tonic, also a mild laxative and diuretic.

Coriandrum sativum

Coriander *Umbelliferae*

Cultivated as a medicinal and culinary herb for at least 3,000 years, coriander is mentioned in Sanskrit texts, on Egyptian papyri, in *Tales of the Arabian Nights*, and in the Bible, where manna is compared with coriander seed. Coriander was brought to northern Europe by the Romans, who, combining it with cumin and vinegar, rubbed it into meat as a preservative.

The Chinese once believed it conferred immortality, and in the Middle Ages it was put into love potions as an aphrodisiac. All coriander parts have a pungent aroma; one Peruvian tribe is so fond of the leaf that they exude its scent. That of the mildly narcotic seed changes considerably when it ripens to a sweet spicy flavour.

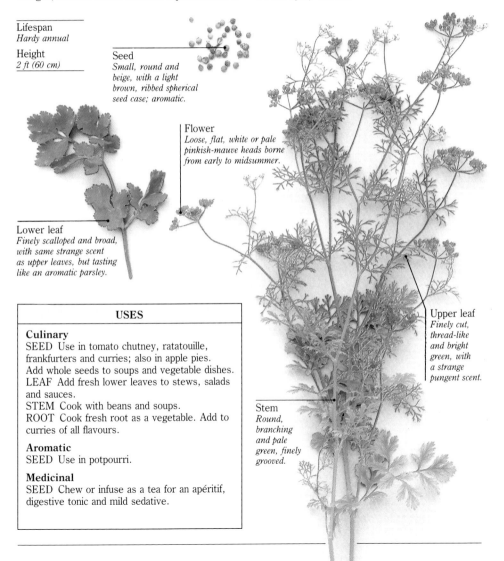

Lifespan
Hardy annual

Height
2 ft (60 cm)

Seed
Small, round and beige, with a light brown, ribbed spherical seed case; aromatic.

Flower
Loose, flat, white or pale pinkish-mauve heads borne from early to midsummer.

Lower leaf
Finely scalloped and broad, with same strange scent as upper leaves, but tasting like an aromatic parsley.

Upper leaf
Finely cut, thread-like and bright green, with a strange pungent scent.

Stem
Round, branching and pale green, finely grooved.

USES

Culinary
SEED Use in tomato chutney, ratatouille, frankfurters and curries; also in apple pies.
Add whole seeds to soups and vegetable dishes.
LEAF Add fresh lower leaves to stews, salads and sauces.
STEM Cook with beans and soups.
ROOT Cook fresh root as a vegetable. Add to curries of all flavours.

Aromatic
SEED Use in potpourri.

Medicinal
SEED Chew or infuse as a tea for an apéritif, digestive tonic and mild sedative.

Dianthus caryophyllus

Clove pink *Caryophyllaceae*

This herb was a flower of divinity to the Greeks, who dedicated it to the "sky father" and called it *dianthus*, meaning flower of flowers. To the Romans, it was *flos Jovis*, Jove's flower. In the making of coronets and garlands, in which both these cultures delighted, pinks were given place of honour. These flowers of love were also floated in the drinks of engaged couples, and in medieval art they indicated betrothal. Pinks have long been used to flavour dainty dishes with their spicy fragrance: flowers were crystallized, and petals were used in soups, sauces, syrups, cordials and wine. In 1699, John Evelyn suggested that the petals had "a more palatable relish infused in vinegar".

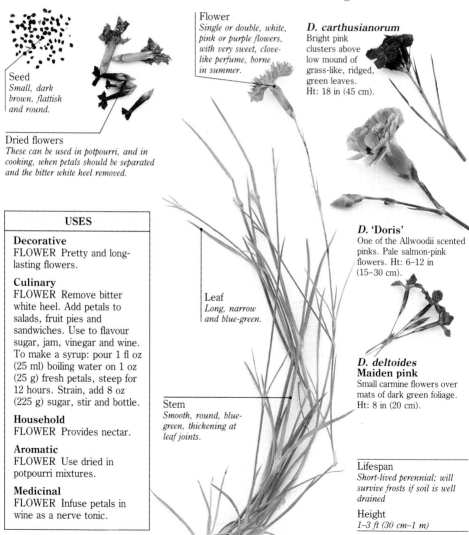

Seed
Small, dark brown, flattish and round.

Flower
Single or double, white, pink or purple flowers, with very sweet, clove-like perfume, borne in summer.

D. carthusianorum
Bright pink clusters above low mound of grass-like, ridged, green leaves.
Ht: 18 in (45 cm).

Dried flowers
These can be used in potpourri, and in cooking, when petals should be separated and the bitter white heel removed.

D. 'Doris'
One of the Allwoodii scented pinks. Pale salmon-pink flowers. Ht: 6–12 in (15–30 cm).

Leaf
Long, narrow and blue-green.

D. deltoides
Maiden pink
Small carmine flowers over mats of dark green foliage.
Ht: 8 in (20 cm).

Stem
Smooth, round, blue-green, thickening at leaf joints.

USES

Decorative
FLOWER Pretty and long-lasting flowers.

Culinary
FLOWER Remove bitter white heel. Add petals to salads, fruit pies and sandwiches. Use to flavour sugar, jam, vinegar and wine. To make a syrup: pour 1 fl oz (25 ml) boiling water on 1 oz (25 g) fresh petals, steep for 12 hours. Strain, add 8 oz (225 g) sugar, stir and bottle.

Household
FLOWER Provides nectar.

Aromatic
FLOWER Use dried in potpourri mixtures.

Medicinal
FLOWER Infuse petals in wine as a nerve tonic.

Lifespan
Short-lived perennial; will survive frosts if soil is well drained

Height
1–3 ft (30 cm–1 m)

Eupatorium purpureum

Sweet Joe Pye *Compositae*

A glorious feature of the herb garden in late summer, the vigorous purple stems of sweet Joe Pye display clouds of rose-pink flowers. This herb was named after a North American Indian called Joe Pye, who cured a grateful New Englander of typhus. The Indian used this plant to induce profuse sweating, which broke the fever. Its Latin name *Eupatorium* is derived from Eupator, a first-century BC king of Persia, famed for his herbal skills. Other species, *E. cannabinum* and *E. perfoliatum*, are very similar in appearance and both also have medicinal properties.

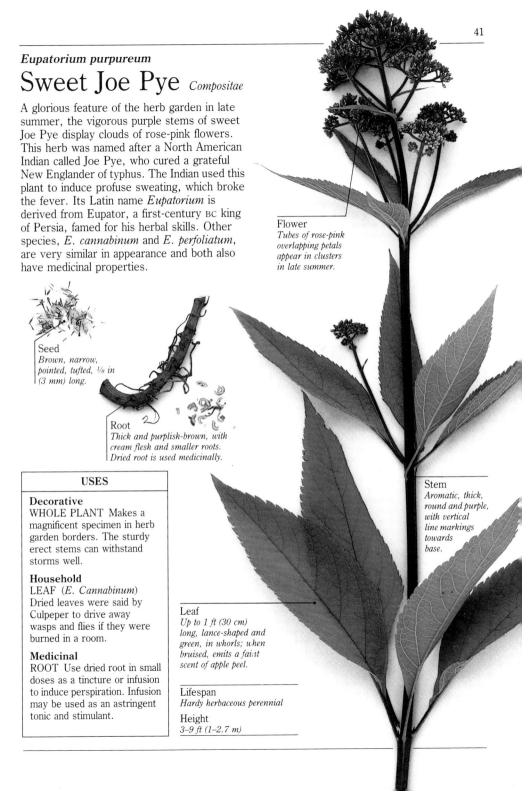

Flower
Tubes of rose-pink overlapping petals appear in clusters in late summer.

Seed
Brown, narrow, pointed, tufted, ⅛ in (3 mm) long.

Root
Thick and purplish-brown, with cream flesh and smaller roots. Dried root is used medicinally.

Stem
Aromatic, thick, round and purple, with vertical line markings towards base.

Leaf
Up to 1 ft (30 cm) long, lance-shaped and green, in whorls; when bruised, emits a faint scent of apple peel.

Lifespan
Hardy herbaceous perennial

Height
3–9 ft (1–2.7 m)

USES

Decorative
WHOLE PLANT Makes a magnificent specimen in herb garden borders. The sturdy erect stems can withstand storms well.

Household
LEAF (*E. Cannabinum*) Dried leaves were said by Culpeper to drive away wasps and flies if they were burned in a room.

Medicinal
ROOT Use dried root in small doses as a tincture or infusion to induce perspiration. Infusion may be used as an astringent tonic and stimulant.

Filipendula ulmaria

Meadowsweet *Rosaceae*

Meadowsweet was the favourite strewing herb of Queen Elizabeth I, and the herbalist Gerard believed it excelled all other strewing herbs because its leaves delighted the senses without causing headaches. Meadowsweet was so frequently in demand for strewing at church weddings and for making into bridal garlands that it was given another name "bridewort". Other qualities unknown to us once made this plant most sacred to the Druids. There is also a gold variegated leaf form, and *F. vulgaris*, which has larger flowers.

USES

Decorative
FLOWER Use in bouquets.

Culinary
FLOWER Flavours herb beers, mead and wines. Gives slight almond flavour to jams and stewed fruit.
LEAF Add to soup.

Household
FLOWERING TOP Use to scent linen.

Aromatic
FLOWER Dry for potpourri.
LEAF Add to potpourri.

Stem
Hollow, furrowed, branching and reddish.

Flower
Cream-coloured clusters of tiny blossoms with sweet almond fragrance throughout summer.

Seed
Light brown and crescent-shaped, ⅛ in (3 mm) long.

Leaf
Wrinkled, deeply indented and dark green with grey-green undersides; exudes pleasant wintergreen fragrance.

Dried leaves
Smell of hay with a hint of wintergreen.

Root
Pinkish-red, sweetly aromatic and creeping.

Dried flowers
Sweet almond fragrance improves with age; used for tea and potpourri.

Lifespan
Hardy perennial

Height
2–4 ft (60 cm–1.2 m)

Foeniculum vulgare

Fennel *Umbelliferae*

Fennel is one of our oldest cultivated plants and was much valued by the Romans. "So gladiators fierce and rude; mingled it with their daily food. And he who battled and subdued; a wreath of fennel wore" (Henry Wadsworth Longfellow). In an age of banquets, Roman warriors took fennel to keep in good health, while Roman ladies ate it to prevent obesity. Every part of the plant, from the seed to the root, is edible. It was one of the nine herbs held sacred by the Anglo-Saxons for its power against evil. With healing properties also to its credit, Charlemagne declared in AD 812 that fennel was essential in every imperial garden.

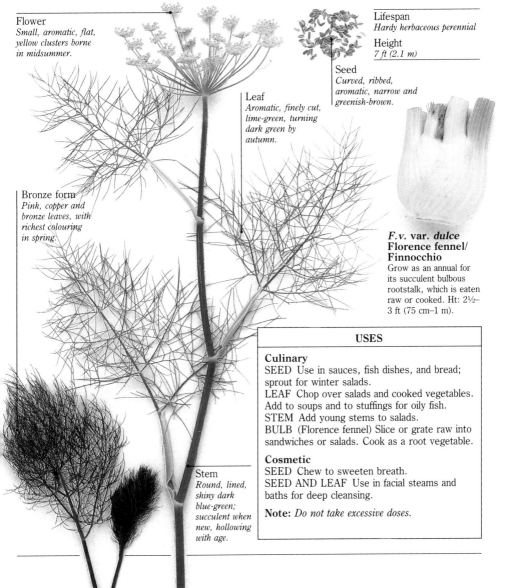

Flower
Small, aromatic, flat, yellow clusters borne in midsummer.

Seed
Curved, ribbed, aromatic, narrow and greenish-brown.

Lifespan
Hardy herbaceous perennial

Height
7 ft (2.1 m)

Leaf
Aromatic, finely cut, lime-green, turning dark green by autumn.

Bronze form
Pink, copper and bronze leaves, with richest colouring in spring.

**F.v. var. *dulce*
Florence fennel/
Finnocchio**
Grow as an annual for its succulent bulbous rootstalk, which is eaten raw or cooked. Ht: 2½–3 ft (75 cm–1 m).

Stem
Round, lined, shiny dark blue-green; succulent when new, hollowing with age.

USES

Culinary
SEED Use in sauces, fish dishes, and bread; sprout for winter salads.
LEAF Chop over salads and cooked vegetables. Add to soups and to stuffings for oily fish.
STEM Add young stems to salads.
BULB (Florence fennel) Slice or grate raw into sandwiches or salads. Cook as a root vegetable.

Cosmetic
SEED Chew to sweeten breath.
SEED AND LEAF Use in facial steams and baths for deep cleansing.

Note: *Do not take excessive doses.*

Fragaria vesca

Wild strawberry *Rosaceae*

"Doubtless God Almighty could have made a better berry but doubtless God never did." Dr Butler's praise sums up most people's feelings about strawberries. Growing in cool, secret woodlands, strawberries are often associated with fairy folk, and in Bavaria, a basket of the fruit is sometimes tied between a cow's horns to please the elves so that they bless the cow with abundant milk. Woodland strawberries were recommended by Sir Hugh Platt in his *Garden of Eden* (1653), as most likely to prosper in gardens. While discussing plants that scent the air, Francis Bacon noted that "the strawberry leaves dying . . . yield a most excellent cordial smell".

Strawberries are one of the fruits dedicated to the Virgin Mary. In Lapland, they are mixed with reindeer milk and blueberries to make a Christmas pudding. Their one unhappy association is with the fateful handkerchief that Othello gave Desdemona, which was embroidered with strawberries.

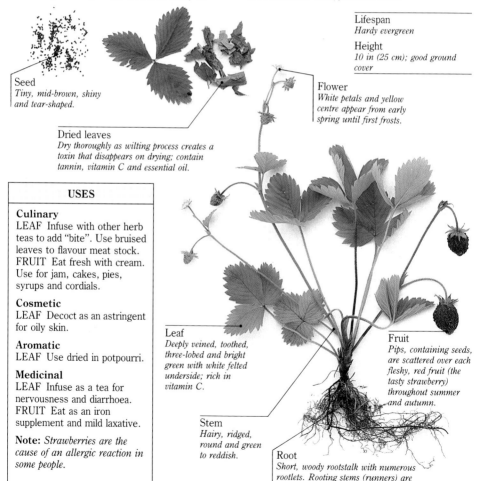

Seed
Tiny, mid-brown, shiny and tear-shaped.

Dried leaves
Dry thoroughly as wilting process creates a toxin that disappears on drying; contain tannin, vitamin C and essential oil.

Lifespan
Hardy evergreen

Height
10 in (25 cm); good ground cover

Flower
White petals and yellow centre appear from early spring until first frosts.

Leaf
Deeply veined, toothed, three-lobed and bright green with white felted underside; rich in vitamin C.

Stem
Hairy, ridged, round and green to reddish.

Fruit
Pips, containing seeds, are scattered over each fleshy, red fruit (the tasty strawberry) throughout summer and autumn.

Root
Short, woody rootstalk with numerous rootlets. Rooting stems (runners) are produced from stem area.

USES

Culinary
LEAF Infuse with other herb teas to add "bite". Use bruised leaves to flavour meat stock.
FRUIT Eat fresh with cream. Use for jam, cakes, pies, syrups and cordials.

Cosmetic
LEAF Decoct as an astringent for oily skin.

Aromatic
LEAF Use dried in potpourri.

Medicinal
LEAF Infuse as a tea for nervousness and diarrhoea.
FRUIT Eat as an iron supplement and mild laxative.

Note: *Strawberries are the cause of an allergic reaction in some people.*

Galium odoratum (Asperula odorata)

Sweet woodruff *Rubiaceae*

This pretty little woodland plant will, when added to a wine-cup, "make a man merrie", wrote Gerard. Sweet-smelling garlands of woodruff were hung in churches, strewn on domestic floors, sprinkled into potpourri and linen and stuffed into mattresses. The coumarin in leaves develops its sweet hay scent only when the plant is dried, so sweet woodruff is invaluable from the appearance of its first flowers for the traditional German May Bowl punch, through to Christmas, when it is used extensively in herb pillows.

Lifespan
Hardy perennial

Height
12 in (30 cm); good ground cover

Dried leaves
Smell like new-mown hay and act as a fixative in potpourri.

Flower
Brilliant white, loose clusters of star-shaped flowers appear in late spring.

Leaf
The shiny green circular spokes of the leaves give the plant its "ruff" name.

Stem
Slender, squarish and smooth.

Root
Small, red-brown creeping rootstalk with hair-like roots.

USES

Decorative
FLOWERING STEM Use in garlands and festive wreaths.

Culinary
LEAF Make "an exhilarating drink to lift the spirits and create a carefree atmosphere": dry a small handful of fresh woodruff leaves in a warm cupboard for 3 hours. Pour over juice of one lemon and half a bottle of hock. Put in a warm place for 3–4 hours. Add 4–6 tbsp (60–90 ml) sugar and one and a half bottles of hock. Chill. Just before serving, add a bottle of sparkling white wine.

Aromatic
LEAF Add dried leaves to potpourri and herb pillows.

Helianthus annuus

Sunflower *Compositae*

This remarkable flower, which was cultivated by American Indians some 3,000 years ago, derives its name from helios, the Greek word for sun. In the fifteenth century, Aztec sun priestesses were crowned with sunflowers, carried them in their hands and wore gold jewellery with sunflower motifs. Sunflowers were introduced into Europe in the sixteenth century. Large-scale cultivation began in Russia, where the seeds are sold on street corners and offered in restaurants.

All parts of the sunflower are usable. The pith, for example, is one of the lightest substances known and is used in scientific laboratories. The plant's ability to absorb water from soil has been utilized in the reclamation of marshy land in the Netherlands.

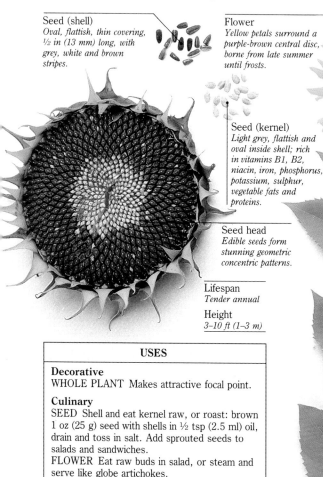

Seed (shell)
Oval, flattish, thin covering, ½ in (13 mm) long, with grey, white and brown stripes.

Flower
Yellow petals surround a purple-brown central disc, borne from late summer until frosts.

Seed (kernel)
Light grey, flattish and oval inside shell; rich in vitamins B1, B2, niacin, iron, phosphorus, potassium, sulphur, vegetable fats and proteins.

Seed head
Edible seeds form stunning geometric concentric patterns.

Lifespan
Tender annual

Height
3–10 ft (1–3 m)

Stem
Thick, hairy, light green and high in potash. Dried stems are very hard and make excellent fuel.

Leaf
Large, rough, toothed, heart-shaped with prominent veins.

USES

Decorative
WHOLE PLANT Makes attractive focal point.

Culinary
SEED Shell and eat kernel raw, or roast: brown 1 oz (25 g) seed with shells in ½ tsp (2.5 ml) oil, drain and toss in salt. Add sprouted seeds to salads and sandwiches.
FLOWER Eat raw buds in salad, or steam and serve like globe artichokes.

Helichrysum italicum (H. angustifolium)

Curry plant *Compositae*

This plant from southern Europe is a relatively new addition to herbal lists. Curry plant's initial attraction lies in the intense silver of its evergreen leaves, which make it and its dwarf form, *H.i.* var. *microphyllum*, a good choice for formal edgings and knot gardens. However, it is the sweet curry scent of its leaves which is so unusual and has caused its recent rise in popularity, especially among adventurous cooks. If the leaves are accidentally disturbed they give off such a spicy aroma that people often look for a nearby picnic group in an attempt to track down the source.

The genus *Helichrysum* also includes *H. bracteatum*, whose pretty everlasting flowers are often added to potpourri.

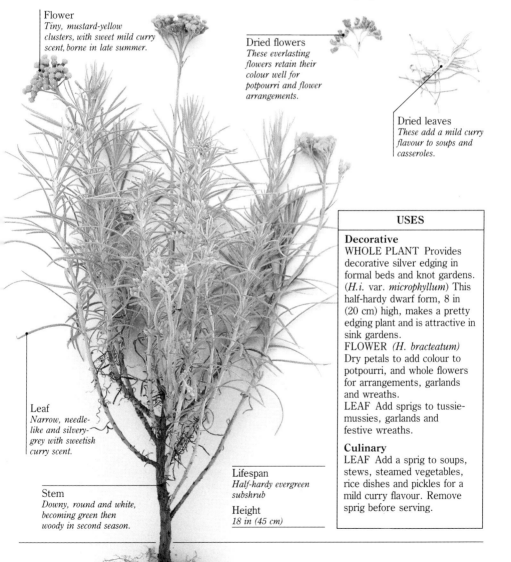

Flower
Tiny, mustard-yellow clusters, with sweet mild curry scent, borne in late summer.

Dried flowers
These everlasting flowers retain their colour well for potpourri and flower arrangements.

Dried leaves
These add a mild curry flavour to soups and casseroles.

Leaf
Narrow, needle-like and silvery-grey with sweetish curry scent.

Stem
Downy, round and white, becoming green then woody in second season.

Lifespan
Half-hardy evergreen subshrub

Height
18 in (45 cm)

USES

Decorative
WHOLE PLANT Provides decorative silver edging in formal beds and knot gardens. (*H.i.* var. *microphyllum*) This half-hardy dwarf form, 8 in (20 cm) high, makes a pretty edging plant and is attractive in sink gardens.
FLOWER (*H. bracteatum*) Dry petals to add colour to potpourri, and whole flowers for arrangements, garlands and wreaths.
LEAF Add sprigs to tussie-mussies, garlands and festive wreaths.

Culinary
LEAF Add a sprig to soups, stews, steamed vegetables, rice dishes and pickles for a mild curry flavour. Remove sprig before serving.

Hesperis matronalis

Sweet rocket *Cruciferae*

This pretty cottage flower has maintained its position in the herb garden because of its sweet-scented flowers as well as its medicinal properties. A native of Italy, it can be found growing wild in much of Europe and northern America as a garden escapee.

Its massed flowers, a glorious sight in midsummer, are sometimes called dame's violet or vesper-flower, since its perfume is strongest in the evening. The young leaves are occasionally eaten as a salad herb, but they are more bitter than salad rocket.

Flower
Sweetly fragrant, purple, mauve and white flowers appear in midsummer.

Seed
Brown, narrow and pointed, 1/8 in (3 mm) long.

Lifespan
Hardy biennial. Sometimes behaves as a perennial, sending out new shoots from old roots.

Height
3 ft (1 m)

Stem
Slender and carries flowers in second year.

USES

Decorative
FLOWER Pick flowers for a pretty, sweet-scented summer bouquet.

Culinary
FLOWER Toss in salads. Use as a decoration for desserts. LEAF Add chopped young leaves sparingly to salads.

Aromatic
FLOWER Add dried flowers to potpourri for their pastel colour and sweet scent.

Medicinal
LEAF Dried leaves were once popular for preventing and curing scurvy. A strong dose may cause vomiting.

Leaf
Spear-shaped and dark green.

Humulus lupulus

Hops *Cannabidaceae*

In the first century AD, the Roman writer Pliny described hops as a popular garden plant and vegetable: in spring, young shoots were sold on markets, to be eaten like asparagus. By the eighth century, this plant was used in brewing throughout most of Europe for its clearing, flavouring and preserving qualities. However, in Britain, brewers continued to rely on traditional herbs such as ground ivy and alecost until the sixteenth century, believing that hops engendered melancholy. In 1670, John Evelyn explained that "hops . . . preserve the drink indeed, but repay the pleasure in tormenting diseases and a shorter life".

USES
Decorative   FLOWERS Attractive in dried arrangements and garlands.
Culinary   SHOOT Steam young side shoots and serve in the same way as asparagus.
Medicinal   FLOWER Infuse as a mild sedative tea for digestive problems.

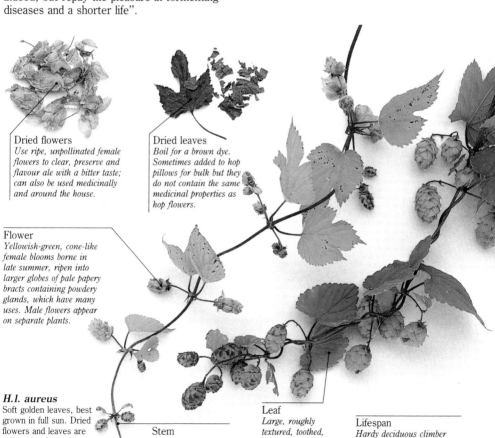

Dried flowers
Use ripe, unpollinated female flowers to clear, preserve and flavour ale with a bitter taste; can also be used medicinally and around the house.

Dried leaves
Boil for a brown dye. Sometimes added to hop pillows for bulk but they do not contain the same medicinal properties as hop flowers.

Flower
Yellowish-green, cone-like female blooms borne in late summer, ripen into larger globes of pale papery bracts containing powdery glands, which have many uses. Male flowers appear on separate plants.

H.l. aureus
Soft golden leaves, best grown in full sun. Dried flowers and leaves are believed to have the same properties as the species.

Stem
Tough, prickly haired, faceted, green tinged with red.

Leaf
Large, roughly textured, toothed, heart-shaped and mid-green, with three or five lobes.

Lifespan
Hardy deciduous climber

Height
23 ft (7 m)

Hyssopus officinalis

Hyssop Labiatae

The Greek *hyssopos* may derive from the Hebrew *ezob*, or holy herb, because it was used for purifying temples and the ritual cleansing of lepers: "Purge me with hyssop, and I shall be clean" (*Psalm* 51 v.7). The biblical plant may not in fact have been common hyssop but rather a form of oregano or savory. However, research now favours common hyssop once again, with the discovery that the mould that produces penicillin grows on its leaf. This could have acted as antibiotic protection when lepers were bathed in hyssop.

A wine called *hyssopites*, made from hyssop, was mentioned by the Roman writer Pliny in the first century AD. This may have influenced the Benedictine monks who, in the tenth century, brought the herb into central Europe to flavour their liqueurs.

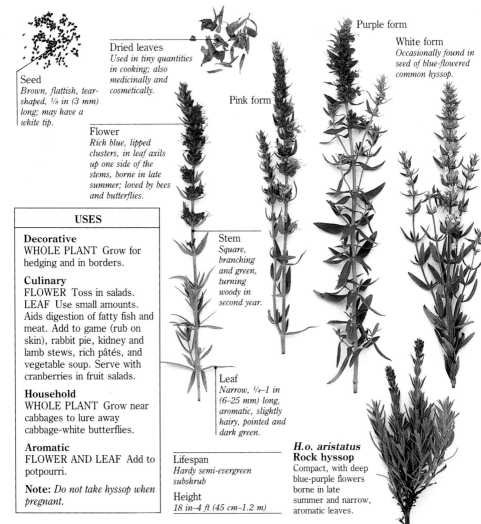

Seed
Brown, flattish, tear-shaped, ⅛ in (3 mm) long; may have a white tip.

Dried leaves
Used in tiny quantities in cooking; also medicinally and cosmetically.

Pink form

Purple form

White form
Occasionally found in seed of blue-flowered common hyssop.

Flower
Rich blue, lipped clusters, in leaf axils up one side of the stems, borne in late summer; loved by bees and butterflies.

Stem
Square, branching and green, turning woody in second year.

Leaf
Narrow, ¼–1 in (6–25 mm) long, aromatic, slightly hairy, pointed and dark green.

Lifespan
Hardy semi-evergreen subshrub

Height
18 in–4 ft (45 cm–1.2 m)

**H.o. aristatus
Rock hyssop**
Compact, with deep blue-purple flowers borne in late summer and narrow, aromatic leaves.

USES

Decorative
WHOLE PLANT Grow for hedging and in borders.

Culinary
FLOWER Toss in salads.
LEAF Use small amounts. Aids digestion of fatty fish and meat. Add to game (rub on skin), rabbit pie, kidney and lamb stews, rich pâtés, and vegetable soup. Serve with cranberries in fruit salads.

Household
WHOLE PLANT Grow near cabbages to lure away cabbage-white butterflies.

Aromatic
FLOWER AND LEAF Add to potpourri.

Note: *Do not take hyssop when pregnant.*

Inula helenium

Elecampane *Compositae*

Helen of Troy was believed to be gathering elecampane when she was abducted by Paris, and its botanic name has captured this association. Its root contains a sweet starchy substance called inulin, which is responsible for elecampane's popularity as a crystallized sweet. According to the Roman writer Pliny, the Empress Julia Augusta "let no day pass without eating some of the roots candied, to help the digestion and cause mirth". In the Middle Ages, apothecaries sold the candied root in flat, pink, sugary cakes, which were sucked to alleviate asthma and indigestion and to sweeten the breath.

Lifespan
Hardy herbaceous perennial

Height
5–8 ft (1.5–2.4 m)

Dried petals
Dry the shaggy, daisy-like, yellow flowers and use the petals in potpourri for colour.

Seed
Mid-brown, torpedo-shaped, 3/16 in (4 mm) long, with short tufts of hair at one end, in velvety, dark brown seed heads.

USES
Decorative SEED Use velvety seed heads for winter arrangements.
Culinary ROOT Eat dried pieces or cook as a root vegetable. Be prepared for its sharp bitter flavour. Crystallize as a sweet.
Household ROOT Burn over embers to scent a room.
Cosmetic ROOT Apply a decoction to alleviate acne.
Medicinal ROOT Decoct as a general tonic, as an expectorant to ease bronchitis and coughs, and as a digestive.

Leaf
Up to 18 in (45 cm) long, pointed, coarsely toothed and green, with downy grey underside.

Stem
Thick, hairy, ridged, round and green, filled with white spongy pith.

Root
Thick, dark brown, tuberous and aromatic with creamy, edible flesh smelling of bananas.

Dried root
This smells of violets and is used medicinally.

Lavandula angustifolia (L. officinalis or L. spica)

Lavender *Labiatae*

Tranquillity and purity are inherent in the unique fragrance of lavender, as reflected by the seventeenth-century angling author Izaak Walton, "I long to be in a house where the sheets smell of lavender." Its fresh clean scent was the favourite bathwater additive of the Greeks and Romans, and its name derives from the Latin *lavare* "to wash".

A popular strewing herb both for its insect-repellent properties and its long-lasting fragrance, lavender was also distilled for liberal use in masking household smells and stinking streets. Stories that the glovers of Grasse, who used lavender oil to scent their fashionable leather, were remarkably free of plague, encouraged other people to carry lavender.

Lavender has long been used medicinally. The herbalist Gerard, for example, prescribed it to bathe the temples of those with a "light migram or swimming of the braine". One Sir James Smith also told of an alcoholic tincture created "for those who wished to indulge in a dram under the appearance of elegant medicine".

Its healing powers are now mainly obtained from the essential oil. This is distilled from shining oil glands embedded among the tiny star-shaped hairs which cover the flowers, leaves and stems. The best-quality oil is extracted from *L. angustifolia* and *L. stoechas*.

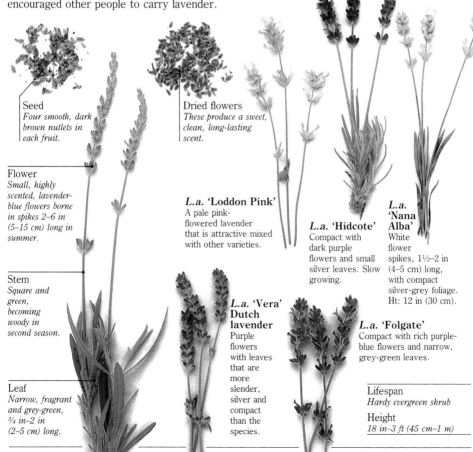

Seed
Four smooth, dark brown nutlets in each fruit.

Dried flowers
These produce a sweet, clean, long-lasting scent.

Flower
Small, highly scented, lavender-blue flowers borne in spikes 2–6 in (5–15 cm) long in summer.

L.a. 'Loddon Pink'
A pale pink-flowered lavender that is attractive mixed with other varieties.

L.a. 'Hidcote'
Compact with dark purple flowers and small silver leaves. Slow growing.

L.a. 'Nana Alba'
White flower spikes, 1½–2 in (4–5 cm) long, with compact silver-grey foliage. Ht: 12 in (30 cm).

Stem
Square and green, becoming woody in second season.

L.a. 'Vera' Dutch lavender
Purple flowers with leaves that are more slender, silver and compact than the species.

L.a. 'Folgate'
Compact with rich purple-blue flowers and narrow, grey-green leaves.

Leaf
Narrow, fragrant and grey-green, ¾ in–2 in (2–5 cm) long.

Lifespan
Hardy evergreen shrub

Height
18 in–3 ft (45 cm–1 m)

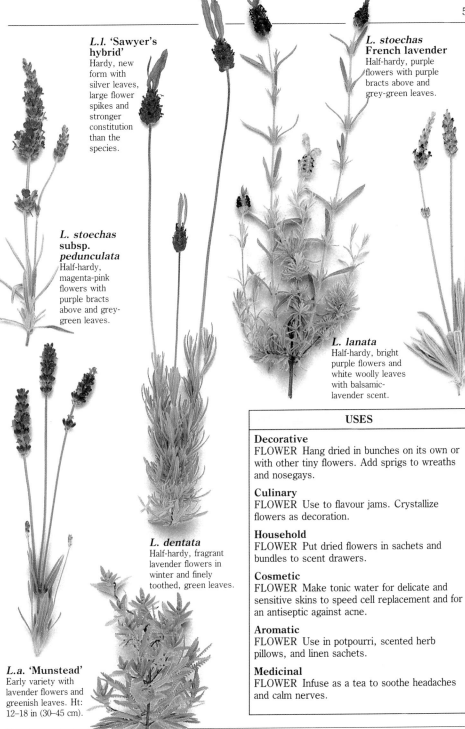

L.l. 'Sawyer's hybrid'
Hardy, new form with silver leaves, large flower spikes and stronger constitution than the species.

L. stoechas subsp. pedunculata
Half-hardy, magenta-pink flowers with purple bracts above and grey-green leaves.

L. stoechas French lavender
Half-hardy, purple flowers with purple bracts above and grey-green leaves.

L. lanata
Half-hardy, bright purple flowers and white woolly leaves with balsamic-lavender scent.

L. dentata
Half-hardy, fragrant lavender flowers in winter and finely toothed, green leaves.

L.a. 'Munstead'
Early variety with lavender flowers and greenish leaves. Ht: 12–18 in (30–45 cm).

USES

Decorative
FLOWER Hang dried in bunches on its own or with other tiny flowers. Add sprigs to wreaths and nosegays.

Culinary
FLOWER Use to flavour jams. Crystallize flowers as decoration.

Household
FLOWER Put dried flowers in sachets and bundles to scent drawers.

Cosmetic
FLOWER Make tonic water for delicate and sensitive skins to speed cell replacement and for an antiseptic against acne.

Aromatic
FLOWER Use in potpourri, scented herb pillows, and linen sachets.

Medicinal
FLOWER Infuse as a tea to soothe headaches and calm nerves.

Laurus nobilis

Bay/Sweet bay/Laurel *Lauraceae*

The bay tree was sacred to Apollo, the Greek god of prophecy, poetry and healing. His prophecies were communicated through his priestess at Delphi, who, among other rituals, ate a bay leaf before expounding her oracle. As bay leaves are slightly narcotic in large doses, they may have induced her trance state. Apollo's temple at Delphi had its roof made entirely of bay leaves for protection against disease, witchcraft and lightning. A wreath of bay leaves became the mark of excellence for poets and athletes and, to the Romans, bay was a symbol of wisdom and glory. The Latin *laurus* means "laurel" and *nobilis* "renowned".

Bay has been used against disease, especially the plague, for many centuries.

Dried leaves
Use within a few days of drying to capture optimum flavour. Old dried leaves lack pungency.

Lifespan
Evergreen tree. When mature, roots are hardy but leaves die in freezing winds

Height
23 ft (7 m)

Leaf
Fragrant, leathery, pointed, oval, glossy dark green, with olive-green underside and bitter flavour.

**L.n. aurea
Golden bay**
Golden leaves; a slightly hardier variety than the species when both are small plants.

L. nobilis

**L.n. angustifolia
Willow leaf bay**
This narrow-leaved variety was promoted as less susceptible to wind damage – an aim not achieved.

Stem
Solid, round, rich purple-brown, becoming woody, and grey.

USES
Decorative WHOLE PLANT Clip for topiary hedges.
Culinary LEAF Include in bouquet garni for stews, soups and sauces. Add to marinades, stock, potato soup, stuffing, pâté, curry, game and poached fish liquid. Remove leaf before serving. Boil in milk to flavour custards and rice pudding. Use as a garnish.
Aromatic BRANCH Hang to freshen and perfume the air. LEAF Crumble leaves into potpourri.
Medicinal LEAF Infuse as a digestive aid and to stimulate the appetite.
Note: *All laurels except sweet bay are poisonous.*

Levisticum officinale (Ligusticum levisticum)

Lovage *Umbelliferae*

Lovage is a handsome plant with a powerful flavour and numerous uses, both traditional and modern. Its leaves used to be laid in shoes to revive the weary traveller, and at inns it was served in a popular cordial, which was flavoured with tansy and a variety of yarrow known as *Achillea ligustica*, as well as lovage. A modern form of this cordial is made by steeping fresh lovage seed in brandy, sweetening it with sugar and then drinking it to settle an upset stomach. Lovage also adds a strong flavour to savoury dishes.

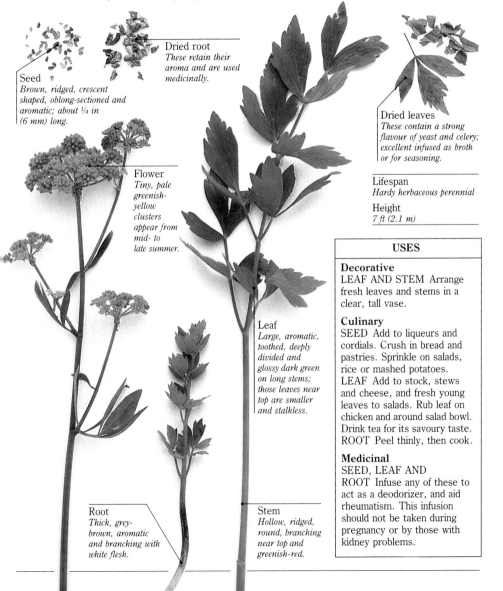

Dried root
These retain their aroma and are used medicinally.

Seed
Brown, ridged, crescent shaped, oblong-sectioned and aromatic; about ¼ in (6 mm) long.

Dried leaves
These contain a strong flavour of yeast and celery; excellent infused as broth or for seasoning.

Lifespan
Hardy herbaceous perennial

Height
7 ft (2.1 m)

Flower
Tiny, pale greenish-yellow clusters appear from mid- to late summer.

Leaf
Large, aromatic, toothed, deeply divided and glossy dark green on long stems; those leaves near top are smaller and stalkless.

Root
Thick, grey-brown, aromatic and branching with white flesh.

Stem
Hollow, ridged, round, branching near top and greenish-red.

USES

Decorative
LEAF AND STEM Arrange fresh leaves and stems in a clear, tall vase.

Culinary
SEED Add to liqueurs and cordials. Crush in bread and pastries. Sprinkle on salads, rice or mashed potatoes.
LEAF Add to stock, stews and cheese, and fresh young leaves to salads. Rub leaf on chicken and around salad bowl. Drink tea for its savoury taste.
ROOT Peel thinly, then cook.

Medicinal
SEED, LEAF AND ROOT Infuse any of these to act as a deodorizer, and aid rheumatism. This infusion should not be taken during pregnancy or by those with kidney problems.

Marrubium vulgare

Horehound *Labiatae*

For thousands of years, horehound has been much valued as a cough remedy. Egyptian priests honoured its medicinal properties and called it "seed of Horus", "bulls' blood" and "eye of the star". The Greek physician Hippocrates and other physicians down the ages have also held this herb in high esteem as a cure for many ills. It was also thought to break magical spells.

Horehound's botanical name comes from the Hebrew *marrob*, which translates as bitter juice. Its common name is derived from the Old English term for downy plant, *har hune*.

Lifespan
Hardy perennial

Height
18 in (45 cm)

Flower
Small, white clusters borne from midsummer to early autumn from second year.

Seed
Shiny, dark brown, tear-shaped, ¹/₁₂ in (2 mm) long.

Dried leaves
Use as a medicinal infusion for chest, nasal and sinus congestion.

Stem
Downy, square, branching and white.

Leaf
Wrinkled, heart-shaped and green, with white woolly covering most pronounced towards tip; fruit-scented but bitter flavour; contains vitamin C.

USES

Decorative
FLOWERS Use dried in flower arrangements.

Household
FLOWER Attracts bees to the garden.
LEAF Infuse as a spray for cankerworm in trees. Infuse in fresh milk and set in a dish as a fly killer.

Medicinal
LEAF At the first sign of a cold: finely chop nine small horehound leaves, mix with 1 tbsp (15 ml) honey and eat slowly to ease sore throat or cough. Repeat several times if necessary. Drink a cold infusion to ease digestion and heartburn, and to destroy intestinal worms.

Melilotus officinalis

Melilot/Sweet clover *Leguminosae*

The name melilot derives from *meli* meaning honey, and *lotos* meaning fodder or clover, hence its other name, sweet clover. A native of Europe, Asia and North America, it was once a popular strewing herb and fodder crop, until replaced by common clover.

   M. albus with white flowers originates from the Mediterranean and also decorates the highways of northern Alberta. There it is called Canadian sweet clover, and it is a valued honey plant. Near Gruyère, the Swiss pick a local blue form (*M. caeruleus*) to flavour cheese.

Flower
Yellow, honey-scented, pea-like flowers throughout summer and autumn.

Dried flowers
Provide colour and a little scent for potpourri; use in eye lotion.

Seed
Small, brown, egg-shaped fruit-pod, wrinkled and one-seeded.

Dried leaves
Drying process develops coumarin – a long-lasting scent of new-mown hay – in the leaves.

USES

Culinary
LEAF Use dried leaves in a "cordial" and add small amounts to sausages, pork marinades and rabbit stuffings. Gives an original flavour to beer and cheese.

Household
FLOWER Attracts bees to the garden.
LEAF Scatter dried leaves among clothes to deter moths.

Aromatic
LEAF Add to potpourri.

Stem
Hollow, ridged, round, branching and green – occasionally red.

Lifespan
Hardy biennial. Behaves as an annual if sown in early spring

Height
M. officinalis 2–4 ft (60 cm–1.2 m)
M. albus 7 ft (2.1 m)

Leaf
Unevenly toothed and mid-green, with lighter underside. Faintly aromatic, leaves arranged in threes.

Mentha species

Mints *Labiatae*

In Greek mythology, Minthe was a nymph beloved by Pluto, who transformed her into this scented herb after his jealous wife took drastic action. Mint has been highly esteemed ever since, its value being epitomized by biblical references to the Pharisees collecting tithes in mint, dill and cumin. The Hebrews laid it on synagogue floors, and this idea was repeated centuries later in Italian churches.

Mint as a symbol of hospitality is mentioned by the Roman poet Ovid, who wrote of two peasants, Baucis and Philemon, who scoured their serving board with mint before feeding guests. Gerard enlarged on this theme in 1597, "they use it to strew in places of recreation, pleasure and repose, where feasts and banquets are made". The Romans also used mint to flavour wines and sauces. However, when women who drank wine were threatened with death, secret drinkers would mask their breath by chewing a paste of mint and honey.

Many mint varieties had been introduced into Europe by the ninth century. A monk writing during this time said that there were so many he would rather count the sparks of Vulcan's furnace.

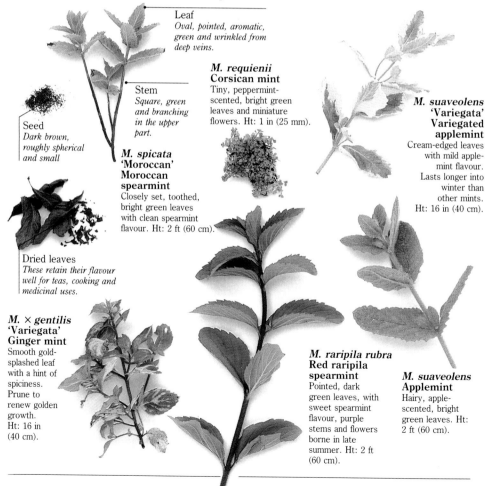

Leaf
Oval, pointed, aromatic, green and wrinkled from deep veins.

Stem
Square, green and branching in the upper part.

Seed
Dark brown, roughly spherical and small

M. requienii
Corsican mint
Tiny, peppermint-scented, bright green leaves and miniature flowers. Ht: 1 in (25 mm).

M. spicata
'Moroccan'
Moroccan spearmint
Closely set, toothed, bright green leaves with clean spearmint flavour. Ht: 2 ft (60 cm).

M. suaveolens
'Variegata'
Variegated applemint
Cream-edged leaves with mild apple-mint flavour. Lasts longer into winter than other mints. Ht: 16 in (40 cm).

Dried leaves
These retain their flavour well for teas, cooking and medicinal uses.

M. × gentilis
'Variegata'
Ginger mint
Smooth gold-splashed leaf with a hint of spiciness. Prune to renew golden growth. Ht: 16 in (40 cm).

M. raripila rubra
Red raripila spearmint
Pointed, dark green leaves, with sweet spearmint flavour, purple stems and flowers borne in late summer. Ht: 2 ft (60 cm).

M. suaveolens
Applemint
Hairy, apple-scented, bright green leaves. Ht: 2 ft (60 cm).

M. pul. 'Upright'
Upright pennyroyal
Smooth, bright green leaves, with strong peppermint scent. Ht: 12 in (30 cm).

M. pulegium
Creeping pennyroyal
Bright green, peppermint-scented leaves, lax stems, which root where they contact earth. Ht: 6 in (15 cm).

M. × villosa
'Alopecuroides'
Bowles' mint
Large, round, hairy, apple/spearmint-scented, mid-green leaves, pink flowers. Ht: 3 ft (1 m).

M. aquatica
'Citrata'
Lemon mint
Smooth, lemon-scented, mid-green leaves. Ht: 16 in (40 cm).

M. spicata
'Crispa'
Curly mint
Crinkled, deep green leaves, with savoury apple scent. Ht: 16 in (40 cm).

M. × piperita
'Crispa'
Crinkle-leaved black peppermint
Vibrant green leaves with strong peppermint scent, purple stems. Ht: 2½ ft (75 cm).

M. piperita
'Citrata'
Eau de Cologne mint
Smooth, bergamot-scented, purple-tinged, dark green leaves, purple stems. Ht: 18 in (45 cm).

Lifespan
Hardy herbaceous perennial

Height
1 in–3 ft (25 mm–1 m); smaller species make good ground cover

USES

Culinary
LEAF Infuse either individual or blended mints as a refreshing tea. (Spearmint and peppermint) Use for mint sauce and with chocolate in rich desserts. Crystallize as decoration.

Household
WHOLE PLANT (Spearmint and peppermint) Grow near roses to deter aphids.
LEAF Scatter fresh or dried leaves around food to deter mice. (Pennyroyal) Strew in cupboards and beds to deter ants and fleas.

Aromatic
LEAF Use in potpourri and herb bags.

Medicinal
LEAF (Peppermints) Infuse as a tea to help digestion, colds and influenza.

Note: *Do not take pennyroyal in large doses when pregnant or suffering from kidney problems.*

Melissa officinalis
Lemon balm *Labiatae*

Lemon balm, it was believed, could completely revive a man and the *London Dispensary*, in 1696, claimed: "Balm, given every morning, will renew youth, strengthen the brain and relieve languishing nature."

In the thirteenth century, Llewelyn, Prince of Glamorgan, regularly took lemon balm tea and lived to be 108, while John Hussey of Sydenham, England, lived to be 116 after 50 years of breakfasting on the same infusion, laced with honey. Its virtue of dispelling melancholy has long been praised by herbal writers and it is still used today in aromatherapy to counter depression.

Seed
Shiny dark brown with white tip, tear-shaped, 1/16 in (1 mm) long.

Dried leaves
Drying lemon balm reduces its scent and medicinal properties.

Leaf
Lemon-scented, hairy, strongly veined, toothed, oval and light green. Leaves turn yellow and harsh-scented when grown in full sun and dry soil.

M.o. 'Aurea' Variegated lemon balm
Gold-splashed, lemon-scented leaves. Grow in light shade, as hot sun scorches leaves, creating pale spots. Ht: 1 ft (30 cm).

Lifespan
Hardy herbaceous perennial

Height
3 ft (1 m)

Flower
Small, two-lipped, pale yellow blooms in clusters, maturing through white to pale blue, borne from summer to autumn.

Stem
Hairy, square, branching and light green, with occasional purple markings.

USES

Decorative
LEAF Use in invalid posies.

Culinary
LEAF Finely chop fresh leaves into salads, white sauces for fish, mayonnaise, sauerkraut, pickled herrings, poultry and pork. Add to fruit salads, jellies, custards, fruit drinks and wine cups. Infuse fresh leaves for melissa tea or float in Indian tea. Add to blended vinegars: try lemon balm with tarragon.

Household
LEAF Add juice to furniture polish. Once a strewing herb.

Aromatic
LEAF Use in potpourri and pillows.

Medicinal
LEAF Infuse as a tea for relief from chronic bronchial catarrh, feverish colds and headaches.

Monarda didyma

Bergamot/Bee balm *Labiatae*

This North American native became a popular garden and tisane plant in Europe after settlers sent back seed. The name *Monarda* honours the Spanish medical botanist Dr Nicholas Monardes of Seville, who wrote his herbal on the flora of America in 1569. He probably called this herb bergamot because its leaf scent resembles that of the Italian bergamot orange, *Citrus medica* var. *bigarradia*, which produces the oil used in aromatherapy and cosmetics. Bergamot became a popular tea substitute in New England after the Boston Tea Party in 1773. Several Indian tribes used wild bergamot for colds.

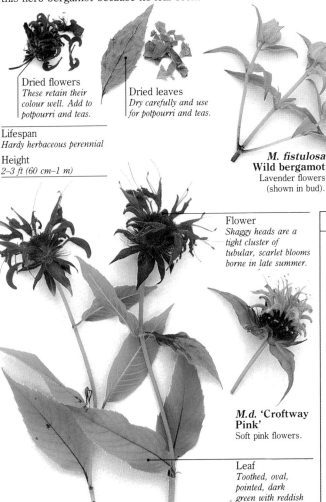

Dried flowers
These retain their colour well. Add to potpourri and teas.

Dried leaves
Dry carefully and use for potpourri and teas.

Lifespan
Hardy herbaceous perennial

Height
2–3 ft (60 cm–1 m)

M. fistulosa
Wild bergamot
Lavender flowers
(shown in bud).

M.d. 'Blue Stocking'
Purple-blue flowers. Leaves are slightly less aromatic than the species.

Flower
Shaggy heads are a tight cluster of tubular, scarlet blooms borne in late summer.

M.d. 'Croftway Pink'
Soft pink flowers.

Leaf
Toothed, oval, pointed, dark green with reddish veining, exuding eau de Cologne scent strongest in young leaves.

Stem
Hairy, hard, ridged, square, branching and tinged red at leaf joints.

USES

Decorative
FLOWER Use fresh and dried in flower arrangements.

Culinary
LEAF Infuse, or simmer for 10 minutes in an enamel saucepan for greater flavour, as a tea. Put fresh leaf into China tea for an Earl Grey flavour. Add sparingly to salads, stuffings, pork.

Household
FLOWER Attracts bumble bees (honey bees are unable to reach nectar unless holes have been made by other insects).

Aromatic
FLOWER AND LEAF Use in potpourri mixtures.

Medicinal
LEAF Infuse as a tea to relieve nausea, flatulence, menstrual pain and insomnia.

Myrrhis odorata
Sweet cicely/Myrrh *Umbelliferae*

The attractive fern-like leaves of sweet cicely are among the first to appear in spring and the last to depart in autumn. The soft green leaves have a myrrh-like scent with overtones of moss and woodland and a hint of aniseed.

An extra bonus of sweet cicely is the cluster of large, upstanding green seeds or, more properly, fruits, which appear in early summer. They have a delicious nutty flavour and characteristic scent and are excellent when eaten raw and with fruit.

A similar North American plant, *Osmorhiza longistylis*, flowers in early summer and has a sweet, aniseed-flavoured root.

Ripe seed
Dark brown, glossy, ridged, ¾ in (19 mm) long.

Unripe seed
Green, ridged, ¾ in (19 mm) long appear late spring. Eat raw.

Flower
Small white flowers appear in late spring. One of the earliest nectarous flowers for bees.

Lifespan	Dried leaves
Hardy herbaceous perennial	*These retain a little scent; occasionally used medicinally, also to decorate paper and candles.*
Height	
3 ft (1 m)	

USES

Culinary
SEED Toss unripe seeds into fruit salads. Chop into ice cream. Use ripe seed whole in cooked dishes such as apple pie; otherwise use crushed.
LEAF Chop finely and stir into salad dressing and omelettes. Add to soups, stews and to cabbage when cooking.
ROOT Chop, peel and serve raw with salad dressing. Cook as a root vegetable.

Medicinal
WHOLE PLANT Considered to be a "wholesome" tonic (especially the root in brandy); aids digestion.

Leaf
Up to 18 in (45 cm) long, downy beneath, green above. White markings may appear as season progresses.

Stem
Hollow, furrowed, downy surface; branching.

Root
Thick brown taproot, occasionally branching, with white, aromatic flesh.

Myrtus communis
Myrtle *Myrtaceae*

In Greek legend, Myrrha was a favourite priestess of Venus, who transformed her into this fragrant evergreen to preserve her from too ardent a suitor. Venus wore a myrtle wreath when Paris awarded her the Golden Apple for beauty. Representing Venus and love, myrtle is often woven into bridal wreaths. An Arabian story tells of Adam, bringing a sprig of myrtle from the bower where he declared his love to Eve, and Shakespeare planned that Venus and Adonis should meet under myrtle shade. In 1640, the apothecary John Parkinson wrote, "we nourish Myrtles with great care for their beautiful aspect, sweet scent and rarity."

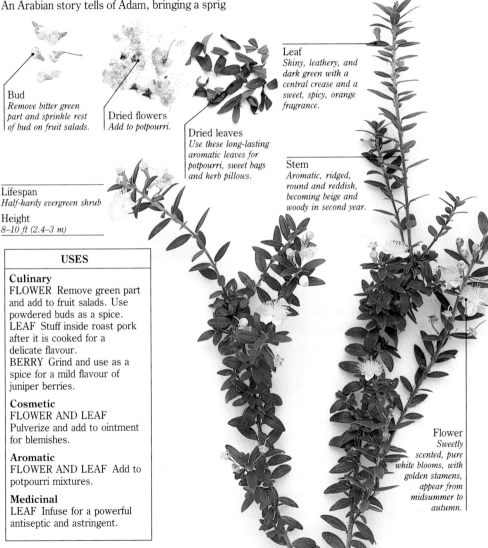

Bud
Remove bitter green part and sprinkle rest of bud on fruit salads.

Dried flowers
Add to potpourri.

Dried leaves
Use these long-lasting aromatic leaves for potpourri, sweet bags and herb pillows.

Leaf
Shiny, leathery, and dark green with a central crease and a sweet, spicy, orange fragrance.

Stem
Aromatic, ridged, round and reddish, becoming beige and woody in second year.

Lifespan
Half-hardy evergreen shrub

Height
8–10 ft (2.4–3 m)

Flower
Sweetly scented, pure white blooms, with golden stamens, appear from midsummer to autumn.

USES

Culinary
FLOWER Remove green part and add to fruit salads. Use powdered buds as a spice.
LEAF Stuff inside roast pork after it is cooked for a delicate flavour.
BERRY Grind and use as a spice for a mild flavour of juniper berries.

Cosmetic
FLOWER AND LEAF Pulverize and add to ointment for blemishes.

Aromatic
FLOWER AND LEAF Add to potpourri mixtures.

Medicinal
LEAF Infuse for a powerful antiseptic and astringent.

Nepeta cataria

Catnip/Catmint *Labiatae*

The name *Nepeta* may derive from the Roman town Nepeti, where catnip was cultivated when it was more highly valued than today. It had a reputation as a seasoning and medicinal herb, and in less favourable times the mildly hallucinogenic dried leaves were smoked to relieve the pressures of life. Set in a border, catnip can be a pretty plant, with its whorls of lavender or white flowers attracting the bees, if it is not damaged by cats. These animals will lie in the centre of the plant, rubbing the leaves in a state of sheer bliss, thus giving catnip its common name.

The smaller catmint *N. mussinii*, receives less attention from cats, and is traditionally planted in front of lavender and roses.

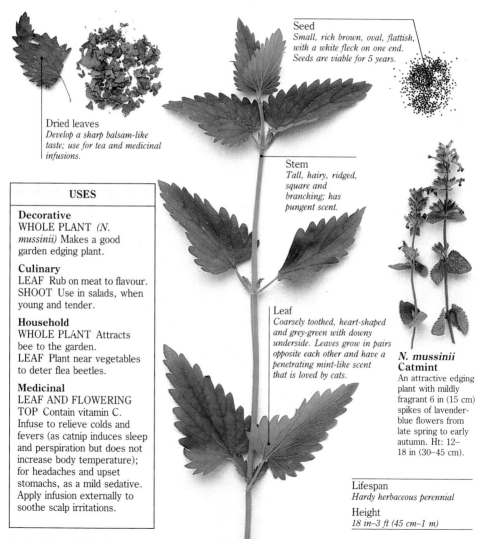

Seed
Small, rich brown, oval, flattish, with a white fleck on one end. Seeds are viable for 5 years.

Dried leaves
Develop a sharp balsam-like taste; use for tea and medicinal infusions.

Stem
Tall, hairy, ridged, square and branching; has pungent scent.

Leaf
Coarsely toothed, heart-shaped and grey-green with downy underside. Leaves grow in pairs opposite each other and have a penetrating mint-like scent that is loved by cats.

N. mussinii Catmint
An attractive edging plant with mildly fragrant 6 in (15 cm) spikes of lavender-blue flowers from late spring to early autumn. Ht: 12–18 in (30–45 cm).

USES

Decorative
WHOLE PLANT *(N. mussinii)* Makes a good garden edging plant.

Culinary
LEAF Rub on meat to flavour.
SHOOT Use in salads, when young and tender.

Household
WHOLE PLANT Attracts bee to the garden.
LEAF Plant near vegetables to deter flea beetles.

Medicinal
LEAF AND FLOWERING TOP Contain vitamin C. Infuse to relieve colds and fevers (as catnip induces sleep and perspiration but does not increase body temperature); for headaches and upset stomachs, as a mild sedative. Apply infusion externally to soothe scalp irritations.

Lifespan
Hardy herbaceous perennial

Height
18 in–3 ft (45 cm–1 m)

Ocimum basilicum

Basil *Labiatae*

This important culinary herb, with its warm spicy flavour, sends cooks into poetic raptures. A native of India, basil is held in reverence as a plant imbued with divine essence, and therefore the Indians chose this herb upon which to swear their oaths in court. Basil was found growing around Christ's tomb after the resurrection, so some Greek Orthodox churches use it to prepare the holy water, and pots of basil are set below church altars.

There are many varieties of basil, including bush basil, which is a South American native. In Haiti, it belongs to the pagan love goddess Erzulie, as a powerful protector, and in rural Mexico it is sometimes carried in pockets to return a lover's roving eye.

Seed
Dark brown, faceted, tear-shaped, ¹/₁₆ in (1 mm) long.

Dried leaves
Pulverize to release the clove scent and use in potpourri and scented beads.

O.b. 'Citriodorum'
Lemon basil
Lemony scented, green leaves, white flowers.
Ht: 12 in (30 cm).

O.b. 'Purpurascens'
Dark opal basil
Crinkled, purple leaves with good medium flavour, pale pink flowers.

Flower
Small, scented, whitish blooms, in circular clusters of six, appear in late summer.

Leaf
Large, toothed, oval, pointed and bright green, with a warm yet fresh, strong, clove-like scent.

Stem
Hairy, finely ridged, square, branching and light green to reddish at base.

Lifespan
Tender annual

Height
18 in (45 cm)

USES

Culinary
LEAF Pound with oil or tear with fingers rather than chop. Add at last minute to cooked dishes. Sprinkle over salads and sliced tomatoes. Basil's rich pungent flavour complements garlic. Used in pesto sauce and many Mediterranean dishes, and to flavour blended vinegars.

Household
WHOLE PLANT Place pots on windowsills to deter flies.

Medicinal
LEAF Steep a few leaves in wine for several hours as a tonic. Infuse as a tea to aid digestion. Basil has many uses in aromatherapy.

Oenothera biennis

Evening primrose *Onagraceae*

A plant for a moonlit garden: the clear yellow flowers unclasp their hooked cover at twilight and open their blossom to the moon. As the season progresses, the flowers often stay open all day as well.

Though probably grown in nineteenth-century monastery gardens, the evening primrose was overlooked by the Austrian monk Gregor Mendel when choosing plants for his famous experiments into inheritance. However, it is now grown by geneticists to demonstrate the principles of heredity. Medical research is also currently exploring ways in which the seeds, which contain the rare gamma-linoleic acid, may alleviate premenstrual tension, menopausal discomfort,

psoriasis, reduce thrombosis and control multiple sclerosis and other degenerative diseases. The increasing uses of this seed may well signal a time when whole fields billow with these glorious yellow flowers.

Lifespan
Hardy biennial

Height
3–6 ft (1–2 m)

Flower
Fragrant clear yellow flowers, 3 in (8 cm) across, open from early summer to mid-autumn.

Seed
Beige, round, oily; contains gamma-linoleic acid and unknown anti-coagulant compounds of interest to medical researchers.

Leaf
Long, oval, pointed and mid-green, arranged in rosettes the first year; along the stem in the second.

Root
Thick and conical, with yellow outside and white inside.

USES

Culinary
ROOT Boil root, which tastes like sweet parsnip. Pickle and toss in salads.

Medicinal
SEED Take evening primrose oil capsules for premenstrual tension, menopausal discomfort and psoriasis.
LEAF AND STEM Infuse peeled "bark" and leaves to soothe cough spasms.

Stem
Sturdy, rough, hairy and reddish.

Onopordum acanthium

Cotton thistle *Compositae*

Readers of A.A. Milne's *Winnie the Pooh* will know how fond donkeys are of thistles, and the botanic name of this herb derives from the Greek *onos*, meaning "an ass", and *perdon*, meaning "I disperse wind". This perhaps provides a clue as to why the character Eeyore led such a solitary and sorrowful existence.

   O. acanthium is thought to be the true Scotch thistle, the emblem of Scotland. This symbol was firmly fixed by 1503, when the poet Dunbar wrote "The Thrissill and the Rose" on the union of the Scottish James IV and the English Princess Margaret. The Order of the Thistle was instituted in 1540.

Flower
Magenta-purple, tufted blooms, 2 in (5 cm) across, borne in second summer.

Stem
Spiny, winged stem of triangular section; covered with fine silvery down.

Dried leaves
These were once used medicinally. Down used to be collected for stuffing pillows.

Seed
Dark brown, oval, faceted, ¼ in (6 mm) long.

Leaf
Long, narrow, toothed with prickles, green with white down.

First-year plant
Clusters of silvery leaves appear in first season; tall, flowering stems then grow in second season.

Lifespan
Hardy biennial

Height
9 ft (2.7 m)

Root
Dark brown taproot, with beige side roots and white astringent flesh.

USES

Culinary
FLOWER Prepare and cook large disc containing the florets in the same way as globe artichokes: remove petals and tough outer bracts and boil or steam until tender.
STEM Blanch and peel young stems. Eat raw with oil and vinegar, or steam and serve in the same way as asparagus.

Medicinal
ROOT Decoction diminishes mucous discharges.

Origanum species

Marjorams & Oregano *Labiatae*

The Greeks have given us the legends and the name of this ancient culinary herb: *oros ganos*, joy-of-the-mountain. Those who have visited Greece, where oregano (wild marjoram) covers the hillsides and scents the summer air, would probably endorse the name. The sweet spicy scent of sweet marjoram was reputedly created by Aphrodite as a symbol of happiness. The Greeks enjoyed its scent after a bath, when marjoram oil was massaged into their foreheads and hair. Even in ancient Egypt oregano's power to heal was well known.

Sweet marjoram was introduced into Europe in the Middle Ages and was in demand by ladies "to put in nosegays, sweet bags and sweet washing waters". Its leaves were also rubbed over heavy oak furniture and floors to give a fragrant polish. In thundery weather, dairymaids would place marjoram by pails of fresh milk in the curious belief that this plant would preserve its sweetness. This task might well have been followed by marjoram tea – advised by the herbalist Gerard for those who "are given to overmuch sighing".

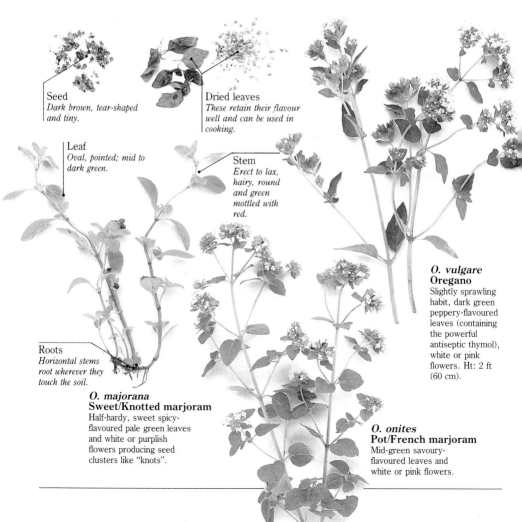

Seed
Dark brown, tear-shaped and tiny.

Dried leaves
These retain their flavour well and can be used in cooking.

Leaf
Oval, pointed; mid to dark green.

Stem
Erect to lax, hairy, round and green mottled with red.

**O. vulgare
Oregano**
Slightly sprawling habit, dark green peppery-flavoured leaves (containing the powerful antiseptic thymol), white or pink flowers. Ht: 2 ft (60 cm).

Roots
Horizontal stems root wherever they touch the soil.

**O. majorana
Sweet/Knotted marjoram**
Half-hardy, sweet spicy-flavoured pale green leaves and white or purplish flowers producing seed clusters like "knots".

**O. onites
Pot/French marjoram**
Mid-green savoury-flavoured leaves and white or pink flowers.

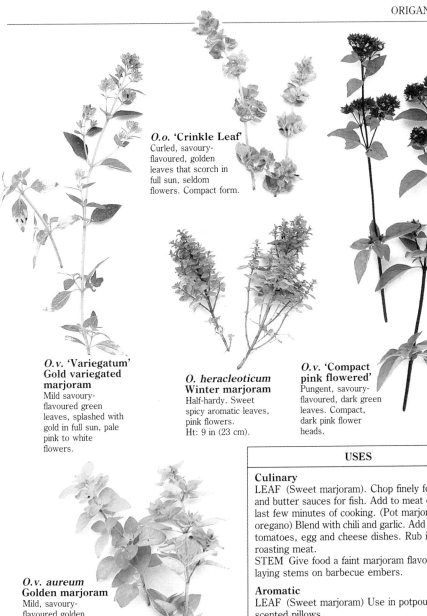

O.o. 'Crinkle Leaf'
Curled, savoury-flavoured, golden leaves that scorch in full sun, seldom flowers. Compact form.

O.v. 'Variegatum' Gold variegated marjoram
Mild savoury-flavoured green leaves, splashed with gold in full sun, pale pink to white flowers.

O. heracleoticum Winter marjoram
Half-hardy. Sweet spicy aromatic leaves, pink flowers.
Ht: 9 in (23 cm).

O.v. 'Compact pink flowered'
Pungent, savoury-flavoured, dark green leaves. Compact, dark pink flower heads.

O.v. aureum Golden marjoram
Mild, savoury-flavoured golden leaves that scorch in full sun.

Lifespan
Hardy herbaceous or shrubby perennial

Height
6 in–2 ft (15–60 cm)

USES

Culinary
LEAF (Sweet marjoram). Chop finely for salads and butter sauces for fish. Add to meat dishes in last few minutes of cooking. (Pot marjoram, oregano) Blend with chili and garlic. Add to pizza, tomatoes, egg and cheese dishes. Rub into roasting meat.
STEM Give food a faint marjoram flavour by laying stems on barbecue embers.

Aromatic
LEAF (Sweet marjoram) Use in potpourri and scented pillows.

Medicinal
FLOWERING TOP (Sweet marjoram) Infuse as a tea for colds and headaches. Add a decoction or essential oil to bathwater as relaxant.
(Oregano) Infuse as a tea for coughs, nervous headaches and irritability.

Papaver species

Poppies *Papaveraceae*

Around 3000 BC, the Sumerians revered
poppies as cult plants. The species gives us
flowers described as the handmaidens of
cornfields, voluptuous garden plants, an oil,
edible seed and opium.

The laboratory analysis of the opium poppy
is historically the transition from the magical
and religious use of plants to scientific use. It
also highlights the dangers of reducing plants to
their chemical components. The opium poppy
gives us morphine and codeine, our most
important painkillers, and also heroin, which is
addictive and results in much human misery.
Many countries strictly control its growth.

Seed
*Minute, blue-grey
and kidney shaped
(called maw seed).
Indian or white
flower seed is cream
and smaller; flavours
are similar.*

**P. rhoeas
Field poppy/Corn
poppy**
Long, slender stem
with solitary, dark-
centred, red flower.
Ripe seed capsule
has ring of pores
near top.

Flower
*White, pink, purple or dull red flowers
appear in late summer.
There is also a
double form
(below).*

**P. somniferum
Opium poppy**

Stem
*Tall, slightly
hairy, rigid and
occasionally
branching.*

Leaf
*Smooth, deeply lobed,
unsymmetrical and
pale grey-green. Upper
leaves clasp the stem.*

Seed head
*Bulbous, flat-capped,
hairless capsule, becoming
woody.*

Lifespan
Hardy annual

Height
*2½–4 ft
(75 cm–1.2 m)*

USES

Decorative
WHOLE PLANT (Field poppy) Make a "poppy
doll": bend back petals and tie around stem with
grass; use dried stalk for arms.

Culinary
SEED Sprinkle on bread, cake and biscuits.

Note: *All parts of opium poppy except ripe seed are
dangerous and should be used only by trained
medical staff.*

Pelargonium species

Scented geraniums *Geraniaceae*

Most pelargoniums originate from the Cape of Good Hope in Africa and although they were introduced to Britain in 1632, it was not until 1847 that the French perfume industry realized their aromatic potential. From the leaf of the rose-scented geranium, *P. graveolens*, the French distilled an oil which is popular in cosmetics and important in aromatherapy.

However, it is an easy oil to adulterate, so purchase it from a reputable supplier.

In winter, the Victorians brought pot-grown pelargoniums indoors, and positioned them so that their long skirts would brush against the plants, thus scenting a room. In summer, they moved the pots outdoors and put them along paths for a similar effect.

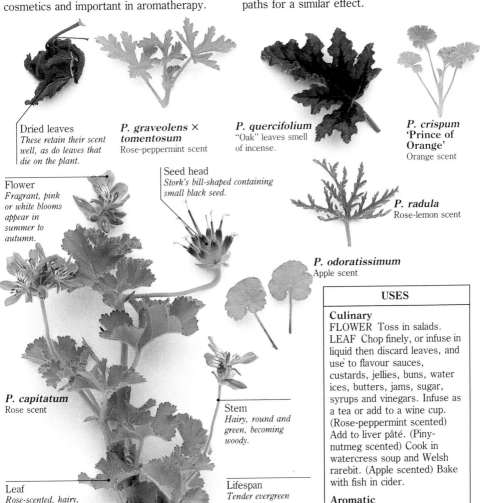

Dried leaves
These retain their scent well, as do leaves that die on the plant.

P. graveolens × tomentosum
Rose-peppermint scent

P. quercifolium
"Oak" leaves smell of incense.

P. crispum 'Prince of Orange'
Orange scent

Flower
Fragrant, pink or white blooms appear in summer to autumn.

Seed head
Stork's bill-shaped containing small black seed.

P. radula
Rose-lemon scent

P. odoratissimum
Apple scent

P. capitatum
Rose scent

Stem
Hairy, round and green, becoming woody.

Leaf
Rose-scented, hairy, toothed, mid-green, with five to seven lobes.

Lifespan
Tender evergreen perennial

Height
1–3 ft (30 cm–1 m)

USES

Culinary
FLOWER Toss in salads.
LEAF Chop finely, or infuse in liquid then discard leaves, and use to flavour sauces, custards, jellies, buns, water ices, butters, jams, sugar, syrups and vinegars. Infuse as a tea or add to a wine cup. (Rose-peppermint scented) Add to liver pâté. (Piny-nutmeg scented) Cook in watercress soup and Welsh rarebit. (Apple scented) Bake with fish in cider.

Aromatic
LEAF Use in potpourri and scented pillows.

Petroselinum crispum

Parsley *Umbelliferae*

Held in high esteem by the Greeks, parsley was used to crown victors at the Isthmian Games and to decorate tombs, being linked with Archemorus, the herald of death. The Greeks also planted parsley and rue along the edges of herb beds, but, although they used parsley medicinally, and Homer recorded that warriors fed parsley to their horses, it appears that the Romans were the first to use it as a food. They consumed parsley in quantity and made garlands for banquet guests to discourage intoxication and to counter strong odours.

There are many excellent parsley varieties, including Hamburg parsley (*P.c. tuberosum*). This has flat leaves and a large, edible, well-flavoured root. All parsleys are rich in vitamins, minerals and antiseptic chlorophyll, making it a beneficial as well as attractive garnishing herb.

Seed
Small, grey-brown and sickle-shaped with cream ridges; contains apiole, which can be toxic.

Dried leaves
These retain most flavour when dried quickly. Use in cooking and boil with stem for a yellow-green dye.

**P. crispum
Curled parsley**

USES

Culinary
LEAF Add raw to salads. Finely chop and sprinkle over sandwiches, egg dishes, vegetable soups, fish, and boiled potatoes. Add to mayonnaise and many classic sauces. When cooked, parsley enhances other flavours, but add towards end of cooking time. Use in bouquet garni.
ROOT Use in bouquet garni. Add to soups and stews. (Hamburg parsley) Boil as a root vegetable. To use raw, grate into salads.

Cosmetic
LEAF Infuse as a hair tonic and conditioner.

Medicinal
LEAF Chew raw to freshen the breath and promote healthy skin.

Leaf
Finely cut, curled with toothed margins and bright green, with fresh taste; rich in vitamins A, B and C, salts of iron, calcium, magnesium and chlorophyll.

Root
Thin, brownish-yellow, smooth taproot with tiny hair-like roots; contains strongest parsley flavour.

Stem
Solid, ridged, semi-circular, branching and mid-green; more strongly flavoured than leaves.

**P.c. neapolitanum
Italian, or French, parsley**
Flat, cut, dark green leaves with stronger, coarser flavour than the species, and edible, succulent stems.
Ht: 2 ft (60 cm).

Lifespan
Hardy biennial

Height
15 in (38 cm)

Pimpinella anisum

Anise/Aniseed *Umbelliferae*

This graceful feathery annual has been cultivated for centuries. Around 1500 BC, the Egyptians grew their native anise in quantity to supply food, drink and medicine from its leaves and seed. The fields of Tuscany were planted with anise by the Romans, who developed a special spiced cake, *mustaceus*, as a finishing dish for feasts. It was baked with anise, cumin and other digestive herbs and established a tradition thought to be the precursor of spiced wedding cakes. Charlemagne's edict of the ninth century, that every herb growing in St Gall's monastery should be planted on all his royal estates, spread anise throughout Europe. It became so valued in England that its import was taxed.

Flower
Small, star-like, white blooms, in clusters, appear in late summer.

Stem
Ridged, round, branching and mid-green.

Seed
Aromatic, light grey-brown, ridged, elongated, pointed egg-shape; requires a sunny summer to ripen fully.

Lifespan
Half-hardy annual

Height
12–18 in (30–45 cm); erect or prostrate

Leaf
Aromatic, toothed, round, lobed and mid-green lower leaves; finely divided and feathery upper leaves.

USES

Culinary
SEED Use whole or crushed in breads, cakes, apple pies, apple sauces, creams and confectionery. Add to cream cheese, pickles, curries and water for boiling shellfish.
FLOWER Mix into fruit salads.
LEAF Add to fruit salads with figs, dates and chestnuts. Use to garnish.
STEM AND ROOT Mix into soups and stews.

Aromatic
SEED Use crushed in potpourri.

Medicinal
SEED Infuse as a comforting antiseptic tea for colds and coughs.

Poterium sanguisorba (Sanguisorba officinalis)

Salad burnet *Rosaceae*

The dainty decorative leaves of this refreshing herb belie its hardiness – its leaves often survive a mild winter. Should they fail to do so, they are then among the earliest leaves to appear in spring. Salad burnet, which the Pilgrim Fathers carried to New England, was thought by Gerard to "make the hart merry and glad, as also being put in wine, to which it yeeldeth a certaine grace in the drinking". The young leaves have a pleasant if somewhat sharp cucumber flavour. The green flowering globes expand amid tiny red dots with the unfulfilled promise of an explosion of colour. This pretty plant was recommended by Francis Bacon to be set in alleys with wild thyme and water mint, with the intention that it should "perfume the air most delightfully, being trodden on and crushed".

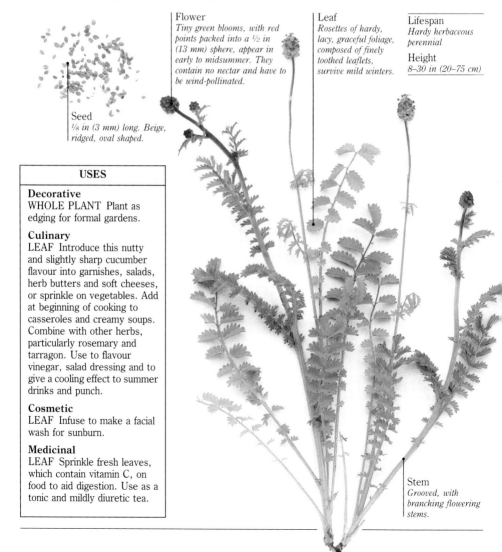

Flower
Tiny green blooms, with red points packed into a ½ in (13 mm) sphere, appear in early to midsummer. They contain no nectar and have to be wind-pollinated.

Seed
⅛ in (3 mm) long. Beige, ridged, oval shaped.

Leaf
Rosettes of hardy, lacy, graceful foliage, composed of finely toothed leaflets, survive mild winters.

Lifespan
Hardy herbaceous perennial

Height
8–30 in (20–75 cm)

Stem
Grooved, with branching flowering stems.

USES

Decorative
WHOLE PLANT Plant as edging for formal gardens.

Culinary
LEAF Introduce this nutty and slightly sharp cucumber flavour into garnishes, salads, herb butters and soft cheeses, or sprinkle on vegetables. Add at beginning of cooking to casseroles and creamy soups. Combine with other herbs, particularly rosemary and tarragon. Use to flavour vinegar, salad dressing and to give a cooling effect to summer drinks and punch.

Cosmetic
LEAF Infuse to make a facial wash for sunburn.

Medicinal
LEAF Sprinkle fresh leaves, which contain vitamin C, on food to aid digestion. Use as a tonic and mildly diuretic tea.

Primula veris and *Primula vulgaris*

Cowslip & Primrose *Primulaceae*

These two flowers of spring never fail to gladden the heart. Favourite of favourites, the primrose is the first to appear. Although picked and used in making both jams and cosmetics, its real attraction is the soft yellow simplicity of its perfect flower. Its leaves are particularly enjoyed by silkworms.

The cheerful, nodding cowslip, the "Keys of St Peter", has a unique milky scent likened to a cow's breath or to that of a new baby. In some areas, it has almost been picked to extinction, mainly to make cowslip wine, but also for the childish delight of sucking the nectar from the flowers.

USES
Culinary
FLOWER (Cowslip) Use for jam and wine. (Primrose) Eat raw in salads.
LEAF (Cowslip) Use in salads and for meat stuffing. (Primrose) Boil as a vegetable.
Aromatic
FLOWER AND ROOT Use in potpourri.
Medicinal
WHOLE PLANT (Primrose) Infuse to make a cough remedy and mild sedative.
LEAF (Primrose) Use for a medicinal tea.

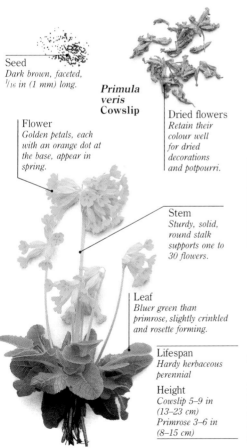

Seed
Dark brown, faceted, $^1/_{16}$ in (1 mm) long.

Primula veris Cowslip

Flower
Golden petals, each with an orange dot at the base, appear in spring.

Dried flowers
Retain their colour well for dried decorations and potpourri.

Stem
Sturdy, solid, round stalk supports one to 30 flowers.

Leaf
Bluer green than primrose, slightly crinkled and rosette forming.

Lifespan
Hardy herbaceous perennial

Height
*Cowslip 5–9 in (13–23 cm)
Primrose 3–6 in (8–15 cm)*

Dried flowers
These make a mild, sedative tea.

Primula vulgaris Primrose

Seed
Dark brown, faceted, $^1/_{16}$ in (1 mm) long.

Flower
Pale yellow, heart-shaped petals with deeper yellow centres. One flower per stalk; multiples are hybrids.

Leaf
Crinkled, oblong and yellow-green.

Root
Tan, aromatic rootstalk with small, pale yellow roots.

Rosmarinus officinalis

Rosemary *Labiatae*

Rosemary, "dew of the sea", holds a special place in the affections of many as the essence of a summer herb garden. It has been used by cooks and apothecaries from earliest times. With a reputation for strengthening the memory, it soon became the emblem of fidelity for lovers.

In times past, resinous rosemary was burned in sick chambers to purify the air and branches were strewn in law courts as a protection from "gaol fever". During the plague, it was carried in neck pouches to be sniffed when travelling through suspicious areas. In some Mediterranean villages, linen is spread over rosemary to dry, so the sun will extract its moth-repellent aroma. Rosemary also makes a good garden hedge.

Apart from common rosemary, there are several named varieties, including a vigorous new upright form, 'Sawyer's Selection', with large, mauve-blue flowers, which can reach 8 ft (2.5 m) within three years. There is a variable gold-tipped form, and ancient texts mention a silver variegated form.

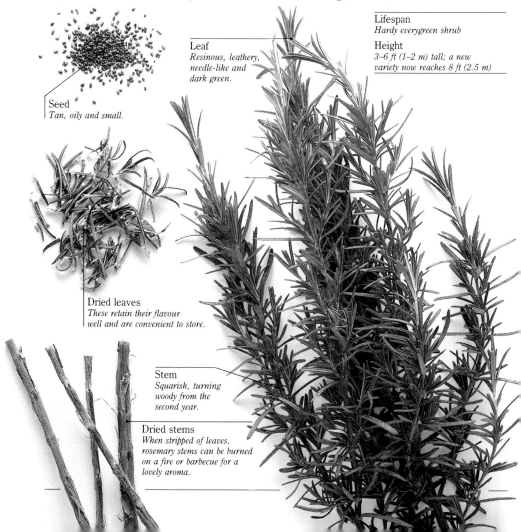

Seed
Tan, oily and small.

Leaf
Resinous, leathery, needle-like and dark green.

Lifespan
Hardy everygreen shrub

Height
3–6 ft (1–2 m) tall; a new variety now reaches 8 ft (2.5 m)

Dried leaves
These retain their flavour well and are convenient to store.

Stem
Squarish, turning woody from the second year.

Dried stems
When stripped of leaves, rosemary stems can be burned on a fire or barbecue for a lovely aroma.

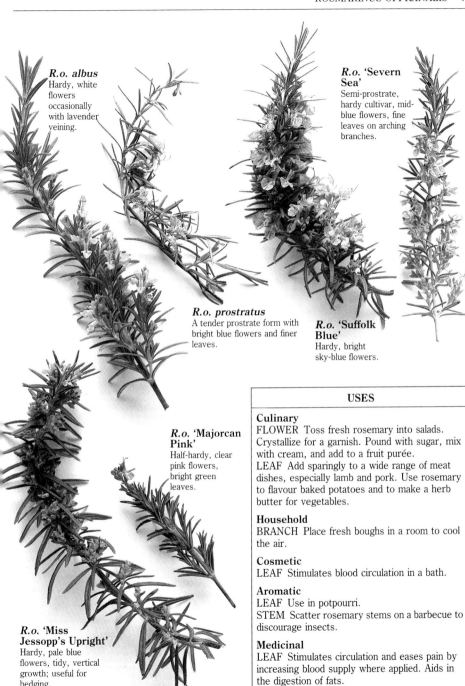

R.o. albus
Hardy, white
flowers
occasionally
with lavender
veining.

**_R.o._ 'Severn
Sea'**
Semi-prostrate,
hardy cultivar, mid-
blue flowers, fine
leaves on arching
branches.

R.o. prostratus
A tender prostrate form with
bright blue flowers and finer
leaves.

**_R.o._ 'Suffolk
Blue'**
Hardy, bright
sky-blue flowers.

**_R.o._ 'Majorcan
Pink'**
Half-hardy, clear
pink flowers,
bright green
leaves.

**_R.o._ 'Miss
Jessopp's Upright'**
Hardy, pale blue
flowers, tidy, vertical
growth; useful for
hedging.

USES
Culinary
FLOWER Toss fresh rosemary into salads. Crystallize for a garnish. Pound with sugar, mix with cream, and add to a fruit purée. LEAF Add sparingly to a wide range of meat dishes, especially lamb and pork. Use rosemary to flavour baked potatoes and to make a herb butter for vegetables.
Household
BRANCH Place fresh boughs in a room to cool the air.
Cosmetic
LEAF Stimulates blood circulation in a bath.
Aromatic
LEAF Use in potpourri. STEM Scatter rosemary stems on a barbecue to discourage insects.
Medicinal
LEAF Stimulates circulation and eases pain by increasing blood supply where applied. Aids in the digestion of fats.

Rosa species

Roses *Rosaceae*

For sheer fragrance and beauty, the rose has no equal. It reigns supreme. Its cultivation has spread from Persia, bringing inspiration to artists, warriors and lovers in every land. Cleopatra seduced Antony knee deep in roses, and Roman banquets were garlanded with petals. In 1187, on entering Jerusalem, the Muslim conqueror Saladin even had the Omar mosque washed in rosewater to purify it.

This "gift of the angels" was also popular for its gentle healing powers. Rose essence is among the safest healing substances known, and the delicate flavour of rosewater is excellent for cooking. Rose wine dates from ancient Persia, and the sweet Turkish delight is made with rosewater. Rose petals were historically valued for jam, vinegar and pies and these delights are now being rediscovered.

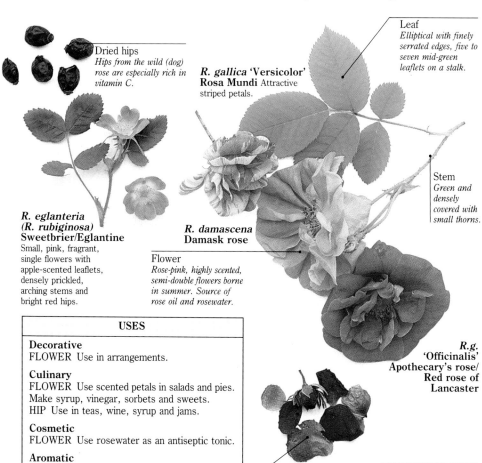

Dried hips
Hips from the wild (dog) rose are especially rich in vitamin C.

R. gallica 'Versicolor'
Rosa Mundi Attractive striped petals.

Leaf
Elliptical with finely serrated edges, five to seven mid-green leaflets on a stalk.

Stem
Green and densely covered with small thorns.

R. eglanteria (R. rubiginosa)
Sweetbrier/Eglantine
Small, pink, fragrant, single flowers with apple-scented leaflets, densely prickled, arching stems and bright red hips.

R. damascena
Damask rose

Flower
Rose-pink, highly scented, semi-double flowers borne in summer. Source of rose oil and rosewater.

R.g.
'Officinalis'
Apothecary's rose/
Red rose of
Lancaster

USES
Decorative
FLOWER Use in arrangements.
Culinary
FLOWER Use scented petals in salads and pies. Make syrup, vinegar, sorbets and sweets. HIP Use in teas, wine, syrup and jams.
Cosmetic
FLOWER Use rosewater as an antiseptic tonic.
Aromatic
FLOWER Add petals to potpourri.
Medicinal
LEAF Infuse for a tonic and astringent tea.

Dried petals and buds
Pick petals once flowers open as a main ingredient in potpourri and sweet bags.

Lifespan
Hardy shrub

Height
4–8 ft (1.2–2.4 m)

Rumex acetosa

Sorrel *Polygonaceae*

Prolific flowering stalks of sorrel, rising above grass on an acid soil, can cause a hay meadow to assume a reddish tint at harvest time. On a hot summer day, haymakers would frequently eat the succulent leaves to quench their thirst. Most sorrel leaves have an intriguing sharp acidic flavour, which is used to advantage in many dishes. However, buckler leaf sorrel (*R. scutatus*) boasts a milder lemony zest but still with an interesting sharpness. It is preferred by the French for sorrel soup. Confusingly, both species have been called French sorrel and garden sorrel.

Flower
Whorled reddish-green spikes borne during summer. Remove to ensure continued supply of succulent young leaves.

Seed
Small, rich brown, shiny, pointed and ridged with three curved facets.

R. scutatus
Buckler leaf sorrel
Silvery patches on light green leaves, which have sharp flavour; a "more grateful acidity" than broad leaf sorrel.

R. acetosa
Broad leaf sorrel
Fresh sap-green leaves that are almost tasteless in early spring: acidity develops as season progresses.

Leaf
Lance-shaped with broad base, containing potassium and vitamins A, B1 and C.

Stem
Juicy, ridged and reddish.

Lifespan
Hardy perennial

Height
R. acetosa 2–4 ft (60 cm– 1.2 m); R. scutatus 6–18 in (15–45 cm)

USES

Culinary
LEAF Eat raw young leaves (especially *R. scutatus*) in salads (reducing vinegar or lemon in dressing) and in sorrel soup. Cook like spinach, changing the cooking water once to reduce acidity. Use to season vegetable soups, omelettes, lamb and beef dishes, and in sauces.

Household
LEAF Use juice to bleach rust, mould and ink stains from linen, wicker and silver.

Ruta graveolens

Garden rue *Rutaceae*

Leonardo da Vinci and Michelangelo both claimed that, owing to rue's metaphysical powers, their eyesight and creative inner vision had been improved. Branches of rue were used to sprinkle holy water before high mass, and it was an important strewing herb and anti-plague plant. Robbers who stripped plague victims protected themselves with "Vinegar of the four thieves", rue being an ingredient. Rue is shown on the heraldic Order of the Thistle and inspired the design of the suit of clubs in playing cards.

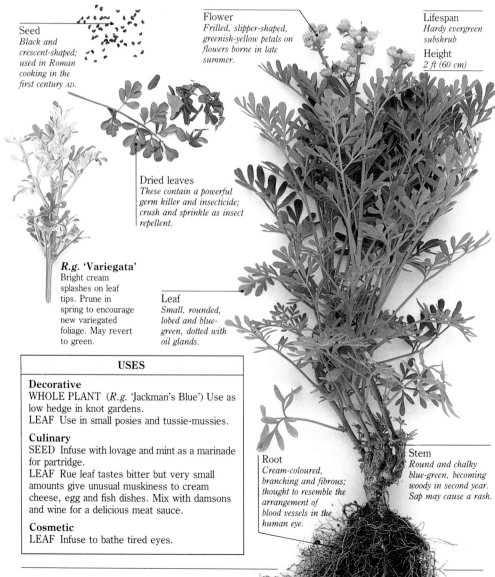

Seed
Black and crescent-shaped; used in Roman cooking in the first century AD.

Flower
Frilled, slipper-shaped, greenish-yellow petals on flowers borne in late summer.

Lifespan
Hardy evergreen subshrub

Height
2 ft (60 cm)

Dried leaves
These contain a powerful germ killer and insecticide; crush and sprinkle as insect repellent.

R.g. 'Variegata'
Bright cream splashes on leaf tips. Prune in spring to encourage new variegated foliage. May revert to green.

Leaf
Small, rounded, lobed and blue-green, dotted with oil glands.

Root
Cream-coloured, branching and fibrous; thought to resemble the arrangement of blood vessels in the human eye.

Stem
Round and chalky blue-green, becoming woody in second year. Sap may cause a rash.

USES

Decorative
WHOLE PLANT (*R.g.* 'Jackman's Blue') Use as low hedge in knot gardens.
LEAF Use in small posies and tussie-mussies.

Culinary
SEED Infuse with lovage and mint as a marinade for partridge.
LEAF Rue leaf tastes bitter but very small amounts give unusual muskiness to cream cheese, egg and fish dishes. Mix with damsons and wine for a delicious meat sauce.

Cosmetic
LEAF Infuse to bathe tired eyes.

Santolina chamaecyparissus (S. incana)

Santolina *Compositae*

Although it has long been known as cotton lavender, santolina is not a lavender but a member of the daisy family. The whole plant is highly aromatic and has been used to sweeten the air in Mediterranean regions for centuries. Santolina was probably brought into Britain in the sixteenth century by French Huguenot gardeners, who were skilled in creating the popular knot gardens. The three colour forms available make it still a popular plant today for edging and hedging.

Lifespan
Hardy evergreen subshrub

Height
1–2 ft (30–60 cm)

S. rosmarinifolia subsp. canescens
Yellow flowers and small, rosemary-like, willow-green leaves, which have a less pungent, sweeter scent than *S.c.*

Santolina chamaecyparissus

Flower
Bright yellow button flowers, one on each stalk, borne from mid- to late summer.

**S. virens
S. rosmarinifolia subsp. rosmarinifolia (S. viridis)**
Bright yellow button flowers and thread-like, pungent, vivid green leaves.

Leaf
Pungent, finely divided, silver-grey, evergreen foliage forming low mounds.

S. pinnata neapolitana
Bright yellow button flowers and silver-grey leaves which are longer, more feathery and slightly fruitier scented than *S.c.*
Ht: 2½ ft (75 cm)

Stem
Soft, round and white felted; greenish-brown and woody in second season.

USES

Decorative
WHOLE PLANT Use for hedges, edging and knot gardens. Create patterns with the three colours available.
FLOWER Dry for decorations.

Household
BRANCH To deter moths and other insects, lay in drawers, under carpets, hang in closets and place among books.

Aromatic
LEAF Add to potpourri.

Medicinal
FLOWER AND LEAF A decoction is thought to kill intestinal worms and to give mild stimulation to menstrual flow.
LEAF Mix in herbal tobacco with chamomile and coltsfoot.

Salvia officinalis

Sage *Labiatae*

The sage plant has been praised highly throughout history and on many continents for its powers of longevity. "How can a man grow old who has sage in his garden?" is the substance of an ancient proverb much quoted in China and Persia and parts of Europe. It was so valued by the Chinese in the seventeenth century that Dutch merchants found the Chinese would trade three chests of China tea for just one of sage leaves.

The name *salvia*, from the Latin *salvere*, to be in good health, to cure, to save, reflects its benevolent reputation. To the Romans it was a sacred herb gathered with ceremony. The appointed person would make sacrifices of bread and wine, wear a white tunic and approach well washed and with feet bare. Roman instructions advised against using iron tools, a sensible edict as iron salts are incompatible with sage.

This powerful healing plant is also a strong culinary herb, often best used on its own. As one chef wrote: "In the grand opera of cooking, sage represents an easily-offended and capricious prima donna. It likes to have the stage almost to itself." However, it is valuable as an aid to digesting fatty foods.

Dried leaves
*Highly aromatic
and pungent.*

Flower
Deep-throated, two-lipped, generally mauve-blue. The white and pink forms are less common.

Seed
Dark brown, ovoid and tiny; form in fruits at the base of each flower.

Leaf
Set in pairs, grey-green often with yellow blotches on old leaves. Thick, downy and "pebbly" with pronounced veining on underside.

Lifespan
Hardy evergreen shrub

Height
1–2 ft 6 in (30–75 cm)

Stem
Square, green with fine hairs; woody from the second year.

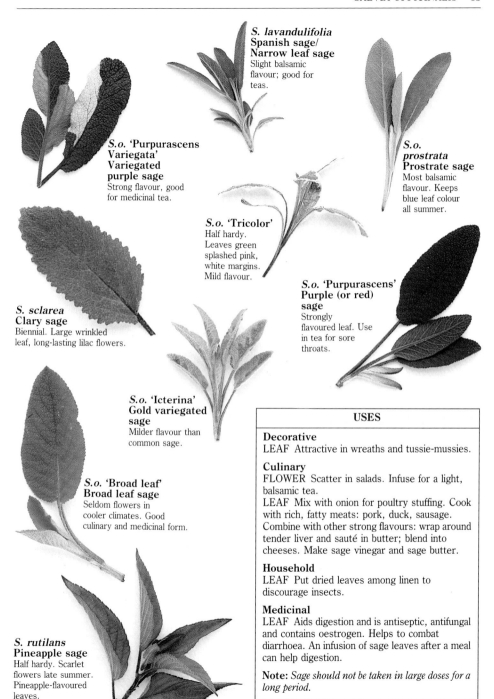

S. lavandulifolia
Spanish sage/
Narrow leaf sage
Slight balsamic
flavour; good for
teas.

S.o. 'Purpurascens
Variegata'
Variegated
purple sage
Strong flavour, good
for medicinal tea.

S.o.
prostrata
Prostrate sage
Most balsamic
flavour. Keeps
blue leaf colour
all summer.

S.o. 'Tricolor'
Half hardy.
Leaves green
splashed pink,
white margins.
Mild flavour.

S. sclarea
Clary sage
Biennial. Large wrinkled
leaf, long-lasting lilac flowers.

S.o. 'Purpurascens'
Purple (or red)
sage
Strongly
flavoured leaf. Use
in tea for sore
throats.

S.o. 'Icterina'
Gold variegated
sage
Milder flavour than
common sage.

S.o. 'Broad leaf'
Broad leaf sage
Seldom flowers in
cooler climates. Good
culinary and medicinal form.

S. rutilans
Pineapple sage
Half hardy. Scarlet
flowers late summer.
Pineapple-flavoured
leaves.

USES

Decorative
LEAF Attractive in wreaths and tussie-mussies.

Culinary
FLOWER Scatter in salads. Infuse for a light,
balsamic tea.
LEAF Mix with onion for poultry stuffing. Cook
with rich, fatty meats: pork, duck, sausage.
Combine with other strong flavours: wrap around
tender liver and sauté in butter; blend into
cheeses. Make sage vinegar and sage butter.

Household
LEAF Put dried leaves among linen to
discourage insects.

Medicinal
LEAF Aids digestion and is antiseptic, antifungal
and contains oestrogen. Helps to combat
diarrhoea. An infusion of sage leaves after a meal
can help digestion.

Note: *Sage should not be taken in large doses for a*
long period.

Saponaria officinalis

Soapwort *Caryophyllaceae*

Soapwort is worth searching for, as it is a lovely garden herb. It yields a soapy sap which is excellent for revitalizing precious fabrics, and is now used in museums for this purpose. It also exudes the most delicious raspberry-sorbet scent with a hint of clove, thus revealing its family connection with pinks.

In the Middle East, soapwort has been used both as a cleaning agent and as a medicinal herb for skin problems such as eczema, acne and those caused by venereal diseases. For these qualities, as well as for its believed ability to help eliminate toxins, especially from the liver, and soothe poison ivy rashes, soapwort was grown on the nineteenth-century herb farms of the American Shakers.

USES

Culinary
FLOWER Toss on green and fruit salads.

Household
LEAF, STEM AND ROOT Just cover in rain or soft water (not chemically-treated tap water) and boil for 30 minutes; then use soapy liquid to wash and miraculously revive delicate old fabrics.

Aromatic
FLOWER Perfume a room with bouquets of soapwort.

Note: *Soapwort root is poisonous and should not be taken internally.*

Flower
Single, pale pink blooms, 1–1½ in (2.5 cm) across, with a sweet fruit scent, borne in late summer.

Leaf
Oval, pointed and pale green with three parallel veins; sap contains saponin, a lathering substance.

Stem
Sturdy, cylindrical and light green to purple-red at base; contains saponin.

Root
Fibrous rootlets grow on pinky-brown runners, ¼–½ in (6–13 mm) thick. These contain the highest concentration of saponin.

Dried leaves
These contain less saponin than fresh leaves; use for household cleaning.

Lifespan
Hardy herbaceous perennial

Height
18 in–3 ft (45 cm–1 m)

Satureja montana (Satureia montana)

Winter savory *Labiatae*

Savory, with its peppery spiciness, is one of the oldest flavouring herbs and has long been considered an antiseptic herb beneficial to the whole digestive tract. It is also a stimulant and was in demand as an aphrodisiac – a possible reason why it was named *Satureia*, meaning satyr. Virgil, in a poem of country life, described savory as highly aromatic and valuable when planted near beehives. The Romans added savory to sauces and to vinegars, which they used liberally as a flavouring. They also introduced savory into northern Europe, where it became a valued disinfectant strewing herb.

S. spicigera (S. repanda) Creeping winter savory
Rockery carpet of strongly flavoured deep green leaves sprinkled with tiny white flowers in late summer. Ht: 3 in (8 cm).

S. hortensis Summer savory
Annual. Sparser, slightly larger and more rounded leaves than winter savory and pale lilac to white flowers in late summer. Ht: 18 in (45 cm).

Seed
Shiny, mid-brown, elongated sphere, halved lengthways, with tiny tip.

Dried flowering tops
These contain an antiseptic that aids digestion and is used medicinally. Crumble leaves for cooking.

Leaf
Small, narrow, pointed and dark green, gland-dotted and aromatic with a distinctive central vein that creates a fold.

Lifespan
Hardy evergreen subshrub

Height
15 in (38 cm)

Stem
Hairy, square, branching and green, turning reddish-brown; woody in second season.

Root
Dark brown, dense and fibrous.

USES
Decorative WHOLE PLANT A useful edging plant.
Culinary LEAF Cook with beans. Make into savory jelly using grape juice.
Cosmetic FLOWERING TOP Use as an astringent and antiseptic in facial steams or baths for oily skin.
Medicinal FLOWERING TOP Infuse as a tea to stimulate appetite, ease indigestion and flatulence; also use as an antiseptic gargle.

Sempervivum tectorum

Houseleek *Crassulaceae*

According to legend, as a gift from Jupiter for protection from lightning, thunder, fire and witchcraft, houseleek has always been considered a form of home fire insurance. Its wild origins are unknown: even in the fourth century BC, the Greek botanist Theophrastus recorded its presence on walls and roof tiles. The Romans planted courtyard urns of houseleek, and Charlemagne ordered one plant to be grown on every roof.

In the language of flowers, houseleek symbolizes vivacity and industry. It is also one of the oldest first-aid herbs, with similar but reduced healing properties to aloe vera. Houseleek's advantage is that it will survive several degrees of winter frost.

Offset
Houseleek produces small rosettes which develop roots and become separate plants. Occasionally, in midsummer, a spray of 1 in (3 cm) rose-purple flowers will appear on an erect round stem covered with scale-like leaves. The rosette that produced the flower stem then dies.

Leaf
Fleshy and mid-green, forming rosettes 2–6 in (5–15 cm) wide, with spiny-pointed maroon tips.

Lifespan
Hardy evergreen perennial succulent

Height
2–3 in (5–8 cm); flowering stem 8 in (20 cm)

Runner
Smooth red rootstalk which extends some of the offsets outward.

Root
Fibrous; clings to surfaces, especially to roofs.

Split leaf
Contains a succulent mucilage which has healing and soothing qualities.

USES

Culinary
LEAF The Dutch, in particular, add it to salads.

Cosmetic
LEAF Soak fresh leaves in a bath or facial steam to heal and nourish the skin. Apply juice (from sliced fresh leaf) or a decoction to warts and other skin blemishes.

Medicinal
LEAF Relieves small injuries; slice open fresh leaves to reveal their succulent interior and apply directly to skin. Apply to minor burns, wasp and nettle stings, cuts and insect bites. To soften skin around corns, bind on leaves for a few hours, soak foot in hot water then attempt to remove corn.

Infuse as a tea for septic throats, bronchitis and mouth ulcers and sores.

Sium sisarum

Skirret *Umbelliferae*

This Chinese pot herb, grown for its aromatic edible root, was brought to Rome by early traders and became so valued by the Emperor Tiberius that he accepted skirret as tribute. In the sixteenth century, skirret was introduced to northern Europe as "the most delicious of root vegetables". As a perennial that multiplies quickly, it was an invaluable crop for peasants. Writing in 1699, John Evelyn praised skirret as "Exceedingly nourishing, wholesome and delicate; of all the root-kind, not subject to be windy. This excellent root . . . is very acceptable to all palates."

Lifespan
Hardy herbaceous perennial

Height
2–4 ft (60 cm–1.2 m) in first two seasons; mature plants can reach 6 ft (2 m)

Flowers
Small clusters of tiny, fragrant, white, five-petalled flowers, fragrant in evening in mid- to late summer.

Seed
Brown, ridged, crescent-shaped, ⅛ in (3 mm) long.

Leaf
One to five pairs of narrow, pointed, finely toothed, mid-green leaflets and one terminal leaflet; older leaflets are more rounded. Some turn red in autumn.

Stem
Sturdy, hollow, ridged, round, branching and light green; red toward the base.

USES

Culinary
SHOOT Steam or stir-fry young shoots.
ROOT Lightly scrub, steam or boil and serve with butter and seasoning or with white sauce; or purée cooked root and serve with butter and nutmeg. Cook whole roots in stews, vegetable pies and Chinese stir-fried dishes.

Medicinal
SHOOT Fresh young shoots said by Culpeper to be a "wholesome food, of a cleansing nature, and easy digestion, provoking urine".

Root
Hair-like roots and numerous light brown, oblong tubers, 4–5 in (10–13 cm) long, with white flesh and pleasant aromatic smell and taste.

Smyrnium olusatrum

Alexanders *Umbelliferae*

This aromatic plant resembles both lovage and angelica, which occasionally leads to mistaken identity, but its bright green glossy leaf has rounded tips and lacks the deep indentations of the other two. However, it is called black lovage by some. The medieval Latin name for this herb was *Petroselinum alexandrinum*, the parsley of Alexandria, illustrating its Mediterranean heritage, and it was one of the many plants introduced by the Romans into northern Europe.

Although listed as an official medicinal plant for two centuries, its historical importance was more as a culinary herb: its leaves, root tops, stems and flower buds all feature in medieval recipes. The dried leaves were taken on long sea voyages to prevent scurvy.

Seed
Two ¼ in (6 mm) long, almost half-globular seeds, ridged, black and aromatic, form in each fruit.

Dried leaves
These retain slight flavour and can be used in cooking or medicinally.

Flower
Greenish-yellow flowers, full of nectar, borne in early to midsummer.

Leaf
Glossy, serrated, and bright green. Lower leaves can reach 12 in (30 cm) in length.

Lifespan
Hardy biennial; sometimes perennial

Height
3–5 ft (1–1.5 m)

Root
Thick at the top, branching to three or four main roots.

Stem
Solid and furrowed.

USES

Decorative
SEED Use dried seed heads for winter arrangements.

Culinary
SEED Grind and use in the same way as pepper.
FLOWER Toss buds in salads and flowers in savoury fritters.
LEAF Eat raw young leaves in salads or use as flavouring in stew. Serve with fish.
STEM Stew, steam or braise young stems, which taste like asparagus; serve with sauce.
ROOT Boil upper part.

Aromatic
SEED Grind coarsely and add to a potpourri.

Symphytum officinale

Comfrey *Boraginaceae*

Among plants, comfrey's claim to be a miracle worker must be preeminent. The list of beneficial substances in its leaves sounds impressive and includes calcium, potassium, phosphorus, vitamins A, C and B12 but not in sufficient amounts to meet our daily requirements. Comfrey has more protein in its leaf structure than any other known member of the vegetable kingdom and is cultivated in many countries. It sends down a 10 ft (3 m) taproot, or longer, to raise moisture and valuable minerals to the upper soil levels.

The leaf and roots contain allantoin, a protein that encourages cell division, and the plant is credited with some remarkable cures, from stubborn leg ulcers to broken bones.

Flower
Blue-mauve bells in drooping clusters open along the spiral flower stem from late spring.

Dried leaves
Infuse for a medicinal tea.

Dried root
Useful medicinally.

Leaf
Oval base, tapering to a point; rough, thick-ribbed and dark green.

Other species
Clockwise from the top:
S. grandiflorum
creamy red flowers; good ground cover.
S. officinale
white and pink flowers.
S. asperum
bright blue flowers.

Stem
Squarish, rough, hairy and branching near top.

USES

Culinary
LEAF Chop young leaves into salads. Cook as spinach.
STEM Blanch; cook in the same way as asparagus.

Cosmetic
LEAF AND ROOT Infuse and add to baths and lotions to soften the skin.

Medicinal
LEAF Put fresh leaves in a poultice for rough skin, aching joints, sores, burns, cuts, sprains and to reduce swelling.
LEAF AND ROOT Drink as a tea to relieve stomach ulcers and coughs.

Lifespan
Hardy herbaceous perennial

Height
3–4 ft (1–1.2 m)

Root
Brown-black, thick, tapering and penetrating.

Tagetes patula

French Marigold *Compositae*

Tagetes offers a unique asset to gardeners: it can deter eelworm. Its root secretions will deaden the detector mechanism of eelworms so that they don't "wake up" to the presence of their host plant. In Holland recent experiments have confirmed that eelworm among roses can be controlled by interplanting with French marigold. Tulip and potato growers also find it invaluable, and the foliage scent deters insects from tomato plants.

African marigold (*T. erecta*) has similar properties to French marigold, but most effective of all is the Inca marigold (*T. minuta*), which can grow to a height of 10 ft (3 m). For hundreds of years, South American Indians have grown potatoes on the same terraces and prevented eelworm attack by interplanting this "sacred weed".

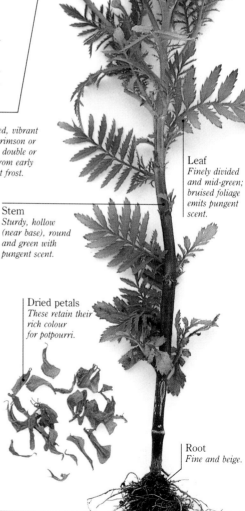

Flower
Pungent-scented, vibrant dark orange, crimson or yellow flowers, double or single, borne from early summer to first frost.

Leaf
Finely divided and mid-green; bruised foliage emits pungent scent.

Stem
Sturdy, hollow (near base), round and green with pungent scent.

Lifespan
Half-hardy annual

Height
T. patula 12 in (30 cm)

Seed
Like miniature paintbrush: cream tipped, shiny, flat, dark "handle", ³⁄₈ in (10 mm) long, with cream "bristles".

Dried petals
These retain their rich colour for potpourri.

Root
Fine and beige.

USES

Decorative
FLOWER Dry for potpourri.

Household
WHOLE PLANT Emits scent which deters white fly from tomato plants.
ROOT Exudes secretions which repel eelworm (*nematodes*).

Aromatic
LEAF (*T. tenuifolia* var. *pumila* 'Tangerine Gem') Plant for its orange scent. (*T. tenuifolia*) Cultivate for its fresh lemon verbena scent. Dry for potpourri.

Tanacetum parthenium (Chrysanthemum parthenium, Matricaria eximia)

Feverfew *Compositae*

Feverfew's ability to aid "melancholy and aches and pains in the head" has been known by herbalists, including Culpeper, for centuries. However, it was not given much attention until recently and, after detailed scientific analysis of the plant, several new healing substances have been discovered and patented. For example, in trials to prevent or reduce migraine, 70 per cent of patients experienced some improvement after eating a number of feverfew leaves every day, while the best drug on the market currently has a 50 per cent cure rate. Feverfew's success in combating migraines may be due to its accumulative effect in slowly reducing the smooth muscle spasms, which are implicated in many forms of migraine.

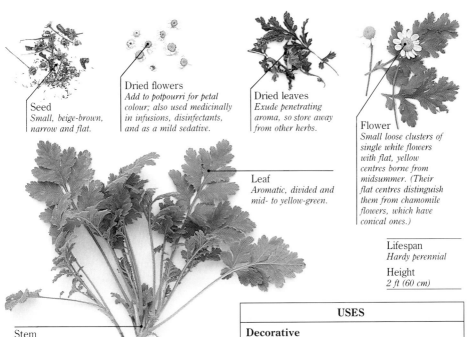

Seed
Small, beige-brown, narrow and flat.

Dried flowers
Add to potpourri for petal colour; also used medicinally in infusions, disinfectants, and as a mild sedative.

Dried leaves
Exude penetrating aroma, so store away from other herbs.

Flower
Small loose clusters of single white flowers with flat, yellow centres borne from midsummer. (Their flat centres distinguish them from chamomile flowers, which have conical ones.)

Leaf
Aromatic, divided and mid- to yellow-green.

Lifespan
Hardy perennial

Height
2 ft (60 cm)

Stem
Slightly downy, ridged, round, branching and green.

**T.p. aureum
Golden feverfew**
Single white flowers and aromatic golden-green leaves; makes an attractive edging plant, especially in winter.
Ht: 12 in (30 cm).

USES

Decorative
WHOLE PLANT Cultivate golden feverfew for year-round colour.
FLOWER Adds colour to potpourri.

Culinary
LEAF Add small amounts to food to "cut" the grease; bitter flavoured.

Household
LEAF Use dried in sachets to deter moths.

Medicinal
LEAF Eat three to five fresh leaves between slices of bread every day to reduce migraines.
LEAF AND FLOWER Infuse as a mild sedative, a tonic to the appetite, and to relieve mild muscle spasms.

Tanacetum vulgare (Chrysanthemum vulgare)

Tansy *Compositae*

Tansy was believed to arrest decay, and its name derives from the Greek *athanatos*, meaning immortality. In some ancient cultures, its strong antiseptic properties were used to preserve the dead and, according to classical legend, a drink made from tansy was given to the beautiful young man Ganymede to make him immortal.

In the 1,100-year-old monastery plan of St Gall in Switzerland, tansy is shown in the physic garden. This monastery garden was Charlemagne's favourite, and he ordered that all its herbs should be grown on his imperial estates. Tansy was also popularly used as an insecticide and disinfectant and, at Easter, was made into "Tansy", a rich custardy pudding. John Evelyn, in 1699, wrote that new leaves, stir-fried and eaten hot with orange juice and sugar, was a most agreeable dish.

Flower
Dense, flat, mustard-yellow clusters borne from late summer to autumn.

Leaf
Aromatic, deeply indented, toothed and dark green; rich in potassium

Dried flowers
These retain their colour well for potpourri, wreaths and garlands.

USES

Decorative
FLOWER Dry as an "everlasting".

Culinary
LEAF Stew with rhubarb. Rub on meat for a rosemary-like flavour.

Household
LEAF Hang indoors to deter flies. Put dried sprigs under carpets. Add to insect-repellent sachets. Sprinkle to deter ants and mice. Mix into the compost heap for its potassium content.

Note: *Use only in moderation, potentially toxic. Do not use at all during pregnancy.*

**T.v. var. *crispum*
Crisp-leaved tansy**
Decorative, fern-like leaves. Less scented and more compact than the species. Ht: 2ft (60 cm).

Stem
Ridged, round, green tinged with red.

Lifespan
Hardy herbaceous perennial

Height
5 ft (1.5 m)

Seed
Minute, greenish-white, ridged and oblong.

Trigonella foenum-graecum

Fenugreek *Leguminosae*

Fenugreek is one of the herbs whose medicinal use and commercial cultivation is at present on the increase. Its seed contains not only mucilage but also diosgenin, which is important in the synthesis of oral contraceptives and sex hormone treatments. Its leaves contain coumarin, which gives them a sweet hay scent when dried, so they are sometimes used to mask inferior hay. *Foenum-graecum*, in fact, is the Latin for Greek hay and it is a well-known fodder crop.

Archaeological evidence suggests that the Egyptians valued fenugreek for eating, healing and embalming. The Greeks and Romans, too, enjoyed the seed as food and medicine. On the Indian subcontinent, its spicy seed has long been included in curry powder and its leafy shoots have been curried as a vegetable.

Lifespan
Tender annual

Height
1–2 ft (30–60 cm); erect or prostrate

Flower
Yellow-white, pea-family-shaped blooms in midsummer. Each matures into a long narrow pod with 10–20 seeds.

Leaf
Slightly toothed and mid-green with three oval leaflets, tasting of fresh French bean when young.

Stem
Slightly hairy, round, light green with very little branching; usually erect, occasionally prostrate.

Seed
Yellow-brown, pebble-shaped, ³⁄₁₆ in (5 mm) long, divided into two unequal parts by a deep furrow. Smells of maple syrup with a hint of celery.

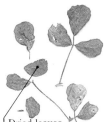

Dried leaves
These often occur in hay mixtures and are well worth adding to "meadow" potpourri mixtures.

USES

Culinary
SEED Used as a spice in curries and chutneys. Sprout and use as a winter salad herb. As sprouts grow, curry flavour recedes.
LEAF Toss sprouted seed leaves into salads. When fenugreek is 8 in (20 cm) tall, eat raw or boil or curry as a vegetable.

Cosmetic
SEED Infuse for a complexion wash.

Medicinal
SEED Grind coarsely, infuse and drink as a tonic tea to stimulate digestion, ease coughing, flatulence and diarrhoea.

Thymus species

Thymes *Labiatae*

Thyme has inspired poetic praise from Virgil to Kipling, who wrote of "wind-bit thyme that smells of dawn in Paradise". Its fragrance is particularly strong on the hillsides of Mediterranean lands. To the Greeks, thyme denoted graceful elegance: "to smell of thyme" was an expression of stylish praise.

Thymus is derived from the Greek word *thymon*, meaning "courage", and many traditions relate to this virtue. Roman soldiers, for example, bathed in thyme water to give themselves vigour. In the Middle Ages,

European ladies embroidered a sprig of thyme on tokens for their knights errant.

The powerful antiseptic and preservative properties of thyme were well known to the Egyptians, who used it for embalming. It is still an ingredient of embalming fluid, and it will also preserve anatomical and herbarium specimens and protect paper from mould. Thyme is the first herb listed in the Holy Herb Charm recited by those with "herb cunning" in the Middle Ages, and it is featured in a charming recipe from 1600 "to enable one to see the Fairies".

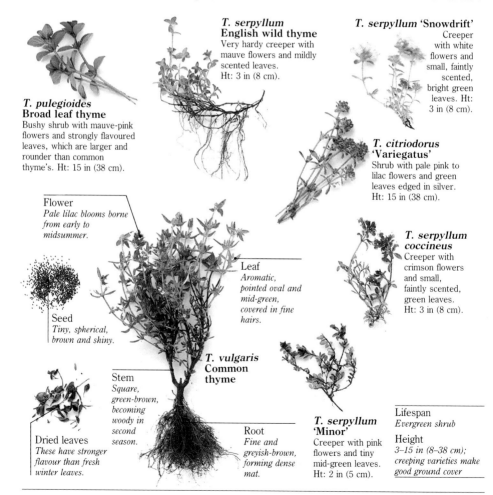

T. pulegioides
Broad leaf thyme
Bushy shrub with mauve-pink flowers and strongly flavoured leaves, which are larger and rounder than common thyme's. Ht: 15 in (38 cm).

T. serpyllum
English wild thyme
Very hardy creeper with mauve flowers and mildly scented leaves.
Ht: 3 in (8 cm).

T. serpyllum 'Snowdrift'
Creeper with white flowers and small, faintly scented, bright green leaves. Ht: 3 in (8 cm).

T. citriodorus
'Variegatus'
Shrub with pale pink to lilac flowers and green leaves edged in silver. Ht: 15 in (38 cm).

Flower
Pale lilac blooms borne from early to midsummer.

Seed
Tiny, spherical, brown and shiny.

Leaf
Aromatic, pointed oval and mid-green, covered in fine hairs.

T. serpyllum coccineus
Creeper with crimson flowers and small, faintly scented, green leaves. Ht: 3 in (8 cm).

T. vulgaris
Common thyme

Stem
Square, green-brown, becoming woody in second season.

Dried leaves
These have stronger flavour than fresh winter leaves.

Root
Fine and greyish-brown, forming dense mat.

T. serpyllum
'Minor'
Creeper with pink flowers and tiny mid-green leaves. Ht: 2 in (5 cm).

Lifespan
Evergreen shrub

Height
3–15 in (8–38 cm); creeping varieties make good ground cover

T. caespititius
(T. azoricus)
Creeper with pink flowers and narrow, pine-scented, green leaves. Ht: 2 in (5 cm).

T. herba-barona
Prostrate subshrub with rose flowers, arching branches and caraway-scented, dark green leaves. Ht: 4 in (10 cm).

T. pallasianus
subsp. pallasianus
(T. odoratissimus)
Shrub with pale pink flowers, long lax branches and citrusy leaves. Ht: 8 in (20 cm).

T.p.a.
'Doone Valley'
Creeper with pale purple flowers and lemon-scented, bright green leaves with gold splashes. Ht: 3 in (8 cm).

T. citriodorus
'Fragrantissimus'
Shrub with pale lilac flowers and sweet, fruity, blue-grey leaves. Ht: 15 in (38 cm).

T.p.a.
'Aureus'
Golden lemon
creeping thyme
Creeper with pink flowers and golden-lemon leaves. Ht: 3 in (8 cm).

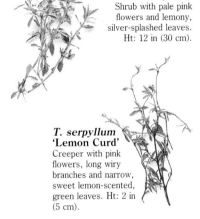

T. × citriodorus
'Silver Lemon Queen'
Shrub with pale pink flowers and lemony, silver-splashed leaves. Ht: 12 in (30 cm).

T. serpyllum
'Lemon Curd'
Creeper with pink flowers, long wiry branches and narrow, sweet lemon-scented, green leaves. Ht: 2 in (5 cm).

T.p.a. 'Citriodorus'
Creeper with pink flowers and large, strongly lemon-scented, green leaves. Ht: 6 in (15 cm).

T × citriodorus
Shrub with pale lilac flowers and lemon-scented, bright green leaves. Ht: 12 in (30 cm).

USES

Culinary
LEAF (Common thyme) Mix with parsley and bay in bouquet garni. Add to stocks, marinades, stuffings, sauces and soups, using cautiously as thyme is extra pungent when fresh. Aids digestion of fatty foods. Suits food cooked slowly in wine – particularly poultry, shellfish and game. (Lemon-scented thymes) Add to chicken, fish, hot vegetables, fruit salads and jams. (T. herba-barona) Use to flavour beef.

Household
FLOWER Thyme is loved by bees. Its honey is esteemed.

Aromatic
LEAF Use in potpourri.

Medicinal
LEAF (English wild thyme) This has the strongest medicinal qualities, although any thyme can be used. Infuse as a tea for a digestive tonic and for hangovers. Sweeten infusion with honey for convulsive coughs, colds and sore throats.

Valeriana officinalis

Valerian *Valerianaceae*

This ancient medicinal herb, whose name derives from the Latin *valere* "to be in health", has long been valued around the world. Nordic, Persian and Chinese herbalists used the root, while the similar *V. sylvatica* was found in the medicine bag of Canadian Indian warriors as a wound antiseptic. Fresh valerian root smells like ancient leather but, when dried, it is nearer to stale perspiration. Its old name, *V. phu*, could be the origin of our expression for an undesirable scent. Valerian was used during the First and Second World Wars for treating shell shock and nervous stress.

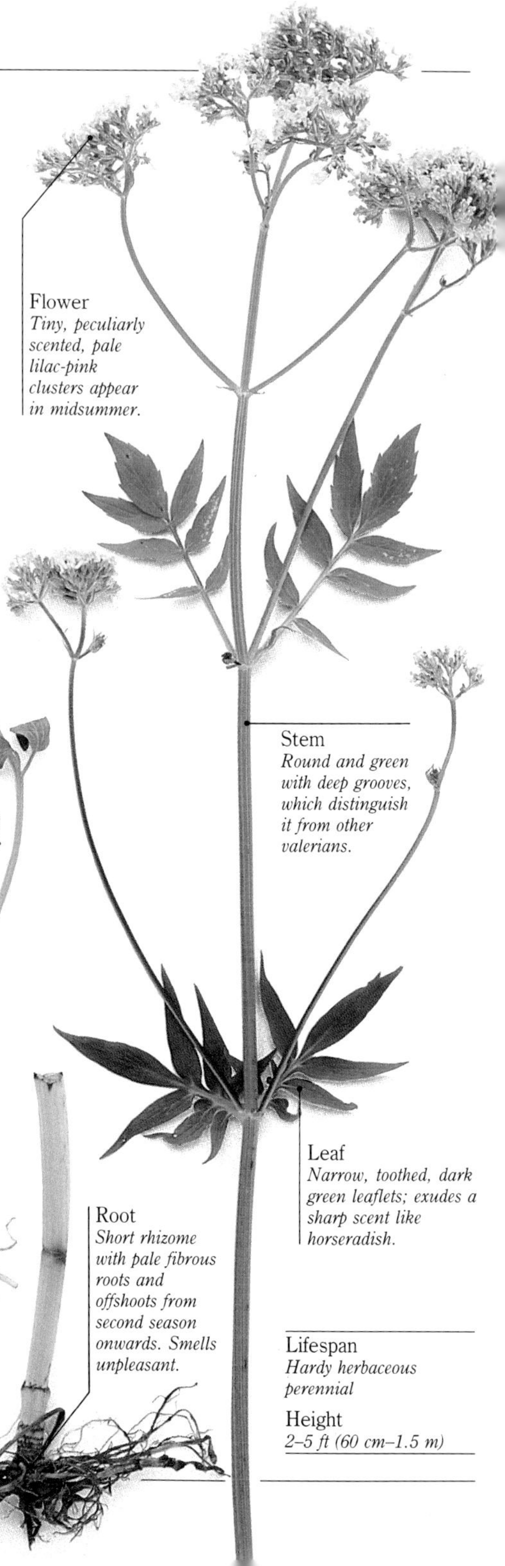

Flower
Tiny, peculiarly scented, pale lilac-pink clusters appear in midsummer.

Young plant
Readily-broken, shiny, light green stems; leaves not yet divided into leaflets.

Seed
Light brown, flat, tear-shaped, $1/10$ in (2 mm) long.

Stem
Round and green with deep grooves, which distinguish it from other valerians.

USES

Decorative
WHOLE PLANT Grow in formal borders.

Culinary
ROOT Add to soups, stuffings and stews.

Household
WHOLE PLANT Boosts growth of nearby vegetables by stimulating phorphorus and earthworm activity.
LEAF Add mineral-rich leaves to raw compost.
ROOT Attracts cats, vermin and worms. Use in rat-traps.

Cosmetic
ROOT Use decoction as a facial wash, for a soothing bath, and in lotion for acne or skin rashes.

Leaf
Narrow, toothed, dark green leaflets; exudes a sharp scent like horseradish.

Root
Short rhizome with pale fibrous roots and offshoots from second season onwards. Smells unpleasant.

Lifespan
Hardy herbaceous perennial

Height
2–5 ft (60 cm–1.5 m)

Verbascum thapsus

Mullein *Scrophulariaceae*

A magical herb of antiquity, mullein was given to Ulysses to protect him from the sorcery of Circe, who changed his crew into pigs. It has attracted over 30 common names, including Aaron's rod, candlewick plant, hag's taper and velvet dock. The soft, fine hairs on the leaves and stem protect the herb from moisture loss, creeping insects and grazing animals, as the down irritates their mucous membranes. This skilfully constructed plant drops rain from its small leaves on to larger leaves and down to the roots.

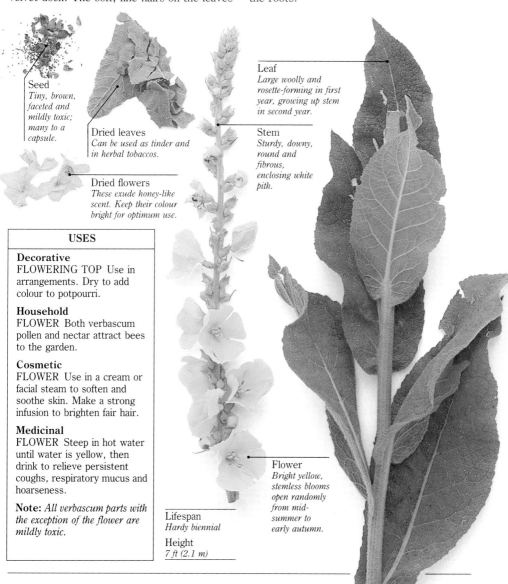

Seed
Tiny, brown, faceted and mildly toxic; many to a capsule.

Dried leaves
Can be used as tinder and in herbal tobaccos.

Dried flowers
These exude honey-like scent. Keep their colour bright for optimum use.

Leaf
Large woolly and rosette-forming in first year, growing up stem in second year.

Stem
Sturdy, downy, round and fibrous, enclosing white pith.

Flower
Bright yellow, stemless blooms open randomly from mid-summer to early autumn.

Lifespan
Hardy biennial

Height
7 ft (2.1 m)

USES

Decorative
FLOWERING TOP Use in arrangements. Dry to add colour to potpourri.

Household
FLOWER Both verbascum pollen and nectar attract bees to the garden.

Cosmetic
FLOWER Use in a cream or facial steam to soften and soothe skin. Make a strong infusion to brighten fair hair.

Medicinal
FLOWER Steep in hot water until water is yellow, then drink to relieve persistent coughs, respiratory mucus and hoarseness.

Note: *All verbascum parts with the exception of the flower are mildly toxic.*

Verbena officinalis

Vervain *Verbenaceae*

It is curious that such an unassuming plant as vervain should have become sacred to so many cultures. In Egypt, for example, vervain was believed to have originated from the tears of Isis, and Greek priests wore its root with their vestments. Being sacred to Venus, vervain was used in love potions. The Chinese names for this herb, "dragon-teeth grass" and "iron vervain" suggest hidden powers.

Vervain was the Roman word for altar plants used for spiritual purification, and the Druids, too, washed their altars with a flower infusion and used vervain in their lustral water for visions. To the Anglo-Saxons, vervain was a powerful protector and part of the Holy Salve against demons of disease.

Flower
Small, tubular, pale lilac blooms appear on spikes from midsummer.

Stem
Slightly hairy, ridged, squarish, branching near top and shiny dark green.

Dried leaves
These are taken internally for nervous depression and other conditions and used externally to treat wounds.

Leaf
Glossy, slightly hairy, veined, narrow with lobed edges, and dark green; like an elongated oak leaf.

Lifespan
Hardy, herbaceous perennial

Height
2–3 ft (60 cm–1 m)

USES

Culinary
LEAF Because of its reputation as an effective love potion, vervain was sometimes included in dishes and added to homemade liqueurs. Note that vervain does not have a lemon scent and should not be confused with lemon verbena.

Cosmetic
LEAF Infuse as an eye compress for tired eyes and inflamed eyelids.

Medicinal
WHOLE PLANT Infused as a tea for a digestive and for a sedative nightcap after nervous exhaustion.

Note: *Use with caution.*

Viola odorata

Sweet violet *Violaceae*

A delightful herald of spring, this modest spreading plant is the most highly scented violet. It has long been cultivated for its perfume and colour and is added to cosmetics, drinks, sweets and syrups. Its seductive scent suggested strong emotions, and so sweet violet became a plant of Venus and Aphrodite.

The Greeks chose sweet violet as their symbol of fertility, while the Romans enjoyed sweet violet wine; for Napoleon, it was the emblem of the imperial Napoleonic party. It was among the most popular scents in Victorian England, and the last Empress Dowager of China imported bottles of "Violetta Regia" from Berlin. Revered writers from Homer to Shakespeare and the old herbalists all speak with great affection of this charming flower with its soothing properties.

USES
Decorative FLOWER Add to a spring posy.
Culinary FLOWER Use crystallized to decorate cakes, puddings and ice cream. Eat raw in salads.
Aromatic FLOWER Use in potpourri mixtures, floral waters and perfumes.
Medicinal FLOWER Take fresh or dried in an infusion or syrup as a mild laxative; also helpful for coughs and bronchitis, and soothing for nerves, headaches and insomnia. ROOT A decoction or infusion of dried root is said to alleviate catarrh and bronchitis.

Flower
Scented, violet or white blooms from late winter to midspring. Provides nectar for early butterflies.

Lifespan
Hardy perennial

Height
4–6 in (10–15 cm); good ground cover

Seed
Light tan, hard, round and small.

Dried leaves
Culpeper claimed that an infusion "doth purge the body of choleric humours".

Leaf
Heart-shaped, mid- to dark green.

Runners
Horizontal runners root every 3–5 in (8–13 cm).

Root
Yellowy brown, knobbly rootstalk with hair-like roots.

Crystallized petals
A delicious sweetmeat alone or as decoration for cakes.

CHAPTER TWO

COOKING WITH HERBS

Herbs have been described as the soul of cookery and the praise of cooks. Used judiciously, they can transform a routine meal into a sensuous experience of tangy, spicy, refreshing flavours and crunchy textures. Many herbs such as angelica, basil, caraway and dill make foods more palatable by easing digestion.

In the past the range of edible herbs and the number of ways of using them was much greater than today. However, with a fresh interest in the culinary arts, herbs are now enjoying a revival. They enliven any dish, snack or drink and can also supply extra nutrition to everyday meals, as many herbs, such as parsley, watercress and comfrey, contain a small but rich balance of vitamins, minerals and trace elements.

The following pages list a selection of useful culinary herbs with guidelines on their attributes and complementary foods. The emphasis in the recipes is on fresh herbs, but if they are not available 1 tsp (5 ml) dried herb is equivalent to 1 tbsp (15 ml) fresh.

Culinary herbs
Herbs have a wide variety of uses in the kitchen. They enliven butters and other spreads, are a delicious addition to vinegars and oils, and give taste and piquancy to almost any dish.

Popular culinary herbs

Angelica

A strong, clean flavour that pierces through heavy syrup makes angelica an excellent candidate for crystallization. Dilute angelica syrup for summer drinks and use to give character to fruit salads and ice cream. Cook leaves with acidic fruits to reduce tartness and sugar consumption.

Angelica and mint sandwich p. 126

Basil

Indispensable for many Mediterranean dishes, the fresh leaf has a sweet clove-like spiciness and is superb on fresh tomatoes with a little salad oil, and in hot tomato dishes. Basil adds interest to rice salads and combines well with courgettes, marrows, beans and mushrooms. It has a powerful enough flavour to stand up to garlic, and together they make the classic pesto sauce. Basil's pungency increases with cooking. The fresh leaves keep their flavour if preserved in oil or vinegar (see p. 134).

Split pea and basil soup p. 107
Pancakes with basil stuffing p. 120

Bay

Bay is one herb that is better dried than fresh. Use it with parsley and thyme to make a bouquet garni. Add a leaf or two to marinades, stock, pâtés, stuffings and curries. When poaching fish, add a bay leaf to the water. A leaf in a storage jar of rice will impart its flavour to the rice. Bay is also used to flavour milk puddings. Add at the start of cooking and remove before serving.

Game soup with bay p. 108

Chervil

Chervil is one of the classic *fines herbes* much used in French cuisine. It has a delicate flavour and is suitable wherever parsley is used. Chop the fresh leaf into omelettes, salads, dressings and add to chicken before roasting. Add at the end of cooking so its flavour is not lost. The stem can be used raw in salads. Preserve in vinegar and oil (see p. 134).

Carrot and chervil soup p. 107
Chervil stuffed trout p. 109

Chives

Freshly chopped chives lift many foods above the mundane. Sprinkle them on soups, salads, chicken, potatoes, cooked vegetables and egg dishes. Blend chopped chives with butter to garnish grilled meats and fish. Use them in place of raw onion in hamburgers for a milder flavour. Blend with butter (see p. 134), mix in cream cheese, yogurt sauces and baked potatoes. Add at the end of cooking. Chives freeze well but are poor dried.

Potato salad with dill and chives p. 125
Cheese balls p. 126
Cheese bread with chives p. 131

Coriander

The leaves and ripe seeds have two distinct flavours. The seeds are warmly aromatic and indispensable in tomato chutney and curries. They provide an excellent flavouring for vegetables and in soups, sauces and biscuits. The leaves have an earthy pungency, delicious in salads, vegetables and poultry dishes.

Lentil and coriander soup p. 108
Persian chicken with herbs p. 116
Mediterranean vegetables p. 123
Mixed salad with chili and coriander p. 125

Dill

Frequently described as similar in flavour to caraway, aniseed and fennel, dill is like none of these. It has a totally unique, spicy green taste. Add whole seeds to potato salad, pickles, bean soups, salmon dishes, and apple pies. Ground, they can flavour herb butter, mayonnaise and mustard. The leaves go well with fish, cream cheese and cucumber.

Gravlax p. 109
Potato salad with dill and chives p. 125
Pickled cucumbers p. 135

Fennel

With its pronounced aniseed flavour, fennel is an excellent digestive and reputed to be a slimming aid. Chop the stems when tender into salads. Stuff the leaves into oily fish such as mackerel, and sprinkle finely chopped on salads and cooked vegetables. Add the seeds to

sauces, breads, savoury biscuits and the water for poaching fish. The swollen bulb of Florence fennel can be eaten raw in salads or cooked.
Fennel with Roquefort sauce p. 122
Fennel salad with orange p. 125

Garlic
A strong flavouring for all savoury dishes, hot and cold. Rub a clove around a salad bowl to subtly flavour salads; add one or two cloves to dressings and marinades, or make garlic vinegar and oil (see p. 134). Mash with butter and bake in a French loaf or on grilled meat or fish. Insert sliced cloves into joints of meat before roasting. It can even be baked as a vegetable. The leaves have a lighter flavour.
Pork chops marinated with juniper and garlic p. 116
Mediterranean vegetables p. 123
Spicy aubergines p. 121

Juniper
The crushed berries of the juniper tree have an aromatic resinous flavour often featured in pâtés, marinades and stuffings for pork, venison and other game. They are also a popular flavouring for sauerkraut, sauces, ham and cabbage.
Pork chops marinated with juniper and garlic p. 116
Baked cabbage with juniper p. 121
Mulled pears with juniper p. 129

Lemon Balm
Use the refreshing, lemon-flavoured leaves fresh in salads, to make a pleasant herbal tea or to give a lemon flavour to Indian tea. Add generously to a white sauce for fish and spread over chicken before roasting. Finely chopped leaves add a lemony sweetness to sauerkraut, mayonnaise, sauces, and stuffings as well as fruit salads and custards. Freeze in ice cubes to add to drinks.
Spicy lemon balm kebabs p. 113
Lemon balm cheesecake p. 129

Lovage
The leaves and stems have a meaty flavour, but use sparingly until familiar with their potency. Fresh leaves make an interesting base on which to serve strong-flavoured pâté.

Young leaves and blanched stems are good steamed as a vegetable and served with a white sauce. A brew of the leaves is like a yeast extract broth.
Lovage soup p. 108
Stuffed lovage and vine leaves p. 114

Mints
With their clean, sharp flavours, the mints are an aid to the digestion and can be used individually or blended. Excellent in mint sauce, syrups, vinegar and in teas. Add to new potatoes, to a garlic and cream cheese dip and to a yogurt dressing or drink. Delicious in fruit salads and punches. Also mix with chocolate cakes, rich desserts and bake with raisins or blackcurrants in pastry. Crystallize the leaf for a sweet decoration.
Persian chicken with herbs p. 116
Melon, tomato and mint salad p. 124
Angelica and mint sandwich p. 126
Raspberry and mint yogurt drink p. 137

Oregano and Marjoram
Marjoram has a distinctive savoury flavour, while oregano is slightly stronger. Both dry well. Marjoram is suitable for thick vegetable soups, pasta, fish, game, beef, chicken and meat loaf. Tomatoes, courgettes, potatoes and peppers are enhanced by its flavour. It is also used in omelettes and cheese dishes. Marjoram leaf also makes an aromatic tea. Oregano is good with pizzas; it can be used like marjoram, but more sparingly.
Oregano cheese pie p. 118

Parsley
The mild flavour and bright green leaves of parsley make it the most useful and popular kitchen herb. Add it to a bouquet garni with bay and thyme. When cooked, it serves to enhance the flavour of other foods and herbs. To increase its potency, use generous amounts and include the stems, which are more strongly flavoured. Feature it in bland dishes and add towards the end of cooking. Use in salads, sandwiches, soups, sauces, mayonnaise and egg dishes. Fry whole sprigs briefly to serve with fish.
Green herb omelette p. 117
Mediterranean vegetables p. 123

Green mayonnaise p. 126
Parsley and chive butter p. 134

Rosemary

This aromatic resinous leaf aids the digestion of
fats, and traditionally is sprinkled on roast lamb
and pork or added to chops, pigeon, sausage
meats, pâtés and stuffings. Crumble dried
leaves and chop fresh, or remove them before
serving as they can be tough. Put a whole sprig
in the oven to flavour baking bread. Put a sprig
in oil or vinegar. Add leaves, pre-soaked in hot
water, to oranges soaked in wine.
Rosemary kebabs p. 113
Rosemary cheese fingers p. 130
Sweet rosemary slices p. 132

Saffron

Saffron is our most expensive seasoning due to
the labour required for harvesting the
individual stamens. Fortunately, only a pinch is
needed to colour and flavour a large dish. Good
saffron should be less than a year old and a
brilliant orange colour. It has a strong aroma
and a pungent, warmly bitter flavour. When
using threads, crush the required number and
infuse in hot milk or liquid from the recipe. If
using powder, infuse in liquid; alternatively add
it with the flour for cakes.
Mussels in saffron p. 110
Saffron fruit bread p. 130

Sage

Sage is a strongly flavoured, pungent herb
which complements strongly flavoured foods
and aids the digestion of fats. Use leaves in
onion soup, with stewed tomatoes, omelettes,
herb scones and bread. Try them in a sage
jelly, butter or vinegar (see p. 134). If dried,
sage must be of top quality as otherwise it
acquires an unpleasant musty flavour.
Hazelnut and sage pâté p. 117
Leek and sage croustade p. 120
Herb leaf fritters p. 123
Sage oat cakes p. 131

Summer and Winter Savory

The two savories have a similar flavour to
thyme, with winter savory being marginally
milder. Cook with fresh or dried beans and

lentils, or in a white sauce for bean dishes. Mix
with parsley and chives for roasting duck.
Sprinkle finely chopped leaves on soups and
sauces. Use to flavour vinegar (see p. 134).

Scented Geraniums (Pelargoniums)

The many scented geranium leaves can flavour
teas and drinks (see p. 136), cakes, custards,
fruit and sorbets. Experiment with them in
savoury dishes too.
Sweet rice with rose geranium p. 129
Scented geranium leaf sponge p. 132

Sorrel

A sharp-flavoured leaf with the tangy zest of
lemon, sorrel adds piquancy to bland dishes
and sauces. Sorrel soup is a classic, and sorrel
is often cooked and served like spinach.
Pork and sorrel terrine p. 114
Sorrel and parsnip mousses p. 122

Sweet Cicely

This is a mild-flavoured leaf with a hint of
aniseed. Add to tart fruit when stewing or
making jam to reduce acidity and cut sugar
requirements. Use fresh chopped leaves in
salads, avocado dressing and punches. Add
green, unripe seeds to fruit salads. Boil the
root, slice and serve cold with salad oil or add
chopped root to stir-fried dishes.

Tarragon

An aristocratic herb with a savoury flavour and
hidden tang; one of the *fines herbes* with chervil
and parsley. It is indispensable for béarnaise
and hollandaise sauces, soups, fish dishes and
any delicate vegetables. Add to egg dishes and
stuff in a roasting chicken.
Tarragon baked chicken p. 113

Thyme

Common thyme is used in a bouquet garni with
parsley and bay. It stimulates the appetite and
aids digestion of fatty food; useful with meat,
shellfish, poultry and game. It is very pungent
when fresh, so use with discretion. Try the
lemon thymes in fish and poultry dishes.
Sole en croûte with thyme p. 110
Rabbit with mustard and thyme p. 112
Pheasant pot roast with thyme p. 112

Herbs and their uses

Herbs for soups

General: chervil, garlic, juniper berries, lemon balm, lovage leaf and seed, marjorams, mint, onion green and bulb, parsley leaf, stem and root, rosemary, savories, smallage, sorrel, tarragon, thyme.
Minestrone: basil, rosemary, thyme.
Pea: basil, borage, dill, marjoram, mint, parsley, rosemary, savory, thyme.
Potato: bay, caraway, parsley.
Tomato: basil, dill, marjoram, oregano, tarragon, thyme.

Herbs for fish

General: alexanders, basil, bay, caraway, chervil, chives, dill, fennel, lemon balm, lemon thyme, lovage, marjoram, mint, parsley.
Baked or grilled: all the above, savory, tarragon, thyme.
Oily fish: fennel, dill.
Salmon: dill seed, rosemary.
Seafood: basil, bay, chervil, chives, dill, fennel seed, marjoram, rosemary, tarragon, thyme.
Soups: bay, lovage, sage (though this should be used sparingly), savory, tarragon, thyme.

Herbs for game and poultry

Venison: bay, juniper, lovage seed, rosemary, sage, savory, sweet marjoram.
Rabbit/Hare: basil, bay, lovage seed, marjoram, rosemary, sage.
Pigeon: juniper berries, rosemary, thyme.
Chicken: chervil, chives, fennel, lemon balm, marjoram, mint, parsley, savory, tarragon, thyme.
Duck: bay, rosemary, sage, sweet marjoram, tarragon.
Goose: fennel, sage, sweet marjoram.
Turkey: parsley, sage, sweet marjoram, tarragon, thyme.

Herbs for meat

Beef: basil, bay, caraway seed, chervil, lovage seed, marjoram (pot roasts), mint, oregano, parsley, peppermint, rosemary, sage, savory, tarragon, thyme.
Lamb: basil, chervil, cumin, dill, lemon balm, lovage seed, marjoram, mints, parsley, rosemary, savory, thyme.
Pork: chervil, coriander, fennel, lovage seed, marjoram, rosemary, sage, savory, thyme.
Liver: basil, dill, marjoram, sage, tarragon.
Ham: juniper berries, lovage, marjoram, mint, mustard, oregano, parsley, rosemary, savory.

Herbs for casseroles

Borage, bay, chicory, chives, coriander seed, dill seed, fennel, garlic, good King Henry, lemon balm, lovage, marjoram, mint, oregano, parsley, sage, savory, smallage, thyme.

Herbs for marinades

Basil, bay, coriander seed and leaves, cumin, dill, fennel, garlic, juniper berries, lemon balm, lovage, mint, onion greens and bulbs, parsley stems, rosemary, tarragon.

Herbs for eggs and cheese

Eggs, general: basil, chervil, chives, dill, parsley, tarragon.
Devilled eggs: the above, marjoram, rosemary.
Scrambled eggs and omelettes: the above, sweet marjoram, oregano.
Cheeses, hard: caraway, dill seed, rosemary, sage.
Cheeses, soft: caraway, chervil, chives, dill seed, fennel, marjoram, mints, rosemary, sage, savory, thyme.
Fondues: basil, garlic, mint.
Welsh rarebit: basil, parsley, sweet marjoram, tarragon.

Herbs for vegetables

Artichokes: bay, savory, tarragon.
Asparagus: chervil, chives, dill, lemon balm, salad burnet, tarragon.
Avocado: dill, marjoram, tarragon.
Brussels sprouts: dill, sage, savory.
Cabbage: borage, caraway, dill seed, marjoram, mint, oregano, parsley, sage, savory, sweet cicely, thyme.
Carrots: chervil, parsley.
Cauliflower: chives, dill leaf and seed, fennel, rosemary.
Celeriac: chervil, parsley, tarragon.

Green beans: dill, marjoram, mint, oregano, rosemary, sage, savory, tarragon, thyme.
Lentils: garlic, mint, parsley, savory, sorrel.
Marrow: basil, dill, marjoram, rosemary, tarragon.
Mushrooms: basil, dill, lemon balm, marjoram, parsley, rosemary, salad burnet, savory, tarragon, thyme.
Onions: basil, marjoram in soup, oregano, sage, tarragon, thyme.
Peas: basil, chervil, marjoram, mint, parsley, rosemary, sage, savory.
Potatoes: basil, bay, chives, dill, lovage, marjoram, mint, oregano, parsley, rosemary, savory, thyme.
Sauerkraut: dill, fennel seed, lovage, savory, tarragon, thyme.
Spinach: borage, chervil, marjoram, mint, rosemary for soup, sage, sorrel, tarragon.
Tomatoes: basil, bay, chervil, Chinese chives, chives, dill seed, garlic, marjoram, mint, oregano, parsley, sage, savory, tarragon.
Turnips: dill seed, marjoram, savory.

Salad herbs

General: alexanders, angelica, basil, bistort, borage leaves, caraway, chervil, chicory, Chinese chives, chives, coriander leaves, corn salad, dill, fennel, lemon balm, lovage, marjoram, mint, mustard seedlings, nasturtium leaves, orach, parsley, purslane (summer and winter), salad burnet, salad rocket, savory, smallage, sorrel, sweet cicely, tarragon, thyme, watercress.
Floral additions: bergamot, borage, marigold (calendula), chives, nasturtium, primrose, rose petals, sweet rocket, violet.

Herbs for desserts

General: angelica, aniseed, bergamot, elderflower, lemon balm, lemon verbena, pineapple sage, rosemary, saffron, sweet cicely leaves and green seeds.
Custards: bay, lemon thyme, mint, rose petals, scented geraniums (pelargoniums).
Fruit salads: aniseed, lemon balm, mints, rosemary, sweet cicely leaves and green seeds.
Fruit compotes: dill, mint with pears; aniseed, caraway, dill with apples; savory with quinces; angelica, sweet cicely with acidic fruits.

Herbs for breads

Aniseed, basil, caraway, chives, dill, fennel, lovage seed, poppy seed, rosemary, sunflower seed, thyme.

Herbs for oils

Savoury: basil, garlic, fennel, marjoram, mint, rosemary, tarragon, thyme, savory.
Sweet: clove pinks, lavender, lemon verbena, rose petals.

Herbs for vinegars

Basil, bay, chervil, dill leaves, fennel, garlic, lemon balm, marjoram, mint, rosemary, savory, tarragon, thyme.

Flowers for vinegars

Carnations, clover, elderflower, lavender, nasturtiums, primroses, rose petals, rosemary flowers, thyme flowers, sweet violets.

Herbs for jelly

Savoury: basil, mint, rosemary, sage, savory, thyme.
Sweet: bergamot, marigold (calendula), lavender flower petals, lemon balm, lemon verbena, scented geranium leaves (rose, apple, peppermint, lemon), sweet violet.

Herbs for wine cups

Angelica leaves, bergamot leaves and flowers, borage leaves and flowers, clary sage leaves, lemon balm leaves, lemon verbena leaves, mint leaves (all varieties), rosemary leaves, salad burnet leaves, sweet woodruff leaves.

Soups

A good, hearty soup often owes much of its flavour to the careful choice of complementary herbs. Bay makes the perfect foil for rich game in a thick, hearty soup while sorrel, with its lemony flavour, adds a tangy bite to a lighter soup, giving a taste of French country cooking. Try substituting one herb for another, but do not be tempted to throw in handfuls of mixed herbs as their subtle flavours will be lost. Use fresh herbs to garnish cream soups.

Carrot and chervil soup

2 oz (50 g) butter
10 oz (275 g) carrots, chopped
2 oz (50 g) plain flour
2 pints (1 litre) chicken stock
salt and black pepper
½ cup (100 ml) chopped chervil

GARNISH
cream or natural yogurt
sprigs of chervil

Serves 4–6

1 Melt the butter in a saucepan and gently sauté the carrots for 5 minutes. Stir in the flour, then the stock and seasoning. Bring the soup to the boil, cover the pan and simmer gently for 30 minutes.

2 Allow to cool slightly, then purée the soup in a blender. Return to the pan with the chopped chervil and slowly bring back to the boil. Serve hot or chilled with a swirl of cream or yogurt and sprigs of chervil.

Split pea and basil soup

1 tbsp (15 ml) vegetable oil
1 large onion, chopped
1 clove garlic, crushed
8 oz (225 g) split peas, soaked overnight
1 tsp (5 ml) tomato purée
1 tbsp (15 ml) vegetable stock concentrate
1 large potato, diced
4 pints (2.3 litres) water
3 tbsp (45 ml) basil leaves
salt and black pepper

GARNISH
4 fl oz (110 ml) single cream
8 basil leaves

Serves 8

1 Heat the oil in a large saucepan and sauté the onion and garlic for 5 minutes. Add the drained split peas, tomato purée, stock concentrate, potato and water.

2 Bring to the boil, add the basil leaves and seasoning, cover and simmer for 40 minutes until the peas soften.

3 Allow to cool slightly, then purée the soup in a blender. Return to the pan to reheat for serving. Garnish with a swirl of cream and a basil leaf.

Game soup with bay

2 pints (1 litre) beef stock
1 pheasant, partridge, pigeon
  or other game bird carcase
1 rabbit or hare
  forequarters
1 medium carrot, quartered
1 medium onion, quartered
4 bay leaves
juice of 1 lemon
salt and black pepper
2 fl oz (50 ml) port

Serves 4–6

1 Place the stock, carcase, forequarters, carrot, onion and bay leaves in a saucepan. Bring to the boil, cover and simmer for about 1 hour until the meat is tender.

2 Strain through a sieve, reserving the carrot, onion and any pieces of meat.

3 Purée the meat, carrot, onion and stock in a blender. Return to a clean pan with the lemon juice, seasoning and port. Reheat and serve with croûtons of bread.

Lentil and coriander soup

1 tbsp (15 ml) vegetable oil
1 large onion, chopped
4 oz (110 g) split red lentils
1 pint (570 ml) tomato juice
½ pint (275 ml) water
salt and black pepper
1 tbsp (15 ml) ground
  coriander seeds
1 tbsp (15 ml) chopped
  coriander

Serves 4

1 Heat the oil in a saucepan and sauté the onion for 5 minutes. Add the lentils and sauté for a few minutes.

2 Stir in the tomato juice, water, seasoning and ground coriander. Bring to the boil, cover and simmer for 20 minutes. Serve very hot, sprinkled with coriander.

Lovage soup

For a sharp lemony soup, try using sorrel instead of lovage.

1 oz (25 g) butter
2 medium onions, finely
  chopped
4 tbsp (60 ml) finely
  chopped lovage leaves
1 oz (25 g) plain flour
1 pint (570 ml) chicken or
  vegetable stock
½ pint (275 ml) milk
salt and black pepper

Serves 4

1 Melt the butter in a saucepan and gently sauté the onions for 5 minutes until soft. Add the lovage, stir in the flour and cook for 1 minute, stirring constantly.

2 Gradually stir in the stock, cover and simmer gently for 15 minutes. Add the milk and seasoning. Reheat slowly; do not boil the soup or it will curdle.

Fish

Parsley is the herb most commonly associated with fish, but there are many other herbs that partner fish exceedingly well. Lemon balm and lemon thyme are obvious choices for most types of fish, but there are others which may not spring so readily to mind, like caraway, lovage and mint. Fresh herbs in butter are delicious with a plain grilled herring.

Chervil stuffed trout

2 oz (50 g) butter
3 oz (75 g) onion, finely
  chopped
4 oz (110 g) soft
  breadcrumbs
3 oz (75 g) mushrooms,
  finely chopped
juice and rind of 1 lemon
1 cup of chopped chervil
salt and black pepper
4 trout, about 8 oz (225 g)
  each, or 1 large fish, 2–4 lb
  (1–2 kg), gutted and cleaned

Serves 4

Illustrated on p. 111.

1 Preheat the oven to 350°F (180°C) Gas 4.

2 Melt the butter and gently sauté the onion until golden but not brown.

3 Combine the breadcrumbs, mushrooms, lemon rind and juice, chervil and seasoning in a large bowl. Add the cooked onion and mix together.

4 Divide the stuffing mixture between the trout, spooning it into each stomach cavity. Put a knob of butter on top of each fish and then wrap in a square of lightly greased kitchen foil. Bake for 15 minutes.

5 Remove the fish from the oven, open the foil and grill or barbecue for 5 minutes on each side.

Gravlax

2 lb (900 g) fresh salmon
5 tbsp (75 ml) sugar
5 tbsp (75 ml) sea salt
black pepper
5 tbsp (75 ml) dill leaves

SAUCE
2 tbsp (30 ml) French mustard
1 tsp (5 ml) clear honey
1 egg yolk
2 tbsp (30 ml) white wine
  vinegar
salt and black pepper
6 tbsp (90 ml) olive oil
2 tbsp (30 ml) chopped
  dill leaves

Serves 6

Illustrated on p. 111.

1 Cut the salmon in half lengthways and remove all the bones.

2 Mix together the sugar, salt and black pepper. Rub the mixture over the fish.

3 Place a layer of dill in the bottom of a dish and lay half the salmon, skin side down, on the dill. Cover with more dill and lay the other half of salmon on it skin side up. Coat with the rest of the dill and any of the remaining sugar mixture.

4 Cover the dish with cling film and a weighted plate. Leave in a cool place for 24 hours.

5 Make the sauce by putting all the ingredients except the oil and dill in a bowl and beating with a whisk. Slowly beat in the oil and then add the chopped dill.

6 Scrape the marinade off the salmon. Slice the flesh away from the skin, across the grain, and serve with the sauce and a garnish of lemon and dill leaves.

Sole en croûte with thyme

4 fillets of sole
1 oz (25 g) butter
salt and black pepper
5 fl oz (150 ml) dry white wine
8 oz (225 g) puff pastry
1 egg, beaten

STUFFING
1 oz (25 g) butter
1 medium onion, finely chopped
2 oz (50 g) mushrooms,
    finely chopped
4 oz (110 g) soft breadcrumbs
3 oz (75 g) raisins
1 tbsp (15 ml) chopped thyme
1 egg, beaten
salt and black pepper

Serves 4

Illustrated opposite.

1 Preheat the oven to 325°F (170°C) Gas 3.

2 Put the sole fillets in a baking dish, dot with butter, season and pour over the wine. Bake gently for about 15 minutes. Drain, retaining the fish juices.

3 Melt the butter and sauté the onion. Add the finely chopped mushrooms and fry for a few minutes until just soft.

4 Mix the onion and mushrooms with the rest of the stuffing ingredients and set aside.

5 Turn up the oven to 375°F (190°C) Gas 5.

6 Divide the puff pastry into four portions. Roll out each one to the size of a small plate. Place one sole fillet with a quarter of the stuffing on each round of pastry. Roll over, moisten the pastry edges with beaten egg and seal.

7 Glaze with beaten egg and bake for about 20 minutes, or until golden brown. Delicious served with a thyme-flavoured cream sauce.

Mussels in saffron

6 pints (2 kg) mussels
1 tbsp (15 ml) olive oil
1 tbsp (15 ml) oats
2 small onions, sliced
2 tbsp (30 ml) finely
    chopped parsley
2 fl oz (50 ml) dry white wine
1 oz (25 g) butter
1 oz (25 g) plain flour
¼ pint (150 ml) milk
¼ tsp (1.25 g) saffron,
    infused in 1 tbsp (15 ml)
    hot water
2 oz (50 g) breadcrumbs

Serves 4–6

Illustrated opposite.

1 Soak the mussels for about 2 hours in a bowl of fresh water with the oats added to plump them up. Carefully scrub all the mussels under running water and remove their beards.

2 Heat the oil in a large saucepan and sauté the onion until soft. Add the parsley, mussels and wine. Cover the saucepan and leave the mussels to steam open (about 5 minutes), stirring occasionally. As the mussels open, remove them from the pan.

3 Preheat the oven to 400°F (200°C) Gas 6.

4 Melt the butter in a saucepan and stir in the flour to make a roux. Add the milk and liquid from the cooked mussels and the saffron infusion. Stir well to make a smooth sauce and remove from the heat.

5 Stir the cooked mussels into the sauce, then pour into a deep 10 in (25 cm) square ovenproof dish. Sprinkle with breadcrumbs and bake for about 10 minutes. Delicious served with garlic bread.

Clockwise from the top: Chervil stuffed trout (p. 109); Sole en croûte with thyme (above); Mussels in saffron (above); Gravlax (p. 109).

Meat

In the past herbs were used to preserve meat and disguise the fact that it might not be as fresh as it should be. Cooks would wrap meat in tansy, both to add a spicy flavour and to deter flies. Fortunately, herbs are used nowadays to enhance the flavour of the meat. Many of the more robust herbs, like thyme, tarragon and rosemary, can be used either to counteract the richness or, in small quantities, to add a subtle flavour to a leaner meat.

Pheasant pot roast with thyme

This is a succulent way of cooking any type of game, just adjust the cooking time accordingly.

2 tbsp (30 ml) vegetable oil
1 pheasant
2 oz (50 g) streaky bacon, cut into 2 in (5 cm) pieces
8 oz (225 g) carrots, cut into 2 in (5 cm) chunks
4 oz (110 g) celery, cut into 2 in (5 cm) lengths
4 oz (110 g) button mushrooms
1 medium onion, thickly sliced
6 large sprigs of thyme
2 tbsp (30 ml) plain flour
½ pint (275 ml) red wine
½ pint (275 ml) water
salt and black pepper

Serves 4

1 Preheat the oven to 350°F (180°C) Gas 4.

2 Heat the oil in a heavy-based casserole and quickly brown the pheasant on all sides. Remove the pheasant from the casserole and set aside.

3 Add the bacon to the casserole and fry until lightly browned. Add the carrots, celery, mushrooms, onion and 3 sprigs of thyme and gently sauté until browned.

4 Stir in the flour, then add the red wine and water. Stir well and gently bring to the boil. Add the pheasant and remaining thyme. Season to taste.

5 Cover and pot roast for 1½ hours. When cooked, remove the pheasant from the casserole and place it on a serving dish. Strain the sauce into a sauce boat.

Rabbit with mustard and thyme

The mustard and thyme coating forms a delicious crust. For chicken, try savory or chives instead of thyme.

2 tbsp (30 ml) mustard powder
2 tbsp (30 ml) plain flour
1 tbsp (15 ml) chopped thyme
salt and black pepper (optional)
about 6 tbsp (90 ml) water
1 rabbit, jointed

Serves 4

1 Preheat the oven to 350°F (180°C) Gas 4.

2 Mix the mustard powder, flour and thyme together in a bowl. Season if liked. Gradually add the water, mixing the mustard and flour to a smooth paste. Using a pastry brush or the back of a spoon, spread the paste all over the surfaces of the jointed rabbit.

3 Arrange the joints on a greased baking tray. Bake for 1–1½ hours or until tender. Serve hot or cold.

Spicy lemon balm kebabs

1 clove garlic
1 leg of lamb, about 3 lb
  (1.5 kg), boned and cut into
  1 in (2.5 cm) cubes
1 large onion, sliced into
  chunks
2 good handfuls of lemon
  balm leaves

MARINADE
2 fl oz (50 ml) wine vinegar
1 tsp (5 ml) ground coriander
1 tsp (5 ml) ground cumin
½ tsp (2.5 ml) chili powder
1 tsp (5 ml) ground turmeric
1 tbsp (15 ml) brown sugar
1 tbsp (15 ml) mango chutney
2 bay leaves
2 chilies (optional)
salt and black pepper

Serves 6

Illustrated on p. 115.

1 Rub the surface of a deep dish with the cut clove of garlic. Arrange the lamb cubes on the base of the dish. Cover with a layer of onion and top with the lemon balm leaves.

2 For the marinade, boil the vinegar, coriander, cumin, chili, turmeric, brown sugar, chutney and bay leaves together for 5 minutes. Leave to cool. Pour the cooled marinade over the meat. Add the chilies and seasoning. Cover and leave overnight in the refrigerator.

3 Drain the lamb and onion pieces and thread them on to metal skewers. Barbecue or grill for 15–20 minutes until browned, basting with the marinade. Discard the bay leaves before serving. Serve with hot garlic bread or on a bed of rice accompanied by a crisp green salad.

Rosemary kebabs

To make a marinade for 1 lb (450 g) chopped lamb or pork, mix 4 tbsp (60 ml) olive oil, the juice of 2 lemons and the grated peel of 1 lemon, a crushed garlic clove and 4 sprigs of rosemary, or 2 tsp (10 ml) dried leaves. Marinade the meat for at least 4 hours, then thread it on to skewers, or woody rosemary stalks, alternating it with chunks of red and green pepper and onion. Use the marinade to baste the meat as it grills.

Tarragon-baked chicken

Parsley, chives, thyme or chervil can be substituted for the tarragon.

8 chicken thighs or
  drumsticks, 3 oz (75 g) each
2 oz (50 g) butter
2 tbsp (30 ml) chopped
  tarragon
salt and black pepper

Serves 4

1 Preheat the oven to 375°F (190°C) Gas 5.

2 To remove the bones from the chicken pieces, use a sharp knife and run it downwards between the bone and the flesh until the bone comes loose. Gently twist the bone with your hands and it will come out easily.

3 Soften the butter a little and work to a paste with a wooden spoon. Mix in the tarragon and seasoning.

4 Divide the flavoured butter between the chicken pieces, filling each cavity with a generous amount. Seal the open ends of each piece using a wooden cocktail stick or small skewer.

5 Lay the pieces in a 9 in (23 cm) square ovenproof dish and cover with foil. Bake for 40 minutes, removing the foil for the last 10 minutes. Alternatively, finish off over a barbecue.

Stuffed lovage and vine leaves

about 8 large stalks of
  lovage
1 tbsp (15 ml) olive oil
1 small onion, finely chopped
2 oz (50 g) pine kernels
1 oz (25 g) raisins
1 tsp (5 ml) chopped
  rosemary
salt and black pepper
8 oz (225 g) lean minced lamb
8 vine leaves

Serves 4

Illustrated opposite.

1 Cut the lovage leaves as close to the small groups of leaves as possible and lay them in a large heatproof dish. Cover with boiling water, leave for 10 minutes, drain and rinse under cold water. Set aside to cool.

2 Preheat the oven to 400°F (200°C) Gas 6.

3 Heat the oil in a large saucepan and gently sauté the onion for about 5 minutes until soft. Add the pine kernels, raisins, rosemary and seasoning. Remove from the heat and set aside to cool.

4 Mix the lamb into the cooled onion mixture.

5 Lay out the vine leaves and put 2–3 lovage leaves in the centre of each one.

6 Place about 1 tbsp (15 ml) of the lamb stuffing on the leaves and roll them up. Place the rolls in a greased 8 in (20 cm) square ovenproof dish. Cover and bake for about 30 minutes.

Pork and sorrel terrine

1½ lb (700 g) lean pork
4 oz (110 g) fresh
  breadcrumbs
1 medium onion
2 cloves garlic
salt and black pepper
about 60 sorrel leaves,
  washed and drained

Serves 8

Illustrated opposite.

1 Mince or blend the pork with the breadcrumbs, onion and garlic. Mix very well and season to taste.

2 Preheat the oven to 375°F (190°C) Gas 5.

3 Grease a 2 lb (1 kg) loaf tin and press a third of the pork mixture into the base. Next make a layer of half the sorrel leaves. Add another third of the pork mixture, then the rest of the sorrel leaves, pressing each layer down well. Finish with a layer of the remaining pork mixture.

4 Cover with foil and stand the tin in a roasting tin half filled with water. Bake for 1½ hours.

5 Let it cool in the tin; slice and serve with hot toast.

Clockwise from the top: Spicy lemon balm kebabs (p. 113); Rosemary kebabs (p. 113); Stuffed lovage and vine leaves (above); Pork and sorrel terrine (above); Persian chicken with herbs (p. 116).

Pork chops marinaded with juniper and garlic

2 tbsp (30 ml) olive oil
6 juniper berries, crushed
2 cloves garlic, crushed
salt and black pepper
4 pork chops, ¾ in (2 cm)
   thick, about 8 oz (225 g) each
1 oz (25 g) plain flour
½ pint (275 ml) dry cider

Serves 4

1 Mix the oil, juniper berries, garlic and seasoning together in a bowl.

2 Lay the pork chops in the base of a shallow dish and cover them with the marinade, making sure all the surfaces are coated. Cover and leave in a cool place for at least 3 hours, preferably overnight.

3 Drain the chops and reserve the marinade.

4 Heat a large frying pan and add the reserved marinade. When hot, add the pork chops and cook over a moderate heat for about 10 minutes on each side. To test if the chops are cooked, insert a sharp knife between the thickest part of the meat and the bone; all traces of pink should have gone. Remove the chops from the pan.

5 Leave the frying pan over the heat and stir the flour into the remaining juices. Add the cider and bring to the boil. Return the chops to the sauce in the pan. Heat through and serve.

Persian chicken with herbs

4 oz (110 g) butter
2 medium onions, sliced
1 boiling chicken
¾ pint (425 ml) chicken stock
salt and black pepper
1 cup (225 ml)
   chopped parsley
1 cup (225 ml) chopped chives
¼ cup (50 ml) chopped mint
¼ cup (50 ml) chopped
   coriander leaves
2 oz (50 g) walnuts,
   chopped
6 fl oz (175 ml) orange juice
grated rind of 2 oranges
2 eggs, beaten (optional)

Serves 4–6

Illustrated on p. 115.

1 Melt 1 oz (25 g) of the butter in a large saucepan and sauté the onions until golden.

2 Add the chicken to the pan with the stock and seasoning. Cover and simmer for 1 hour until tender.

3 Melt the remaining butter in a pan and lightly cook the parsley, chives, mint and coriander to flavour the butter. Add to the chicken, then stir in the chopped walnuts, orange juice and rind. Simmer for 30 minutes.

4 If liked, stir in the beaten eggs just before serving. Accompany with noodles or rice.

Vegetarian main dishes

The increased interest in vegetarian cookery and the attendant abundance of new cookery books has led even confirmed carnivores to enjoy a meatless meal once or twice a week. There is no doubt that the increased availability of fresh herbs can take some of the credit for the vegetarian upsurge.

A savoury dish is always further enhanced by the addition of the right herb, as in Leek and sage croûstade or Oregano cheese pie.

Green herb omelette

6–8 eggs
2 leeks, washed and chopped
4 spring onons, chopped
4 oz (110 g) spinach,
    washed and chopped
3 tbsp (45 ml)
    chopped parsley
3 tbsp (45 ml) chopped
    herbs, such as tarragon,
    coriander, chives,
    chervil, dill
1 tbsp (15 ml) chopped
    walnuts
salt and black pepper

Serves 4

Illustrated on p. 119.

1 Heat the oven to 350°F (180°C) Gas 4.

2 Beat the eggs in a large bowl. Add the chopped vegetables, herbs and walnuts. Season to taste and mix the ingredients together thoroughly.

3 Butter a large ovenproof dish and pour in the mixture. Cover and bake for 30 minutes. Remove the cover and bake for a further 15 minutes until the top is golden. Serve hot or cold.

Hazelnut and sage pâté

5 oz (150 g) hazelnuts
2 oz (50 g) sesame seeds
8 oz (225 g) cream cheese
2 cloves garlic, crushed
⅓ tsp (2 ml) salt
⅓ tsp (2 ml) black pepper
1 tbsp (15 ml) chopped sage
2 tbsp (30 ml) olive oil
about 4 tbsp (60 ml) milk

Serves 4–6

1 Preheat the oven to 350°F (180°C) Gas 4.

2 Place the hazelnuts and sesame seeds on separate baking trays. Lightly roast in the oven for 5–10 minutes. When the nuts are cool, rub off the skins.

3 Grind the nuts and seeds together until they resemble fine crumbs. Or, if you prefer a coarse pâté, grind half the nuts and seeds finely and half coarsely.

4 Beat the cream cheese, garlic, salt, pepper, sage and oil together in a bowl.

5 Add the nut and seed mixture, combining well. Add the milk to give a moist consistency. The mixture needs to be fairly wet as the nuts will absorb some liquid.

6 Serve chilled in ramekins or on small individual salad plates.

Oregano cheese pie

PASTRY
8 oz (225 g) plain flour
pinch of salt
4 oz (110 g) butter

FILLING
8 oz (225 g) ricotta cheese
1 tbsp (15 ml) chopped onion
2 oz (50 g) Parmesan cheese,
 grated
2 eggs
black pepper
2 tbsp (30 ml) parsley
1 tbsp (15 ml) olive oil
1 clove garlic, crushed
2 tbsp (30 ml) chopped oregano
2 oz (50 g) black olives,
 stoned and sliced
7 oz (200 g) tomato purée
4 oz (110 g) Mozzarella
 cheese, thinly sliced
1 green pepper, sliced
a little beaten egg

Serves 6

Illustrated opposite.

1 For the pastry, sift the flour and salt into a bowl. Rub in the butter until the mixture resembles fine breadcrumbs. Add enough water to bind to a dough.

2 Roll out half the dough and use to line an 8 in (20 cm) greased deep pie dish.

3 Preheat the oven to 400°F (200°C) Gas 6.

4 For the filling, mix the ricotta cheese, onion, Parmesan, eggs, plenty of black pepper and chopped parsley.

5 Heat the oil in a small pan and sauté the garlic with the oregano. Stir in the tomato purée and olives.

6 Spread half the ricotta mixture on the pastry base, cover with half the Mozzarella slices, then half the tomato mixture and half the pepper slices. Repeat.

7 Roll out the remaining dough to make a lid. Seal the edges. Brush the top of the pie with beaten egg and slash 4 times with a knife because the pie rises during cooking. Bake in the preheated oven for 30–40 minutes.

Tagliatelle with marigold sauce aurore

12 fl oz (350 ml) milk
1 large onion, quartered
4 tbsp (60 ml) marigold
 (calendula) petals,
 fresh or dried
2 large carrots, sliced
 lengthwise
1 bay leaf
4 oz (110 g) butter
4 oz (110 g) plain flour
6 oz (175 g) cheese, grated
salt and black pepper
8 oz (225 g) tagliatelle verde

Serves 4

Illustrated opposite.

1 Place the milk, onion, marigold petals, carrots and bay leaf in a saucepan. Cover and simmer gently for about 10 minutes until the carrots are soft.

2 Pour through a sieve into a jug and reserve the carrot and onion pieces.

3 Melt the butter in a pan, add the flour and cook for 2–3 minutes, stirring until smooth. Gradually add the flavoured milk and simmer for 2 minutes, stirring to make a smooth sauce.

4 Press the cooked carrot and onion through a sieve and add to the sauce. Fold in the cheese and seasoning.

5 Cook the tagliatelle in a pan of boiling salted water until al dente. Serve topped with the marigold sauce.

Clockwise from top right: Tagliatelle with marigold sauce aurore (above), Oregano cheese pie (above); Herb leaf fritters (p. 123); Green herb omelette (p. 117).

Leek and sage croustade

4 oz (110 g) fresh breadcrumbs
4 oz (110 g) chopped nuts
1 clove garlic, crushed
1 tsp (5 ml) basil
1 tsp (5 ml) rosemary,
 chopped
1 tsp (5 ml) oregano
2 oz (50 g) butter
4 oz (110 g) cheese, grated

SAUCE
2 oz (50 g) butter
4 leeks, washed and finely
 chopped
1 oz (25 g) plain flour
½ pint (275 ml) milk
2 tomatoes, skinned and
 chopped
2 tbsp (30 ml) chopped sage
salt and pepper

Serves 6

1 Preheat the oven to 350°F (180°C) Gas 4.

2 Mix the breadcrumbs, nuts, garlic and herbs together in a bowl. Rub in the butter, then stir in the cheese. Press this mixture firmly into the base of an 8 in (20 cm) flan dish. Bake for 20 minutes until golden.

3 For the sauce, melt the butter in a saucepan and fry the leeks for about 10 minutes until soft. Stir in the flour, then add the milk and cook for 5 minutes, stirring. Add the tomatoes, sage and seasoning.

4 Spread the leek sauce over the cooked croustade. Bake for a further 20 minutes.

Pancakes with basil stuffing

BATTER
4 oz (110 g) plain flour
4 fl oz (110 ml) beer
4 fl oz (110 ml) milk
2 eggs
2 oz (50 g) butter, melted
salt

FILLING
1 oz (25 g) butter
1 small onion, finely chopped
1 clove garlic, crushed
8 oz (225 g) button
 mushrooms, chopped
8 oz (225 g) cream cheese
2 eggs, beaten
1 tbsp (15 ml) shredded
 basil
salt and black pepper

TOPPING
3 tbsp (45 ml) grated
 Parmesan cheese
¼ pint (150 ml) single cream

Serves 4

1 Put all batter ingredients in a blender and blend for about 1 minute. Leave to stand for at least 1 hour.

2 For the stuffing, melt the butter in a pan and sauté the onion and garlic for about 5 minutes. Add the mushrooms and sauté for 1 minute. Leave to cool. Mix with the remaining filling ingredients. Chill.

3 Preheat the oven to 350°F (180°C) Gas 4.

4 For the pancakes, melt a little butter in a small frying pan. Add about 2 tbsp (30 ml) of batter and swirl round the pan. Cook for about 2 minutes until the underside is golden, then turn the pancake and cook the other side for about 1 minute. Put the pancake on a tea towel. Use the remaining batter to make 7 more pancakes.

5 Fill the 8 pancakes with the cream cheese and mushroom mixture. Roll up and place in an ovenproof dish. Sprinkle with Parmesan cheese and pour over the cream. Bake in the preheated oven for 20 minutes.

Vegetable side dishes

A plain roast, grilled chops or cutlets will all benefit from the addition of a well-flavoured vegetable side dish. Try cabbage with juniper, mint or caraway to persuade the younger members of the family that this vegetable *is* fun. They will doubtless enjoy also the novelty of herb fritters and tarragon stuffed mushrooms. Many vegetables like fennel, leeks and kohlrabi are improved by coating them in a herby white sauce.

Spicy aubergines

2 large aubergines
1 tbsp (15 ml) olive oil
1 tsp (5 ml) cumin seeds
1 tsp (5 ml) fennel seeds
1 lb (450 g) tomatoes, skinned and chopped
1 in (2.5 cm) fresh ginger, grated
4 cloves garlic, crushed
1 tsp (5 ml) ground coriander
1 tsp (5 ml) ground cardamom
½ pint (275 ml) water
salt and black pepper

GARNISH
fresh coriander leaves

Serves 4

1 Wipe the aubergines, remove the stalks and cut into finger-sized pieces. Fry them in the oil for about 5 minutes until brown. Drain on kitchen paper.

2 Fry the cumin and fennel seeds for about 2 minutes, stirring all the time, until they turn a shade darker. Stir in the chopped tomatoes, grated ginger, crushed garlic, coriander, cardamom and the water. Simmer for about 20 minutes until the mixture is a thick sauce.

3 Return the aubergines to the pan and heat through, turning them carefully. Garnish with coriander leaves.

Baked cabbage with juniper

1½ lb (700 g) white cabbage
1 tbsp (15 ml) olive oil
1 onion, finely chopped
1 clove garlic, crushed
8 juniper berries, crushed
salt and black pepper

Serves 4–6

1 Preheat the oven to 400°F (200°C) Gas 6.

2 Remove and discard the outer leaves from the cabbage and cut out the centre stalk. Finely shred the cabbage, then rinse in a colander. Drain well.

3 Heat the oil in a flameproof casserole and gently fry the onion and garlic for about 10 minutes until soft. Stir in the juniper berries, then add the cabbage and mix well. Add salt and pepper to taste.

4 Cover with a tight-fitting lid. Bake for about 35 minutes. Check that the cabbage is cooked but still crisp before serving.

Sorrel and parsnip mousses

1 lb (450 g) parsnips, peeled
and cut into large pieces
about 36 sorrel leaves
2 oz (50 g) butter
2 oz (50 g) plain flour
½ pint (275 ml) milk
1 egg, separated
1 tbsp (15 ml) chopped chives
salt and black pepper

Serves 6

1 Place the parsnips in a saucepan, cover and simmer for 20 minutes until tender.

2 Preheat the oven to 375°F (190°C) Gas 5.

3 Very quickly dip each sorrel leaf into a bowl of boiling water to blanch. Use these leaves to line the bases and sides of 6 ramekin dishes. (You will need about 6 leaves for each dish.)

4 When the parsnips are cooked, drain and mash them into a smooth purée.

5 Melt the butter in a pan, add the flour and cook for 2 minutes, stirring until smooth. Gradually add the milk and simmer for 2 minutes, stirring to make a smooth thick sauce.

6 Beat the egg yolk into the sauce. Whisk the egg white in a bowl until soft peaks form.

7 Mix the sauce and parsnip together. Add the chives and seasoning. Fold in the egg white.

8 Divide the mixture between the lined ramekin dishes. Place the dishes in a deep roasting tin half filled with hot water.

9 Bake for 50 minutes until golden and puffy. Turn out and serve hot.

Fennel with Roquefort sauce

4 bulbs of Florence fennel

SAUCE
1 oz (25 g) butter
1 oz (25 g) plain flour
½ pint (275 ml) mixed milk
and fennel stock
3 oz (75 g) Roquefort
cheese, grated
black pepper
1 tbsp (15 ml) plain yogurt

GARNISH
1 tbsp (15 ml) chopped
parsley
1 tbsp (15 ml) chopped
fennel leaves

Serves 4

1 Halve the fennel bulbs vertically, put in a saucepan and cover with water. Bring to the boil and simmer for about 15–20 minutes or until tender. Drain, reserving ¼ pint (150 ml) of the cooking liquid.

2 For the sauce, melt the butter, add the flour and cook for 2 minutes, stirring until smooth. Gradually add the milk and stock and simmer for 2 minutes, stirring to make a smooth sauce.

3 Add the grated cheese and black pepper to taste. Do not allow the sauce to boil. Stir in the yogurt and cook gently for a few minutes, stirring.

4 Place the fennel in a serving dish and pour over the Roquefort sauce. Garnish with the parsley and fennel.

Herb leaf fritters

*Any of the stronger-tasting herb leaves can be used. Salad burnet
leaves have a delicate shape and good flavour, or try sage,
basil or sorrel.*

20–30 herb leaves
  depending on size
oil for deep frying

BATTER
4 oz (110 g) plain flour
pinch of salt
2 tbsp (30 ml) olive oil
4 tbsp (60 ml) warm water
1 large egg white

Serves 4

Illustrated on p. 119.

1 Carefully rinse and dry the herb leaves.

2 For the batter, mix the flour and salt together in a bowl.
Blend in the oil and water until smooth and creamy. Leave to
stand for 1–2 hours in a cool place.

3 Whisk the egg white until stiff, then fold it carefully into the
cool batter.

4 Heat the oil until a drop of batter crisps and browns quickly
but does not burn. Dip the leaves, one at a time, into the
batter. Fry, several at a time, for 2–3 minutes until they are
golden brown.

5 Carefully remove the fritters and drain on kitchen paper.
Keep warm in the oven until all the fritters are cooked. Serve
immediately.

Mediterranean vegetables

4 fl oz (110 ml) olive oil
2 cloves garlic, chopped
8 oz (225 g) potato, cubed
8 oz (225 g) green beans
8 oz (225 g) courgettes,
  sliced
8 oz (225 g) okra, trimmed
4 oz (110 g) onion, sliced
1 tbsp (15 ml) coriander,
  chopped
juice of 1 lime
juice of 1 lemon

GARNISH
2 tbsp (30 ml) chopped parsley

Serves 4

1 Heat the oil in a large saucepan and sauté all the vegetables,
garlic and the coriander for about 5 minutes.

2 Add the lime and lemon juices, then cover and cook gently
for 30 minutes, stirring occasionally to prevent the mixture
from sticking to the bottom of the pan. Garnish with parsley.

Salads and snacks

Salad herbs can be divided into three groups. First are those selected for their crunchy texture and mild flavour. These include the ornamental lettuces, forced chicory, and blanched leaves such as dandelion and summer purslane. Second are the flavouring herbs. This includes most of the savoury leaves and seeds listed under Salad Herbs on p. 106. Use these in small quantities as they can taste sharp. The third group consists of herb flowers, which have subtle flavours and are used more for their beauty than taste.

Melon, tomato and mint salad

This is equally good with lemon balm and fresh basil leaves to replace the mint.

8 oz (225 g) cantaloupe or ogen melon
8 oz (225 g) firm tomatoes, cut into thin wedges
6 oz (175 g) cucumber, peeled and grated
½ cup (125 ml) finely chopped mint
½ pint (275 ml) yogurt
salt and black pepper

GARNISH
mint leaves

Serves 4

Illustrated on p. 127.

1 Cut the melon flesh into balls with a ball cutter. Alternatively, cut the melon into cubes.

2 Combine the melon, tomato and cucumber well in a large salad bowl.

3 Stir the mint into the yogurt to make a dressing, then pour over the salad. Season to taste and garnish the dressed salad with mint leaves.

Sweet anise salad

3 red apples
3 tbsp (45 ml) lemon or orange juice
1 tsp (5 ml) sugar
6 oz (175 g) anise stalks, sliced
2 bananas, sliced
4 oz (110 g) walnuts, coarsley chopped
4 fl oz (110 ml) mayonnaise
lettuce leaves

GARNISH
parsley

Serves 4

1 Core the apples and dice, leaving the peel on. Reserve some apple to use as a garnish.

2 Mix the lemon juice and sugar together in a bowl, then toss the apple in the mixture.

3 Add the anise stalks, banana and walnuts to the apple. Mix in the mayonnaise and chill.

4 Serve the salad in a lettuce-lined salad bowl and garnish with the reserved apple and parsley.

Fennel salad with orange

1 bulb of Florence fennel,
  thinly sliced
1 lettuce
1 bunch of watercress
fennel leaves, chopped

DRESSING
4 fl oz (110 ml) olive oil
juice of 1 large orange
1 tsp (5 ml) French mustard
1 tsp (5 ml) fennel seeds
salt and black pepper

Serves 6

Illustrated on p. 127.

1 First make the dressing. Put all the ingredients in a screwtop jar and shake well. Leave to stand for at least 30 minutes.

2 Arrange the fennel, lettuce and watercress in a salad bowl. Scatter with the fennel leaves.

3 Shake the dressing again, then pour over the salad just before serving.

Mixed salad with chili and coriander

2 onions
2 radishes
2 large carrots
1 large tomato, chopped
1 small lettuce, shredded
bunch of coriander, chopped
  grated rind and juice of
  1 large lemon
1–2 chilies, chopped
salt and black pepper

Serves 4–6

Illustrated on p. 127.

1 Grate the onions, radishes and carrots and place in a large salad bowl.

2 Add the remaining ingredients and toss together well. Add extra lemon juice to taste.

Potato salad with dill and chives

4 medium potatoes
1 tbsp (15 ml) chopped onion
1 tbsp (15 ml) chopped parsley
1 tbsp (15 ml) chopped chives
1 flowering head of dill
  finely chopped or 1 tsp (5 ml)
  dill seed
3 tbsp (45 ml) mayonnnaise
1 tbsp (15 ml) cream or yogurt
salt and black pepper

Serves 4

1 Boil the potatoes in their skins until just tender. Cool, peel and slice them.

2 Sprinkle on the onion, parsley, chives and dill.

3 Blend the mayonnaise and cream, season with salt and pepper. Add to the potato mixture and stir gently. Leave to stand a few hours so the flavours mingle.

Cheese balls

8 oz (225 g) cream cheese
1 cup (225 ml) finely chopped
herbs: chives, parsley,
rosemary, sage, thyme

Illustrated on p. 133.

Shape the cheese into plum-sized balls and then roll them in the chopped herbs. Serve with salads, on hot vegetables or as a spread for bread or toast.

Green mayonnaise

*Use any combination of the following herbs: garlic, lemon balm,
lovage, salad burnet, tarragon, thyme.*

1 egg yolk
½ pt (275 ml) olive oil
1 tbsp (15 ml) wine vinegar
2 tbsp (30 ml) chopped
parsley
1 tbsp (15 ml) selected herbs

Makes ½ pint (275 ml)

1 Beat the egg yolk for a minute or so, then start adding the oil, drop by drop, beating continuously.

2 When over half the oil has been added and the mixture has started to thicken, beat in the vinegar.

3 Add more oil drop by drop until it thickens again, then slowly pour in the rest. (If the mixture refuses to thicken or curdles, break a fresh egg yolk into a clean basin and slowly stir in the first mixture.)

4 Stir in the chopped herbs.

Angelica and mint sandwich

a good handful of fresh
young angelica leaves
a good handful of fresh
mint leaves
1–2 tbsp (15–30 ml)
mayonnaise
2–4 slices of bread

Serves 2

1 Pass the leaves through a herb mouli or chop very finely by hand. Mix the two herbs together.

2 Toast the bread then spread with mayonnaise.

3 Sprinkle a thick layer of the herb mixture on top. Cut into quarters and serve.

HERB SPREADS

These make a delicious snack served with biscuits or bread, and can be used as dips with sticks of raw vegetables.

Mix equal quantities of mayonnaise with chopped chervil, chives, coriander, dill, fennel, nasturtium petals, parsley, tarragon.

Clockwise from the top: Mixed flower and leaf salads; Mixed salad with chili and coriander (p. 125); Melon, tomato and mint salad (p. 124); Herb spread sandwiches (above); Fennel salad with orange (p. 125).

Desserts

There is no better way to end a summer meal or dinner party than with a delicately scented light dessert. Elderflowers and rose petals have a delicious fresh flavour and never fail to excite comment. They are particularly good in milk dishes. You can elevate a cheesecake above the ordinary by adding a few chopped rose geranium or mint leaves, and lemon balm, sweet cicely or aniseed will make the ever-popular fruit salad even more so.

Gooseberry and elderflower cream

1 lb (450 g) fresh washed gooseberries
½ cup (125 ml) water
5 elderflower heads or 1 tbsp (15 ml) orange-flower water
6 oz (175 g) sugar (or to taste)
2 oz (50 g) butter
3 eggs, beaten
whipped cream for topping

DECORATION
borage flowers

Serves 4

1 Cook the gooseberries and elderflowers in the water until soft. Remove the flowers and purée the fruit.

2 Return the mixture to the saucepan. Add the sugar and heat to dissolve. (At this stage, the mixture can be strained, bottled and kept in the freezer as a delicious muscatel-flavoured syrup for serving on fruit dishes or diluted with soda water as a summer drink.)

3 To make the cream dessert, stir in the butter until melted. Cool a little and slowly add the beaten eggs, stirring constantly until thick. Do not boil.

4 Spoon into serving glasses, top with cream and garnish with borage flowers.

Rose layered dessert

1 cup (225 ml) loosely packed scented rose petals, white heels removed
4 bananas, mashed
approx. 4 oz (110 g) chopped dates (equal volume to banana)
2 tbsp (30 ml) mincemeat
4 tbsp (60 ml) rose petal jam (see p. 135)
juice of 2 oranges
small carton whipped cream

DECORATION
crystallized rose petals
sweet cicely seeds (optional)

Serves 4

1 Cover a dish with pink and red rose petals.

2 Mix the banana, dates and mincemeat and make a layer over the petals, leaving the petals protruding around the edge. Cover with a layer of rose petal jam.

3 When ready to serve, pour over the orange juice. Add a layer of whipped cream and garnish with crystallized rose petals and sweet cicely seeds.

Mulled pears with juniper

4 firm pears
¼ pint (150 ml) red wine
¼ pint (150 ml) fresh
orange juice
2 oz (50 g) dark brown
sugar
4 juniper berries, crushed

Serves 4

1 Either peel the pears whole, leaving the stalks intact, or peel, core and quarter them.

2 Mix the red wine, orange juice, brown sugar and juniper berries together in a saucepan. Bring to simmering point.

3 Add the pears and simmer, uncovered, for 15 minutes or 25 minutes if the pears are whole. Turn and baste from time to time.

Sweet rice with rose geranium

4 oz (110 g) pudding rice
1½ pints (800 ml) milk
8 rose-scented geranium
leaves
1 oz (25 g) desiccated coconut
2 oz (50 g) flaked almonds
2 oz (50 g) raisins
2 oz (50 g) soft brown sugar

Serves 6

1 Mix the rice and milk together in a saucepan. Add 4 geranium leaves to the pan. Cover and simmer very gently for 30 minutes.

2 Remove from the heat and take out the leaves. Preheat the oven to 375°F (190°C) Gas 5.

3 Add the coconut, almonds, raisins and sugar to the milk mixture, stirring well.

4 Transfer the mixture to a large 8 in (20 cm) ovenproof dish. Arrange the remaining 4 geranium leaves across the top. Bake for 45 minutes.

Lemon balm cheesecake

PASTRY
4 oz (110 g) plain flour
pinch of salt
2 oz (50 g) margarine, cut
into pieces

FILLING
2 oz (50 g) margarine
2 tbsp (30 ml) honey
12 oz (350 g) cream cheese
2 eggs, beaten
6 tbsp (90 ml) very finely
chopped lemon balm

Serves 6

1 Preheat the oven to 400°F (200°C) Gas 6.

2 For the pastry, sift the flour and salt into a bowl. Rub in the margarine until the mixture resembles fine breadcrumbs. Add enough water to make a soft dough. Roll out to line a 7 in (18 cm) flan dish. Bake blind for 15 minutes.

3 For the filling, cream the margarine, honey and cream cheese together in a bowl until soft and creamy. Beat in the eggs and fold in the lemon balm. Reduce the oven temperature to 350°F (180°C) Gas 4.

4 Pour the filling into the pastry case. Bake for 45 minutes until the filling is golden and set. Serve with whipped cream or natural yogurt.

Breads, cakes and biscuits

There are just a few herbs that can be used really successfully in bread and cake mixes, but they make such a difference to the traditional tea-time bakes that they are well worth trying. The most popular herbs or, at least, the ones most frequently used, are rosemary, poppy seed, chives and caraway, but you can also confidently use aniseed, basil, dill, fennel, lovage seed, sunflower seed and thyme. All add a deliciously natural flavour.

Saffron fruit bread

8 fl oz (225 ml) milk, warmed
1 oz (25 g) fresh yeast
1 tsp (5 ml) sugar
¼ tsp (1.25 ml) saffron powder or strands
¼ pint (150 ml) boiling water
1 lb (450 g) plain flour
4 oz (110 g) butter
2 oz (50 g) caster sugar
6 oz (175 g) currants
4 oz (110 g) chopped mixed peel
1 tsp (5 ml) dried thyme

Serves 10

Illustrated on p. 133.

1 Place the milk in a bowl and dissolve the yeast and the sugar in it. Leave in warm place for about 10 minutes until frothy.

2 Steep the saffron in the boiling water, then leave the mixture to cool.

3 Sift the flour into a large bowl. Rub in the butter. Add the caster sugar, the currants, peel and thyme, mixing well.

4 Add the yeast liquid and saffron liquid to the flour mixture. (Strain the saffron mixture if using strands.) Mix until smooth with a wooden spoon; it should look like a very thick batter.

5 Pour the batter into a greased and lined 10 in (25 cm) round cake tin. Cover with a damp cloth and leave in a warm place for about 1 hour until the mixture rises to the top of the tin.

6 Preheat the oven to 375°F (190°C) Gas 5.

7 Bake the bread for 1 hour. Leave to cool in the tin. Slice and serve with butter.

Rosemary cheese fingers

2 oz (50 g) butter
5 oz (150 g) oat flakes
6 oz (175 g) Cheddar cheese, grated
1 egg, beaten
1 tbsp (15 ml) chopped rosemary
pinch of cayenne
salt

Makes 12 slices

1 Preheat the oven to 350°F (180°C) Gas 4.

2 Melt the butter in a saucepan. Place the remaining ingredients in a bowl and mix in the butter.

3 Press the mixture into a greased 8 in (20 cm) square tin. Bake for 30–40 minutes. Cut into fingers.

Sage oat cakes

1 oz (25 g) lard
6 tbsp (90 ml) boiling water
8 oz (225 g) medium oatmeal
½ tsp (2.5 ml) dried sage
¼ tsp (1.25 ml) bicarbonate
    of soda
pinch of salt

Makes 8 slices

Illustrated on p. 133.

1 Preheat the oven to 350°F (180°C) Gas 4.

2 Place the lard and water in a small pan and heat until the lard has melted. Cool.

3 Mix the oatmeal, sage, bicarbonate of soda and salt together in a bowl. Stir in the cooled liquid and mix to a soft dough, adding a little more water if necessary.

4 Pat the dough into a round about 8 in (20 cm) in diameter. Place on an ungreased baking tray.

5 Bake for about 40 minutes. Cut into 8 wedges, then leave to cool slightly before turning on to a wire rack.

Cheese bread with chives

½ oz (15 g) fresh yeast or
    1 oz (25 g) dried yeast and
    1 tsp (5 ml) sugar
2 fl oz (50 ml) water
1 lb (450 g) plain flour
4 oz (110 g) plain
    wholemeal flour
pinch of salt
12 fl oz (350 ml) water,
    heated to blood temperature
2 oz (50 g) butter
9 oz (250 g) cheese, grated
3 tbsp (45 ml) chopped chives
1 egg, beaten

Makes 2 lb (900 g) loaf

Illustrated on p. 133.

1 Put the yeast into a cup and stir in the 2 fl oz (50 ml) water. If using dried yeast, add the sugar. Leave in a warm place until the liquid is frothy.

2 Put the flours and salt into a large bowl. Pour the yeast mixture into the centre of the flour and mix together well with a knife, adding some of the warm water. Add the rest of the water, then knead the dough for 2 minutes.

3 Form the dough into a ball and sprinkle with flour. Cover the dough with a damp cloth and leave to rise in a warm place for 1½–2 hours until doubled in size.

4 Knead the dough lightly. Roll into a rectangle and dot with butter. Fold into 3, then roll out to the same size again. Sprinkle with the cheese and chives to within 1 in (2.5 cm) of the edge. Roll up from the short end, like a Swiss roll.

5 Place in a greased 2 lb (900 g) loaf tin and score the top with a sharp knife. Leave the dough to prove in a warm place for about 30 minutes.

6 Preheat the oven to 425°F (220°C) Gas 7.

7 Brush the loaf with beaten egg. Bake for 35–40 minutes. Best eaten when warm.

Sweet rosemary slices

2 eggs
5 oz (150 g) soft brown sugar
a few drops of vanilla essence
5 oz (150 g) plain flour
1 tsp (5 ml) baking powder
pinch of salt
1 tbsp (15 ml) rosemary leaves
   or 2 tsp (10 ml) dried
8 oz (225 g) raisins and
   candied fruit, such as
   angelica, glacé cherries,
   or candied pineapple
6 oz (175 g) pecan
   nuts, chopped, or
   sunflower seeds

Makes 24 slices

Illustrated opposite.

1 Preheat the oven to 375°F (190°C) Gas 5.

2 Beat the eggs in a bowl, then gradually add the sugar and vanilla essence. Mix well.

3 Sift in the flour, baking powder and salt. Add the rosemary leaves, then fold in the fruit and nuts.

4 Spoon the mixture on to a greased and floured 8 in (20 cm) baking tin and spread evenly.

5 Bake for 30 minutes. Remove from the tin while still warm. Allow to cool, then cut into squares.

Scented geranium leaf sponge

20 scented geranium leaves
8 oz (225 g) butter
8 oz (225 g) caster sugar
4 eggs, beaten
8 oz (225 g) self-raising
   flour, sifted

DECORATION
scented geranium leaves
icing sugar

Serves 6

1 Grease and line two 8 in (20 cm) sandwich tins. Arrange the geranium leaves on the lining paper.

2 Preheat the oven to 375°F (190°C) Gas 5.

3 Cream the butter and sugar together in a bowl until light and fluffy. Add the beaten eggs, a little at a time, to the creamed mixture, beating well. Fold in the flour.

4 Divide the mixture between the prepared tins. Bake for 20–25 minutes until golden.

5 Turn out of the tins and cool on wire racks. Remove the leaves and lining paper.

6 Sandwich the sponges with a filling: sweet geranium jelly and whipped cream are excellent. Arrange some geranium leaves on top of the sponge, then sift over some icing sugar. Carefully remove the leaves before eating.

Clockwise from top centre: Saffron fruit bread (p. 130); Cheese bread with chives (p. 131); Sage oat cakes (p. 131); Herb butter (p. 134); Sweet rosemary slices (above); Cheese balls (p. 126); Scented geranium leaf sponge (above).

Preserves

This section on preserves is just a brief introduction to a truly vast subject. Sample recipes are given for herb-flavoured oil, vinegars, pickles, butters, jellies and jams, but there is an infinite variety of recipes to be discovered and tried. Herb oils and vinegars form the bases of salad dressings and marinades while a herb butter spread on hot crusty bread makes a delicious accompaniment to a soup. The flavour of most aromatic herbs can be captured in a savoury jelly that will add interest to cold meats, roasts and salads.

HERBAL OILS

To make a herb oil, loosely fill a clear jar with freshly picked herbs and cover with unheated safflower or sunflower oil. (Any oil can be used but avoid strongly flavoured ones.) Cover with muslin and place on a sunny window sill. Allow to steep for 2 weeks, stirring daily. Strain through the muslin, and check the flavour. If it is as strong as you wish, bottle and label. If you want a stronger flavour, repeat the process with fresh herbs. Use herb oils in salad dressings, marinades, for browning meats and softening vegetables (see p. 106 for herbs for oils). For sweet oils, use almond oil with scented flowers.

HERBAL VINEGARS

Use cider or wine vinegar as a base. Bruise the freshly picked herbs and loosely fill a clean jar. Pour on warmed but not hot vinegar to fill the jar and cap with an acid-proof lid. Set in a sunny window and shake daily for 2 weeks. Test for flavour; if a stronger taste is required, strain the vinegar and repeat with fresh herbs. Store as it is or strain through double muslin and rebottle. Add a fresh sprig to the bottle for identification and visual appeal. Use in salad dressings, marinades, gravies and sauces.

HERB BUTTERS

Herb butters are a delicious way of adding the full flavours of fresh herbs to savoury snacks and dishes. Spread on sandwiches, toast and biscuits; use to add piquancy to grilled meats and fish, and vegetables. Try the blend below or make up your own.

Choose from well-flavoured herbs such as chervil, chives, garlic, parsley, rosemary, sage, salad burnet, tarragon and thyme.

Follow the same method, substituting soft cheese for the butter to make a flavoursome spread.

Parsley and chive butter

2 tbsp (30 ml) chopped
   parsley
1 tbsp (15 ml) chopped
   chives
8 oz/1 cup (225 g) butter,
   slightly softened
juice of 1 lemon
salt and black pepper

1 Beat the herbs into the butter and then add the lemon juice and seasoning. Mix until smooth.

2 Chill before serving. Shape in a mould if desired. Store in a cool place, or freeze in an ice-cube tray for handy portions.

Pickled cucumbers

about 2½ lb (1 kg) small
  cucumbers, 3–5 in
  (8–12 cm) long
2 cloves garlic
2 dill flower heads with leaves
7 tbsp (105 ml) coarse salt
6 peppercorns
8 fl oz (225 ml) white wine
  vinegar
1¼ pints (750 ml) water

Makes approx. 2 × 1¾ pints
  (1 litre) jars

1 Scrub the cucumbers and soak overnight in salted cold water. Drain. Sterilize the jars.

2 Place 1 clove garlic and a dill flower head in each.

3 Either leave the cucumbers whole or cut into quarters lengthways. Pack them into the jars.

4 Place the salt, pepper, vinegar and water in a saucepan and bring to the boil. Pour over the cucumbers. Seal, label and date. Store in a cool place for 6 weeks before using. Keep in the refrigerator once the jars have been opened.

Savoury herb jelly

4 lb (2 kg) tart cooking
  apples or crab apples,
  roughly chopped
1½ pints (800 ml) water
½ pint (275 ml) wine vinegar
a good handful of fresh herbs
12 oz (350 g) sugar per pint
  (570 ml) of juice

Makes about 4 lb (1.8 kg)

1 Boil the apples with the water and vinegar in a large preserving pan. Add the fresh herbs and simmer. Cook until the apples are soft. Strain through a jelly bag overnight.

2 Measure the juice, return to the saucepan and add the sugar. Stir to dissolve the sugar, then boil until "setting point" is reached, taking care not to let it boil over. Allow to cool a little for 10 minutes.

3 Pour into clean, sterilized jars. Seal, label and date. Store in a cool, dark cupboard.

Rose petal jam

1 lb (450 g) heavily scented,
  red or pink rose petals,
  washed and with the bitter
  white base removed
1 pint (570 ml) water
1 lb (450 g) caster sugar
juice of 2 lemons
1 tbsp (15 ml) rosewater

Makes approx. 2 × 1 lb
  (450 g) jars

1 Bring the water to the boil in a large, heavy saucepan. Reduce to simmering point then add the rose petals. Simmer gently for 5 minutes until the petals are soft.

2 Add the sugar and lemon juice. Bring back to the boil and simmer for 30 minutes. Stir until the sugar has dissolved and the mixture begins to thicken. Add the rosewater.

3 Allow the mixture to bubble up well. When the bubbles have turned more to foam, test for setting point; put a spoonful of the jam on a cold saucer, allow to cool and push the surface; if it wrinkles it is ready.

4 Allow the jam to cool slightly, then pour into sterilized jars, label and seal.

Herbal drinks

Teas made of aromatic leaves, flowers or roots steeped in boiling water are the most ancient consumed liquid after pure water. Most herb teas are infused: the leaves or flowers are put into a warm teapot, boiling water is poured over and the tea is brewed for 3–5 minutes.

Herb-flavoured yogurt drinks can be either savoury or sweet. In addition to being both easy to digest and refreshing, they take just a minute or two to prepare.

Herbs have long been used to improve the flavour of alcoholic drinks. Some of the most exotic and revered liqueurs derive their character from herbal ingredients. Benedictine and Chartreuse, for example, both contain a huge range of herbal flavourings.

CHINA TEA BLENDS

Many people find herbal tea bland by comparison to coffee and black tea, but, by blending china tea with herbs, the taste buds can more easily make the transition.

Herbal 'Earl Grey'

1 tsp (5 ml) China tea
3 tsp (15 ml) young fresh
  bergamot leaves

Infuse the herbs for 5 minutes in 2 cups (450 ml) boiling water and strain before drinking.

Try, also, substituting 1 tsp (5 ml) hibiscus flowers for the bergamot leaves for a pleasant lemony flavour.

SYRUPS

Herb and fruit syrups are a convenient way of capturing a seasonal crop for year-round use. They can be diluted for drinks or poured over ice creams and puddings.

Peppermint syrup

2 pints (1 litre) loosely
  packed peppermint leaves
white sugar
green food colouring
  (optional)

1 Place the leaves in a saucepan with just enough water to cover. Simmer for 30 minutes.

2 Strain through a jelly bag for 1 hour.

3 For each pint (570 ml) liquid, add 12 oz (350 g) sugar. Place the mixture in a pan and simmer for 15 minutes. Add food colouring, if using.

4 Bottle, label and date. Alternatively, freeze in convenient portions.

Loving cup

2 lemons
6 sprigs of lemon balm
6 sprigs and flowers of
    borage or viper's bugloss
4 oz (110 g) sugar
1½ pints (800 ml) water
½ bottle dessert wine
¼ pint (150 ml) French brandy
1 bottle champagne or
    sparkling dry white wine

DECORATION
borage flower ice cubes

1 Remove the thin rind (zest) from one of the lemons with a zester. Peel and thinly slice the lemons.

2 Put the lemon balm, borage, sliced lemon, lemon zest and sugar into a jug. Stir in the water, wine and brandy. Cover and chill for 1 hour.

3 Chill the champagne and mix in just before serving. Decorate with borage flower ice cubes.

Elderflower fizz

Elderflowers must be picked on a dry, sunny day, as the yeast is mainly in the pollen.

1 gallon (4.5 litres)
    water
1½ lb (700 g) sugar
juice and thinly peeled
    rind of 1 lemon
2 tbsp (30 ml) cider or
    wine vinegar
12 elderflower heads

1 Bring the water to the boil. Pour into a sterilized container, add the sugar, stirring until dissolved.

2 When cool, add the juice and rind of the lemon, vinegar and elderflowers. Cover with several layers of muslin and leave for 24 hours.

3 Filter through muslin into strong glass bottles. This drink is ready after 2 weeks. Serve chilled.

Raspberry and mint yogurt drink

8 fl oz (225 ml) natural
    yogurt
4 fl oz (100 ml)
    mineral water
3 oz (75 g) raspberries
    or 1 tbsp (15 ml)
    raspberry syrup
1 tsp (5 ml) mint syrup

DECORATION
2 sprigs of mint

Serves 2

1 Purée all the ingredients in a blender.

2 Pour the drink into 2 glasses and decorate each with a sprig of mint. Serve chilled.

· CHAPTER THREE ·

HERBS
IN THE HOME

One of the most delightful aspects of
growing herbs is the many attractive ways
in which you can display them and
appreciate their fragrance indoors.
Whether fresh or dried, herbs can be
made into striking arrangements, colourful
posies, or decorative garlands to adorn
your home or to present as gifts.
In earlier centuries herbs were more than
just a decorative addition to the home,
they were central to the household
economy. As well as their culinary and
medicinal importance, they were used to
cover floors, to clean and disinfect utensils
and to sweeten the air.
It is not only historical interest or nostalgia
that makes the idea of using herbs
attractive to us today. They may remind
us of the passing seasons or give us a
sense of continuity with the past, but
herbalists have long asserted that fresh
scents will lift our spirits and modern
research has confirmed this.
The following pages show a range of
delightful herbal arrangements that should
tempt you into floral creativity as well as
many practical ways of using herbs around
the home.

A kitchen display
*Dried summer herbs in a thyme basket set alongside
bottles of herb oils and vinegars make an eyecatching
feature in a kitchen corner.*

Fresh herbal arrangements

Often thought of as insignificant plants unworthy of inclusion in floral arrangements, herbs offer a wide choice of foliage and flowers as well as their refreshing aromatic qualities.

As the arrangements on these pages show, some herbal flowers have rich intense colours and intriguing shapes, others are delicate, inviting closer inspection. Use these to add highlights and focal points to arrangements.

Leaves may be feathery, lush, variegated, textured, soft or glossy. They come in all shades of green, and some are evergreen, providing year-round foliage to boost all arrangements. Many, such as the artemisias, have delicate fronds of silvery grey leaves. Fennel provides feathery leaves in green or bronze forms. Varieties of basil and sage offer deep purple-red leaves and there is a range of herbs with yellow variegated leaves, including some of the highly aromatic mints, marjorams, pelargoniums, lemon balm and golden bay. Include such leaves in arrangements for their shape, form and colour as well as their fragrance, which will delight the senses.

Herbs that you grow indoors can also be used for decorative effect. Evergreen shrubs like rosemary, bay and myrtle may be clipped as miniature topiary pieces, and at Christmas you can add colour to their branches with ribbon bows and small trinkets.

Summer colour bowl (*opposite*)
A fragrant arrangement of summer blooms includes pink honeysuckle, red bergamot, blue borage, white double feverfew and sprays of lady's mantle amidst sprigs of foliage, including rosemary and mints.

HERBS FOR DECORATIONS

The following plants will add fragrance and colour to arrangements when used fresh.

Those marked with an asterisk (*) also dry well for use in winter displays.

Flowers

*Alliums	*Elecampane	Lily of the valley	Poppies
*Angelica	Flax	Love-in-a-mist	Primrose
*Bergamot	Forget-me-not	Marigold	Pyrethrum
Betony	Foxglove	Marjorams	Rosemary
Borage	Honeysuckle	Meadowsweet	*Teasel
Chamomile	Jasmine	Melilot	Thymes
Columbine	Lady's mantle	Mints	Valerian
Cowslips	*Larkspur	Peony	Violet
Dill	*Lavender	Pinks	*Yarrow

Foliage

*Artemisias (all	Fennel	Myrtle	Salad burnet
species)	Lungwort	Parsley	*Santolina
Basils	Marjorams	Pelargoniums	*Thymes
*Bay	Mints	Rosemary	
Eucalyptus	Mullein	*Sages	

Seed heads

*Alexanders	*Fennel	Lovage	*Sorrel
*Alliums	Good King Henry	*Love-in-a-mist	Sunflower
*Angelica	*Hops	*Poppy	*Sweet cicely

Tussie-mussies

Fragrant posies of aromatic herbs and flowers were popular accessories in the sixteenth century, carried through the streets to disguise unpleasant smells and protect the owner from the diseases that plagued those times. Consequently, they were named nosegays or, more curiously, tussie-mussies.

Apart from their aromatic and disinfectant attributes, tussie-mussies became increasingly popular for their hidden messages based on the symbolic meanings given to individual plants.

Before making a tussie-mussie, consider its theme and select ingredients for their appearance and symbolism. Start with a central bloom and encircle it with contrasting flowers and leaves. Bind the stems with florist's tape as you go to keep the posy tight. Build up the layers and emphasize the outer rim with a large-leafed herb. Tussie-mussies stay fresh in water for about a week and can be dried by hanging in a warm, dark place. They make a charming and unique personal gift.

Ivy

Forget-me-not

Golden marjoram

Pink rose

Myrtle

Sage

Variegated mint

Lime blossom

Rosemary

Bridal tussie-mussie
Centred around a pale pink 'New Dawn' rose (pure and lovely) are sprigs of mint (virtue); sage (domestic virtue); forget-me-nots (true love); golden marjoram (blushes); myrtle (love); lime blossom (conjugal love); rosemary (remembrance). A rim of variegated ivy (fidelity) completes the posy.

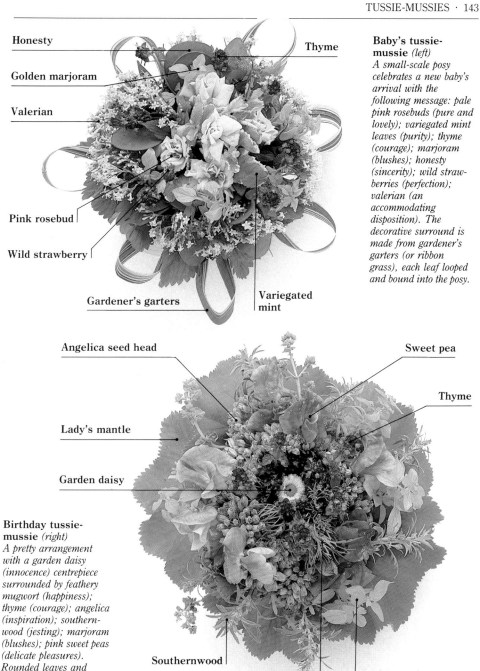

Honesty

Thyme

Golden marjoram

Valerian

Pink rosebud

Wild strawberry

Gardener's garters

Variegated mint

Angelica seed head

Sweet pea

Thyme

Lady's mantle

Garden daisy

Southernwood

Golden marjoram

Mugwort

Baby's tussie-mussie *(left)*
A small-scale posy celebrates a new baby's arrival with the following message: pale pink rosebuds (pure and lovely); variegated mint leaves (purity); thyme (courage); marjoram (blushes); honesty (sincerity); wild strawberries (perfection); valerian (an accommodating disposition). The decorative surround is made from gardener's garters (or ribbon grass), each leaf looped and bound into the posy.

Birthday tussie-mussie *(right)*
A pretty arrangement with a garden daisy (innocence) centrepiece surrounded by feathery mugwort (happiness); thyme (courage); angelica (inspiration); southernwood (jesting); marjoram (blushes); pink sweet peas (delicate pleasures). Rounded leaves and flowering sprigs of lady's mantle (protection) form the edging.

Elder

Angelica seed head

Sorrel

Pink roses

Angelica
leaves

Valerian

Rosemary

Mother's tussie-mussie
A cluster of pink roses (love and beauty) form a posy within a posy in this arrangement. Other ingredients include valerian (accommodating disposition); *angelica (inspiration); sorrel (affection); elder (compassion); rosemary (remembrance); and a feathery collar of angelica leaves.*

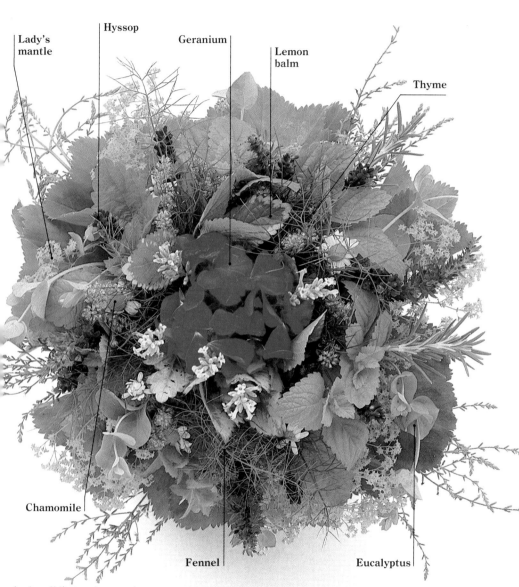

Lady's mantle

Hyssop

Geranium

Lemon balm

Thyme

Chamomile

Fennel

Eucalyptus

An invalid's tussie-mussie
The centrepiece of this sweet-scented posy is a scarlet geranium (comfort), trimmed with lemon balm (sympathy); chamomile (energy in adversity); thyme (courage); hyssop (cleanliness); fennel (strength) and lady's mantle (protection). Disinfectant herbs such as eucalyptus are included to speed the patient's recovery.

Festive wreaths

One of the most traditional and attractive ways of displaying herbs is in a wreath. Hanging from a wall or door, a wreath adds colour and fragrance to any interior. It is also potentially long-lasting and lends itself to an almost infinite variety of styles.

For the base, which you can make yourself or buy from a florist, use plain or moss-covered wire, plaited raffia or twisted vines. On top of this, wire on bunches of selected herbs. Pick from bay, thyme, sage, lavender, rosemary, savory and artemisias for scent and shape. Fresh material is easier to handle than dry, and

you can always make up a wreath and then leave it to dry in a dark, well-ventilated place for later use. For interest, add colourful drying flowers such as yarrow, santolina, roses, bergamot or larkspur; or make a theme-wreath using kitchen herbs such as sage, marjoram, parsley, mint, thyme and rosemary, adding bunches of spices for extra effect. Expand your repertoire by making wreaths for spring, summer, autumn, and winter and festive wreaths for weddings, birthdays, anniversaries and Christmas. The possibilities are endless and always rewarding.

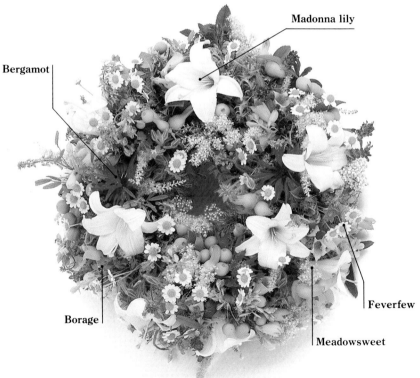

Madonna lily

Bergamot

Feverfew

Borage

Meadowsweet

A fresh summer wreath
Echoing the profusion of a summer garden, this wreath is alive with detail and informality. The base is a circle of florist's foam set in a round plastic container and soaked with water. Madonna lilies form the sweetly-scented focal points, with bergamot, borage, daisy-like feverfew, and other colourful blooms. Set in amidst the flowers are tiny green unripe cherries and filberts.

MAKING A FESTIVE WREATH

1 Cover a wire base with sphagnum moss and bind on with reel wire. When the base is covered, cut the wire and secure the end by bending it back into the moss.

2 Cut small branches of bay to the same length. Place them in overlapping groups all of which face the same way and bind them in place with wire until the entire base is covered.

3 Bunches of buds or berries can be wired together by twisting a medium stub wire over the stems. Leave a length of wire below the stems to pin the bunch in place.

Bay

Rosebuds

A festive wreath
Simple to make, as the steps above show, this stunning wreath has a lush covering of traditional bay, with tiny red rosebuds giving rich points of contrasting colour, accentuated by the red satin ribbon.

Herbal baskets

Baskets make naturally complementary and highly attractive containers for dried herb displays, particularly as they are constructed from plant materials. The texture of woven stems or branches echoes that of many dried herbs, while the natural colours of baskets show off the range of hues found in dried herbs. Baskets made from the aromatic stems of lavender and thyme are also available, as shown below. Alternatively, attach aromatic stems to a basket's rim or handle to give an arrangement extra appeal.

To arrange dried herbs in a basket, you need to prepare a base which will sit in the container area and hold stems in place, as shown opposite. Select herbs for their colours, shapes and textures and incorporate any handles in your design to add height or depth.

Bergamot

Artemisia 'Silver Queen'

Chive flower

A dainty floral basket
Aromatic flowers in delicate shades of pink, lilac, lavender and white make a pretty arrangement in this thyme basket.

Larkspur

Lavender

Thyme

Lavender

Double feverfew

MAKING A HERBAL BASKET ARRANGEMENT

1 Press a block of florist's foam into the basket. Secure in place with wire and cut so that it is higher than the basket's rim.

2 Form a base of colour by lightly covering the foam with leaves and small flowers. Leave space for the feature plants.

3 Add height, texture and solidity with larger seed heads and flowers such as teasel, alexanders, fennel, elecampane, and bergamot.

A basket of contrasts
This striking herbal basket arrangement is packed with bold coloured flowers, delicate florets and interesting seed heads.

Alexander seed head

Teasel

Elecampane

Fennel

Red bergamot

Yarrow

Red roses

Tansy

Blue lavender

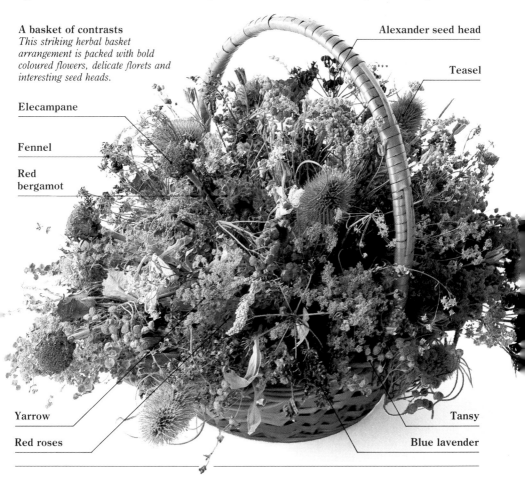

Garlands

Hanging bunches of dried herbs look attractive in their own right: combined into small posies and wired together to form a thick "rope" of foliage, seed heads and flowers, they can look truly spectacular. A garland of herbs such as the one below will transform any room into a setting suitable for a special event. Using dried herbs gives such a garland long-lasting appeal. Drape it over a fireplace or a mirror, around a picture or window frame, over a door, along shelves or beams.

Choose your ingredients to reflect the occasion, selecting items for colour, delicacy, texture and fragrance. Ensure that you have enough materials and assemble them all with the required tools before you start. Experiment with your assembled ingredients, trying out different combinations of colour, texture and shapes. Once you have settled on your scheme, lay out the herbs in groups within arm's reach so they are easy to combine and wire in position.

MAKING A GARLAND

1 Cut string to the required length and knot a loop at one end. Take a length of fine wire and attach one end to the string by wrapping it around a few times. Lay a small bunch of flowers on the string and bind in place.

2 Turn your hand so the first bunch lies under the string and position a second bunch on top, so it overlaps the stems of the first bunch and covers the string loop. Bind in place by wrapping over the wire and pulling it tight.

3 Keep turning your hand and securing bunches one overlapping the other. Follow the procedure until you reach the end of the string. Make a hanging loop with the end piece of wire. Finish with ribbons.

| Thyme | Blue lavender

Lady's mantle

Eucalyptus leaves

Blue larkspur

Love-in-a-mist
seed heads

Peach-coloured roses

Sweet summer garland
*Delicately coloured and highly
fragrant, this striking garland of
dried summer herbs makes a
spectacular decoration. It is scented
with thyme, lavender and eucalyptus.
The curled satin ribbons have a
softening effect and unite the whole
arrangement by their colour.*

Herbal household products

HERBS FOR CONTROLLING PESTS

Herbs can be used effectively to keep unwanted insects and mice at bay. They have the advantage that they are completely safe compared to chemical poisons, which is especially important in the kitchen and other places where food is kept.

Ants Place sprigs of pennyroyal, rue or tansy on shelves or in cupboards to deter ants. Disturb the leaves occasionally to release more scent. This doesn't kill ants but encourages them to go away.

Flies Many herbs help to deter flies, including elder, lavender and mint, mugwort, peppermint, pennyroyal, rue and southernwood. Use them in arrangements, wreaths or potpourri. Hang pieces of sticky elecampane root around windows and doors.

Mice Mint and tansy in your store cupboard will deter mice.

Preserving wraps Wrap dried nettle leaves around stored apples and pears, root vegetables and moist cheeses to preserve them and keep off pests. The wraps will keep vegetables and fruit skins smooth and moist for 2 or 3 months.

Strewing In the Middle Ages, herbs were often strewn on the floor, to repel fleas, lice, moths and insect pests. They also masked unsavoury smells and provided insulation against the cold in winter and the heat in summer. This practice is unsuitable today, but sprigs of herbs can be placed under doormats or carpets, or perhaps on the porch. Choose from the following:
alecost, balm, basil, chamomile, cowslip, daisies, fennel, germander, hop, marjoram, meadowsweet, mint, pennyroyal, pine, rose, rosemary, sage, southernwood, sweet flag, sweet woodruff, tansy, thuja, thyme, sweet violet or winter savory.

Wasps Burn dried leaf of *Eupatorium cannabinum* to drive away wasps.

Weevils Bay leaves in flour and rice bins, and in dried pulses, deter weevils.

HOUSECLEANING

These herbal products make polishing and cleaning an aromatic pleasure. They are also kinder to your skin and to the environment than many chemical household cleansers.

Rosemary disinfectant Simmer leaves and small stems for 30 minutes in water; the less water, the more concentrated the disinfectant will be. Strain and use to clean sinks and bathrooms. The addition of a little washing-up liquid helps to get rid of grease on surfaces. Store any excess in the fridge for up to one week. Disinfectants can also be made with the leaves and flowering stems of eucalyptus, juniper, lavender, sage and thyme and with angelica roots.

Sweet marjoram furniture wax

4 oz (110 g) beeswax	½ oz (15 g) grated
1 pint (570 ml)	olive oil-based soap
turpentine	essential oil of sweet
12 fl oz (350 ml) strong	marjoram (optional)
infusion of sweet	
marjoram	

1 Grate the beeswax into the turpentine and leave to dissolve, which may take a few days. Alternatively, warm the beeswax and turpentine carefully over a flameless heat until the wax melts. Turpentine can easily burst into flames so it's safest to warm it over gently boiling water.

2 In a separate pan, bring the infusion to boiling point and stir in the grated soap until it has melted.

3 Allow both mixtures to cool then blend slowly, stirring until it resembles thick cream. Stir in a few drops of essential oil. Pour into a wide-topped container and label.

Leaves of mock orange, lemon balm, lemon verbena, or rosemary, or lavender flowers can be used instead of sweet marjoram.

Sweet cicely polish Pound fresh, soft sweet cicely seeds in a mortar. Pick up a handful in a cloth and rub on wood as a polish.

Making potpourri

You can use many different herbs and flowers in potpourri, depending on the characteristics you require the finished mixture to have. To blend your own potpourri, select ingredients from each of the categories below. It is probably best to use one of the recipes on page 156 as a guide to quantities initially – experience will soon tell you how much of each is necessary.

Flowers for scent
Pick perfect, whole flowers just before they fully open. Dry by laying as flat as possible on stretched muslin to allow air to circulate. Large-flowered roses and thick-petalled lilies and hyacinths should have their petals separated. Small rosebuds can be dried whole. Make a selection from:
acacia, broom, carnations, elder, freesias, honeysuckle, hyacinth, jasmine, lavender, lilac, lily-of-the-valley, lime, Madonna lily, meadowsweet, Mexican orange blossom, mignonette, mock orange, musk mallow, narcissus, nicotiana, orange blossom, roses, stocks, sweet rocket, violets, wallflowers.

Flowers for colour
Choose from the following for extra colour:
bergamot, borage, calendula, chicory, cornflowers, delphinium, feverfew, forget-me-not, foxglove, larkspur, lawn daisy, poppy, sage, tansy, tulip petals, viper's bugloss, zinnias, and any of the small "everlasting" flowers.

Use pussy willow catkins and sweet myrtle buds to give extra texture.

Aromatic leaves
These represent the second largest group in a potpourri mixture and as their scent is often more powerful than that of flowers, select those that will harmonize. Dry leaves whole, then crush them to release their scent. Choose from the following:
alecost, balm of Gilead, balsam poplar buds, basil, bay, bergamot, lady's bedstraw, lemon balm, lemon verbena, melilot, mints, patchouli, scented pelargoniums, rosemary, sage, southernwood, sweetbrier, sweet cicely, sweet marjoram, sweet myrtle, sweet woodruff, tarragon, thymes and wild strawberry.

Spices, peel, roots and wood chips
These have a strong aroma and are used sparingly; about 1 tbsp (15 ml) to 4 cups (1 litre) of flowers and leaves. Selected spices are usually added in equal proportions. The best scent is obtained by freshly grinding whole spices in a pestle and mortar. To make dried peel, take a thin layer of peel with a zester, grater or potato peeler, avoiding any white pith. Dip in orris root powder to intensify the scent. Dry slowly, then crush or mince if desired. Roots should be cleaned, carefully peeled, sliced and dried slowly. Then chop, crush, mince or powder them. Select from:
alexanders (seed), allspice, aniseed, cardamom, cinnamon, cloves, coriander, dill seed, ginger, juniper, nutmeg, star anise, vanilla pods; dried peel of citrus fruits; roots of angelica, cowslip, elecampane, sweet flag, valerian and vetiver, and shreds or raspings of cedarwood, sandalwood or cassia chips.

Fixatives
These are available as powders and are used to absorb and hold the other scents so they last longer. The most popular vegetable fixative is orris root, as its sweet violet scent doesn't affect a blend strongly: use 1 tbsp (15 ml) per cup (225 ml) of flowers and leaves. Gum benzoin has a sweet vanilla scent; use about ½ oz (15 g) to 4–6 cups (1–1½ litres) of flowers and leaves. The tonka bean from *Dipteryx odorata* also has a strong vanilla scent; use one or two crushed beans per recipe.

Some fragrances also act as fixatives, including oakmoss or chypre, sandalwood, sweet flag root, sweet violet root, and frankincense and myrrh. Use ½ oz (15 g) to 4 cups (1 litre) of potpourri.

Essential oils
These are the concentrated vital essences of aromatic plants. They are a great boon to present-day potpourri blenders, for adding intensity and depth to a fragrant mixture. Oils are particularly good for reviving a potpourri that has lost its scent, but remember that they must be used with discretion to avoid dominating subtler scents.

Potpourri

The traditional way to capture the essence of a summer herb garden is to make a potpourri, a mixture of fragrant, colourful flowers and leaves displayed in a bowl.

Potpourri has become a term for many aromatic mixtures, but the original French means "rotten pot", a moist mixture of pickled flowers and leaves. This older, "moist" method gives a longer-lasting perfume, but it is more difficult to do and visually less attractive. The dry method is popular as it is easier and the colourful result can be displayed in bowls or potpourri balls, and used in herb pillows.

The basic ingredients fall into four categories: flowers for scent or colour; aromatic leaves; spices and peel; and fixatives to preserve the blend. Many herbs are available as essential oils (see below).

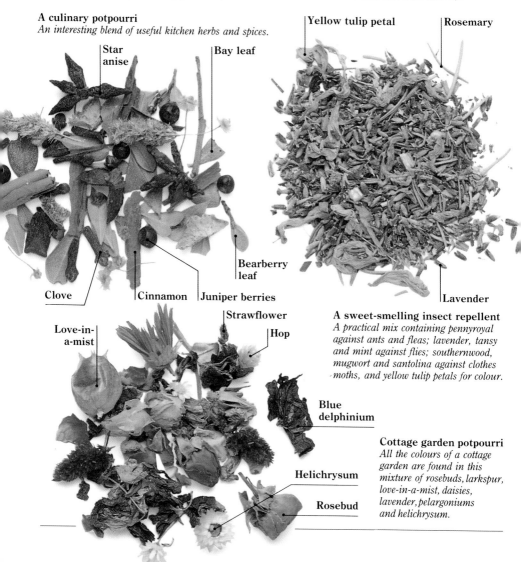

A culinary potpourri
An interesting blend of useful kitchen herbs and spices.

Star anise

Bay leaf

Yellow tulip petal

Rosemary

Bearberry leaf

Clove

Cinnamon

Juniper berries

Lavender

A sweet-smelling insect repellent
A practical mix containing pennyroyal against ants and fleas; lavender, tansy and mint against flies; southernwood, mugwort and santolina against clothes moths, and yellow tulip petals for colour.

Love-in-a-mist

Strawflower

Hop

Blue delphinium

Helichrysum

Rosebud

Cottage garden potpourri
All the colours of a cottage garden are found in this mixture of rosebuds, larkspur, love-in-a-mist, daisies, lavender, pelargoniums and helichrysum.

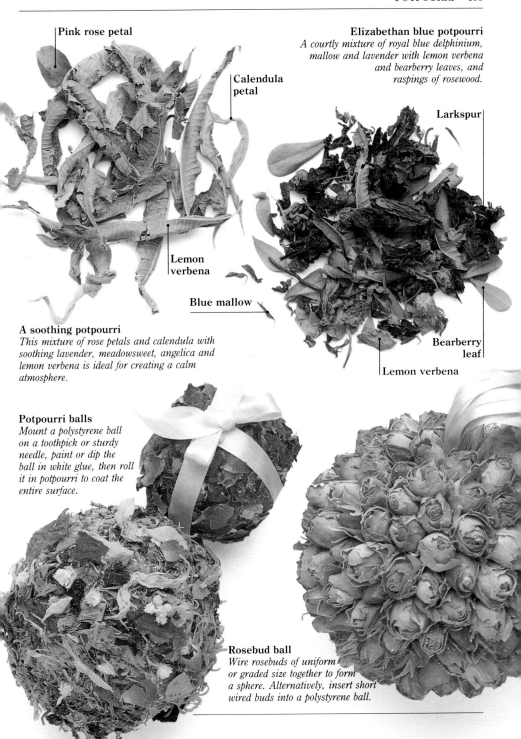

Pink rose petal

Calendula petal

Elizabethan blue potpourri
A courtly mixture of royal blue delphinium, mallow and lavender with lemon verbena and bearberry leaves, and raspings of rosewood.

Larkspur

Lemon verbena

Blue mallow

A soothing potpourri
This mixture of rose petals and calendula with soothing lavender, meadowsweet, angelica and lemon verbena is ideal for creating a calm atmosphere.

Bearberry leaf

Lemon verbena

Potpourri balls
Mount a polystyrene ball on a toothpick or sturdy needle, paint or dip the ball in white glue, then roll it in potpourri to coat the entire surface.

Rosebud ball
Wire rosebuds of uniform or graded size together to form a sphere. Alternatively, insert short wired buds into a polystyrene ball.

Potpourri recipes

Dry potpourri

Select a theme for the scent such as woodland or cottage garden, and assemble paper-dry flowers and leaves. Gently combine the flowers and leaves, then mix the fixative with the spices and blend in with your hands. Sprinkle on essential oils if desired, a drop at a time, stirring between each drop. Seal and store in a warm, dry, dark place for six weeks to "cure". Display in open bowls.

Culinary potpourri

Crush half of each ingredient for scent, leave the other half whole for texture and use.

2 cups (450 ml) sweet marjoram
½ cup (100 ml) lemon thyme flowering tops
½ cup (100 ml) basil
2 tbsp (30 ml) bearberry leaves
20 bay leaves
2 tbsp (30 ml) sweet myrtle leaves

2 tbsp (30 ml) orange peel
20 cardamom seeds
20 star anise pods
20 juniper berries
2 tbsp (30 ml) cloves
2 cinnamon sticks

Cottage garden potpourri

A colourful mixture of well-loved blooms.

2 cups (450 ml) rose petals
1 cup (225 ml) rosebuds
2 cups (450 ml) lavender
1 cup (225 ml) mock orange flowers
1 cup (225 ml) scented pelargonium leaves
1 cup (225 ml) pinks

1 cup (225 ml) bergamot leaves
1 cup (225 ml) larkspur flowers
¼ cup (50 ml) daisies
8 love-in-a-mist seed capsules or hop flowers
8 helichrysum
5 tbsp (75 ml) orris root

Elizabethan mixture

A rich blend of colours and scents.

2 cups (450 ml) lemon verbena
2 cups (450 ml) lavender flowers
1 cup (225 ml) bearberry leaves
1 cup (225 ml) sweet myrtle leaves
1 cup (225 ml) delphiniums

½ cup (100 ml) violets
½ cup (100 ml) blue mallow flowers
½ cup (100 ml) crushed roseroot
1 oz (25 g) rosewood
4 tbsp (60 ml) orris root
1 tbsp (15 ml) gum benzoin

Fly-away potpourri

A sweet scented insect repellent.

2 cups (450 ml) lavender flowers
1 cup (225 ml) rosemary
1 cup (225 ml) southernwood
½ cup (100 ml) spearmint
½ cup (100 ml) santolina

¼ cup (50 ml) pennyroyal
¼ cup (50 ml) tansy
¼ cup (50 ml) mugwort
¼ cup (50 ml) cedarwood chips
10 yellow tulips
3 tbsp (45 ml) orris root

Soothing potpourri

Useful for creating a calming atmosphere.

2 cups (450 ml) lemon verbena
2 cups (450 ml) rose petals
1 cup (225 ml) lavender flowers
1 cup (225 ml) calendula petals

1 cup (225 ml) meadowsweet florets
1 cup (225 ml) chamomile flowers
1 oz (25 g) angelica root
4 tbsp (60 ml) orris root

Woodland blend

Evocative of pleasant wooded walks.

2 cups (450 ml) wild strawberry leaves
1 cup (225 ml) pine needles
½ cup (100 ml) violets
½ cup (100 ml) rosemary
¼ cup (50 ml) cedarwood chippings

¼ cup (50 ml) patchouli
¼ cup (50 ml) rosewood
2 tbsp (30 ml) sweet violet root
3 drops cypress oil
2 drops pine oil
1 oz (25 g) oakmoss

Herbal fragrance in the home

LIVING ROOM

Fresh, scented flowers and herbs arranged in a vase are one of the easiest ways to fill a room with scent. Other ways to freshen or perfume the air are listed below. All are based on simple ideas that have been practised for centuries.

Herbal decorations Generous bunches of fresh herbs will cool and perfume a room. Herbs that sweeten the air include:

alecost, basil, bay, germander, hyssop, lavender, lemon balm, lemon verbena, mints, rosemary, roseroot, santolina, sweet myrtle, thyme, woodruff and wormwood.

Essential oils Add a few drops of lavender oil to a bowl of near-boiling water and place in the room. Alternatively, moisten a sponge with boiling water and add a few drops of an essential oil. Place the sponge in a dish in the room, and moisten it with boiling water twice a day, adding a few drops of oil twice a week.

Potpourri Try out recipes on p. 156 and display in pretty bowls, inviting the potpourri to be touched so the scent is released.

Herb cushions Fill two rectangular muslin bags with favourite potpourri blends. Cover each with material to match your sofa or chair. Join the two bags with two straps of fabric and hang over the back of the sofa so the fragrance is released whenever anyone rests against them. Swap the bags around occasionally.

Scented candles The easiest way to make candles is to buy a candle-making kit. Add small pieces of dried alecost, bergamot, germander, lavender heads, lemon thyme, mint, rosemary, sweet myrtle, powdered cinnamon or a few drops of essential oil to the melted wax just before pouring it into the mould.

HERBS FOR THE KITCHEN

Use herbs in the kitchen to freshen the air and disguise cooking fumes. Make decorative hangings (see pp. 147–9) and incorporate those herbs listed below to deter flies.

Kitchen potpourri Try the recipe on p. 156 to reduce kitchen smells and deter flies.

Fly-away posies Kitchen bouquets of chamomile, hemp agrimony, mugwort, pennyroyal, peppermint, rue, tansy or wormwood also should deter flies.

Oven gloves and pot covers Sew rosemary, thyme or spices into the padding of oven gloves and teapot-covers so they release their scent when warm.

HERBS FOR THE BEDROOM

Fragrant herbs can help you sleep, sweeten the air and your clothes, and are particularly welcome in a bedroom where someone is ill.

Herb pillows Make a small muslin or cotton cover and fill with your favourite potpourri mixture. Keep it under your normal pillow.

Drawer bags (sweet bags) Use lavender, lemon verbena, mint or rose petals to fill sachets of lace, silk or cotton to lay among lingerie, sweaters, gloves and linen.

Scented hangers Add herbs with the padding when making fabric-covered coat hangers.

Lavender bundles To make lavender bundles you need an odd number, 13 or more, of long stems of lavender, freshly picked on a dry day, and about 3 ft (1 m) of lavender or blue ¼ in (6 mm) ribbon. Make a bunch, lining up the base of the flower heads. Leave an 8 in (20 cm) length of ribbon free at one end, then tie the stems together just below the heads. Gently bend back each stem until the flower heads are enclosed by the stems. Take the length of ribbon you saved and weave it under and over each stem, travelling around the bundle several times until the flower heads are covered with ribbon. Tuck in the short end of the ribbon and tie a bow with the other end. Trim the stalks and the ribbon.

Pomanders Press cloves into the skin of an orange allowing a clove space between each to allow for shrinkage as the orange dries. Roll the finished orange in a mixture of orris root and spices – cinnamon or allspice. Tie a ribbon round to suspend the pomander, which should hold its scent for a year or more.

Herbal fragrance for the bedroom

Discover refreshing new ways of using herbs in the bedroom. All the pretty things shown on these pages are enhanced with herbal fragrance of different kinds. A scented sachet can be slipped under your pillow so that turning over in the night produces a soothing drift of bergamot. A lingerie drawer can be perfumed with the sweet scent of rose potpourri. Or a scented hanger can give a shirt the clean, fresh aroma of lemon verbena.

Classic potpourri
Countless possibilities for recipes make concocting potpourri an absorbing art. A classic rose-scented mix has perfume that is very intoxicating.

Lavender bundle
Pretty beribboned bundles of lavender make enchanting presents and are easy to slip into drawers and cupboards. Fresh-cut stalks of lavender are used, and pastel ribbon holds the flower-heads in place.

Pomander
This traditional aromatic pomander is made with an orange, some spicy cloves and a length of ribbon to hang it by.

Lavender bags
Tiny and neat, hand-made lavender bags have a peaceful fragrance. They can be stitched from fabric and lace scraps, or made up to match a scented hanger. Different shapes can be filled with dried lavender or a fragrant mixture of your choice.

Scented hanger
The floral fabric covering this padded coat hanger encloses a selection of fragrant dried herbs, caught beneath muslin strips wound round the hanger. Rose and lavender mixtures are suitable, or, for a man's hanger, a minty citrus blend of spearmint, alecost, lemon verbena and pine-scented thyme.

· Chapter Four ·

Herbs for Beauty

The cosmetic use of plant material runs through all ancient cultures. The Egyptians incorporated beauty preparations in their religious and ceremonial rituals while the ancient Greeks developed a philosophy of all-round health and beauty akin to modern concepts. The Romans indulged further in aromatic rituals and body pampering. Citro, a Roman writer in the first century A.D., produced four books on cosmetics with a comprehensive range of recipes for hair care, avoiding wrinkles and dealing with body odours.

By the time of the Renaissance there was an awareness of skin care as separate from medicinal disorders. Recipes for soaps, creams and herbal waters were collected and recorded in herbals which were handed down from mother to daughter for generations.

Herbal beauty products
As well as facial beauty products, there is a wide range of oils, creams, lotions, floral waters and so on for pampering or refreshing your hands, feet, hair, eyes and teeth.

Preparations and ingredients

During the nineteenth century, cosmetics became an organized industry in America. In 1846 Mr Theron T. Pond offered his "Pond's Extract" to the public and other manufacturers soon followed. The innovative use of preservatives and mass production created an unprecedented choice.

Today's commercial products are often expensive, having vast amounts of money spent on advertising, packaging, distribution and testing (which can involve cruelty to animals). Allergies have increased along with the use of chemical preservatives, synthetic perfumes and artificial colourings. As a result, demand has risen for natural ingredients, and since research has demonstrated the remarkable therapeutic properties of herbs, many firms are rushing to create their own ranges of herbal cosmetics.

By making your own cosmetics, you can be sure of their contents. You select each ingredient and have control over its freshness

and purity. The following recipes combine present-day knowledge with traditional ingredients and methods inherited from past ages, including the first face cream recipe recorded by Galen, a Roman doctor in the second century. This recipe used a formula of oil, water and wax and has formed the basis of day creams ever since. Some preparations take no longer than boiling a kettle, others require heating and blending but are no more complicated or time-consuming than preparing a simple sauce.

NB: Before using any herbal preparations, you are advised to sample a small amount first, particularly if you have had allergic reactions in the past.

USEFUL EQUIPMENT FOR HERBAL COSMETICS

This list is meant as a guide only, but do avoid using aluminium, copper and non-stick pans as their chemical contents can affect the ingredients' beneficial properties.

All containers and utensils must be scrupulously clean. Ideally they should be sterilized by being boiled or placed in a hot oven for 10 minutes. Have a bowl of hot soapy water standing by to wash off wax before it hardens. Otherwise, stand containers over boiling water to remelt traces of contents and wash.

Heatproof glassware or pottery cookware	Electric blender/ grinder
Enamel double boiler	Juice extractor
Wire or electric whisk	Glass dropper
Measuring spoons	Wooden spoons
Measuring jug	Glass rods
Small glass (1 oz (25 ml) measure)	Spatula
Small funnel	Clean dark glass bottles and jars
Nylon sieve	with airtight
Pestle and mortar	lids
Measuring scales	Labels and pen

BASIC HERBAL PREPARATIONS

Most of the recipes in this section use one of these methods to extract the therapeutic properties from herbs.

Infusing Put one and a half handfuls of fresh herbs or 1 oz (25 g) of dried into a heatproof container. Bring 1 pint (570 ml) distilled water to the boil. Pour over the herb immediately and cover. Steep for 30 minutes. Strain and store in a refrigerator for up to three days.

Decocting This method is usually employed for the tougher parts of herbs. Put 1 oz (25 g) of the herb into a saucepan (not aluminium or copper). Add 1 pint (570 ml) distilled water, bring to the boil and simmer for 30 minutes. If more than half the liquid has evaporated, top up with water to make half a pint (275 ml). Cool, strain and bottle. Keep in the refrigerator and use within a few days.

Macerating Use this method for herbs likely to lose some of their therapeutic value if heated. Pack a glass jar with the crushed, fresh herb. Cover with vegetable oil, cider vinegar or pure alcohol. Seal and leave for two weeks, shaking the jar each day. Strain and top up with fresh herbs. Repeat until the liquid smells strongly herbal. Strain, seal and bottle. Keeps well and retains its scent.

Pulverizing Grind, bruise or mash plant fibres and seeds using either a pestle and mortar or an electric blender.

NON-HERBAL INGREDIENTS

The following can be bought from any good pharmacist.

Agar agar Derived from seaweed. Used to make gels.

Alcohol A colourless, flavourless preservative and solvent. The best alcohol for perfumery and least irritating to skin is ethyl alcohol.

Beeswax Acts as an emulsifier for oil and water in creams. Usually sold in blocks.

Benzoin A preservative, astringent and antiseptic.

Borax A white, crystalline mineral powder used as an emulsifier.

Bran Used in face masks, soaps and body scrubs as a cleanser.

Buttermilk Available from health-food shops. Soothing and astringent.

Calamine lotion A soothing alkaline lotion for skin problems.

Castile soap A pure soap with no added colour or perfume.

Cocoa butter A thick fat from the cocoa bean, which makes a rich emollient in creams.

Distilled water Only pure water is suitable for making cosmetics.

Emulsifying wax A wax used to emulsify oil and water in creams.

Fuller's earth A fine grey powder derived from single-cell algae found on sea beds. Its absorbent properties and mineral richness make it an excellent face mask.

Gelatine A colourless, odourless, tasteless glue and a rich source of water-soluble protein, obtained by boiling animal bones. Used in eye ointments and nail hardening lotions. Agar agar is a vegetable substitute.

Glycerine A thick, colourless, odourless syrup and by-product of soap manufacture. It mixes with water, is soluble in alcohol and has softening properties.

Honey Softening, healing and binds other ingredients together.

Iodine Used as an antiseptic.

Kaolin The purest form of clay, useful in face masks.

Lanolin A thick, sticky fat obtained from sheep's wool. Softens and nourishes the skin.

Liquid paraffin A mineral oil which is not absorbed by the skin, making it useful in barrier creams.

Oatmeal See **Bran.**

Oils Almond, avocado, wheatgerm, carrot, coconut and nut kernel oils are particularly skin-enriching.

Oleic acid An emulsifying liquid that can rescue separated creams.

Petroleum jelly A pale yellow translucent mineral jelly insoluble in water. Used in lip salves.

Vinegar Used in cosmetics to soften, cleanse and soothe the skin.

Vitamin capsules A convenient way of adding vitamins to skin creams.

Zinc oxide A white powder derived from zinc with mild antiseptic and astringent qualities. Usually available as an ointment.

Knowing your skin

To ascertain your skin type clean your face thoroughly, then rinse well and pat dry. Allow it to rest for two hours and then press a tissue onto your face. If the tissue comes away full of grease, you have oily skin; if there is grease on only parts of it, you have combination skin. If the tissue comes away unmarked, wash your face with soap and water. If your skin feels supple and smooth afterwards, it's normal; if it feels taut, it's dry.

Normal skin Soft and translucent, normal skin requires only a simple care routine.

Dry skin Taut and dry and with no shine, dry skin requires moisturizer at an earlier age. It should be treated with mild cleansers and with gentle care to avoid further drying of the skin.

Oily skin This has a definite shine and is supple. The pores are open and the skin may look coarse and sallow. It needs thorough cleansing, but this must be gentle to avoid stimulating the sebaceous glands yet further.

Combination skin This is the most common skin type with the pores on the forehead, nose and chin larger than those on the rest of the face. This "T" panel is oily and the remainder of the face is dry. It is best treated as two types of skin as described above.

Skin creams and lotions

All skin creams are based on a combination of melted waxes, oils and scented waters, which must all be at a similar temperature. The waxes are melted together over a low heat, the oils are warmed and beaten into the waxes, then the heated waters are dribbled slowly into the blended wax and oil, and the mixture is stirred until cool. It is like making mayonnaise, only easier – a 10-minute operation.

The proportions of the ingredients govern a cream's consistency and are easy to adjust. To make a cream firmer, add more beeswax; to make it softer, add more oil. Adding more water will make it lighter and fluffier but also makes the ingredients more prone to separation. The addition of herbs such as marsh mallow and houseleek, which contain an emollient mucilage (a sticky substance in the roots, stems or leaves), will tend to make a cream spongier. The incorporation of a few drops of essential oil will add fragrance and its other beneficial properties.

Always label and date products immediately, keeping a record of each recipe and its success. As perishable ingredients are involved, creams should be refrigerated.

Cleansing creams
These are more efficient than soap and water at removing heavy dirt and make-up. Massage into the skin and then wipe off with cotton wool.

Toners
These are important for tightening the pores and refreshing the skin.

Moisturizing creams
After the skin has been cleansed and toned, it is ready for a protective film of moisturizer to maintain the skin's natural moisture level.

NB: Borax has been found to cause a reaction when applied to inflamed skin and can be omitted from any of the recipes.

GLYCERINE AND ROSEWATER CLEANSING CREAM *(for dry and normal skins)*

Most recipes for creams follow this procedure. Waxes are melted in one container while oils are warmed in another. All ingredients should be the same temperature when you mix them together or the mixture may curdle. You can substitute any suitable herbal infusion for the rosewater.

4 tbsp (60 ml) lanolin
2 fl oz (50 ml) almond oil

1 tbsp (15 ml) glycerine
⅛ tsp (0.65 ml) borax
3 tbsp (45 ml) rosewater
1 tsp (5 ml) zinc oxide
   ointment
6 drops essential oil of rose

1 Melt the lanolin and gently heat the almond oil and glycerine together. Slowly pour the oil and glycerine mixture into the lanolin, beating constantly.

2 Dissolve the borax in the warmed rosewater and add gradually to the lanolin and oil mixture, beating all the time. Leave to cool.

3 When cool and creamy, beat in the zinc oxide and rose oil. Spoon into prepared jars and label.

PLANTS TO USE IN CREAMS AND LOTIONS

Many plants and herbs have beneficial cosmetic uses. Those listed here are particularly effective in skin creams. Follow the preparation instructions on p. 164. For equivalent strengths, use half the quantity of dried herbs as fresh. Many of these herbs are also beneficial in face packs, baths and hair treatments and are listed in those sections of the chapter.

Aloe vera The sap from the leaves is soothing and healing.

Avocado An excellent skin food with high vitamin E and A content.

Borage Good for dry, sensitive skins.

Calendula A healing herb for rough or problem skin.

Chamomile A gentle, soothing herb that also softens and whitens skin.

Comfrey A healing and soothing herb that contains allantoin, a protein which speeds up cell renewal. Good for rough and damaged skin.

Cucumber A cleansing agent and toner. Soothing and healing.

Dandelion Contains a rich emollient useful in cleansing lotions for dry, sallow skins.

Elderflower A good tonic for all skins. Reputed to soften skin and smooth wrinkles, fade freckles and soothe sunburn.

Essential oils These are excellent additions to creams and lotions.

Fennel Cleansing and soothing. Add crushed seeds to face packs. Purifies oily skin.

Houseleek A healing, softening and soothing herb especially good for dry, sensitive skins.

Ivy Relieves sunburn; helps to disperse trapped fluids and toxins in the fight against cellulite.

Lady's mantle A healing herb for soothing dry, sensitive skin; a good astringent for large pores.

Lavender A gentle cleanser and tonic for all skin types.

Lemon An astringent that restores the skin's natural acid balance.

Lime tree blossom Softens the skin. Deep cleansing.

Lupin seed A cleanser and pore refiner for oily skin.

Marsh mallow A healing softener for dry skins, chapped hands and sunburn.

Nettle A deep cleanser; very good for oily skin.

Orange flower An excellent skin tonic, said to help restore the skin's acid mantle. Also treats dry skin and broken capillaries and stimulates cell replacement.

Parsley A conditioner for dry, sensitive and troubled skins.

Peppermint An astringent which clears the complexion.

Rose A soothing and gentle cleanser which has a softening effect on the skin.

Rosemary An invigorating antiseptic which boosts circulation and deep cleansing.

Sage A cleansing, stimulating astringent which tightens pores.

Thyme A stimulating but gentle antiseptic cleanser.

Violet A gentle astringent.

Watercress Expressed juice can help to clear blemishes.

Witch hazel Soothing and astringent.

Yarrow A healing and cleansing astringent. Good for oily skin.

SENSITIVE SKIN

No cosmetics can claim to be non-allergenic because every ingredient holds the possibility that someone might be allergic to it. One of the main benefits of making your own cosmetics is that if you do have an allergic reaction you know what ingredients you have used and can soon find the culprit. Test for a reaction by placing a spot of any ingredient on the gauze of a piece of sticking plaster and attaching this to your inner arm, between the wrist and elbow. Leave in place for 24 hours, by which time any reaction you may have will show.

Some essential oils can irritate sensitive skins, particularly on the face. Oils to watch out for are bay, bergamot, geranium, neroli, pennyroyal, peppermint, sage and spearmint.

For those with highly sensitive skins, the following can also cause allergic reactions:

Agrimony	Cucumber	Lanolin	Primrose
Almond oil	Glycerine	Lime blossom	Violet leaves
Cocoa butter	Henna	Lovage	
Cowslips	Ivy	Nettles	

Recipes for skin creams and lotions

Orange-flower cleansing cream
(for dry and normal skins)

Essential oil of neroli (the substance extracted from the orange flower) is used to stimulate the loss of old skin cells and their replacement with new ones.

1 fl oz (25 ml) soya oil	1 fl oz (25 ml) orange-
1 fl oz (25 ml) almond	flower water
oil	⅛ tsp (0.65 ml) borax
1 oz (25 g) cocoa	5 drops essential oil of
butter	neroli
1 tbsp (15 g) beeswax	

1 Mix and warm the oils. Melt the cocoa butter and stir it into the oils. Melt the beeswax then beat it into the oil mixture, a little at a time.

2 Warm the orange-flower water and dissolve the borax in it. Beat this into the main mixture. Leave to thicken and cool.

3 As the mixture starts to thicken, stir in the essential oil. Once cool, spoon into prepared jars and label.

Lemon cleansing cream
(for oily skins)

Lemon has a reputation for clearing greasy skin and smoothing wrinkles, as well as having a mildly antiseptic quality.

1 tbsp (15 ml) beeswax	1 tbsp (15 ml) lemon
1½ tbsp (22 ml)	juice, strained
petroleum jelly	⅛ tsp (0.65 ml) borax
3 tbsp (45 ml) mineral	6 drops essential oil of
oil	lemon
1 tbsp (15 ml) witch	
hazel	

1 Melt the beeswax and petroleum jelly together over a low heat. Warm the mineral oil, then gradually add it to the wax mixture, beating for 3–5 minutes.

2 Add the witch hazel to the lemon juice. Warm gently then stir in the borax until dissolved. Slowly add this to the wax mixture, beating steadily until it is creamy and cool.

3 Once cool, stir in the lemon oil. Spoon into clean jars and label.

Rosewater toner
(for dry skins)

The soothing properties of rose make this a good tonic for dry, sensitive and mature skins.

just over a ¼ pint	just under a ¼ pint
(160 ml) rosewater	(140 ml) witch hazel
6 drops glycerine	

Blend all the ingredients in a bottle and shake well before use.

Fennel cleansing milk
(for oily skins)

½ cup (125 ml)	2 tbsp (30 ml) fennel
buttermilk	seed, crushed

1 Gently heat the milk and seed together in a double boiler for 30 minutes.

2 Leave to stand for a further 2 hours. Strain, bottle, refrigerate and use within 1 week.

Sage astringent
(for oily skins)

4 tbsp (60 ml) dried	¼ tsp (1.25 ml) borax
sage	3 tbsp (45 ml) witch
4 tbsp (60 ml) ethyl	hazel
alcohol (or 6 tbsp	10 drops glycerine
(90 ml) vodka)	

1 Macerate the sage in the alcohol for 2 weeks and then strain.

2 Dissolve the borax in the witch hazel. Stir into the alcohol. Mix in the glycerine and decant into a bottle with a tight-fitting lid. Shake before use.

Clockwise from the top: Light rose moisture cream (p. 168); Ivy cellulite cream (p. 168); Orange-flower cleansing cream (above left); Comfrey and calendula cream (p. 168); Avocado and nettle moisturizer (p. 168); Lemon cleansing cream (above).

Light rose moisture cream

(for all skin types)

A pleasant light cream for daytime use.

1 tsp (5 ml) beeswax	3 tbsp (45 ml)
1 tsp (5 ml) lanolin	rosewater, warmed
1 tbsp (15 ml) almond	6 drops essential oil of
oil	rose, or rose
½ tsp (2.5 ml) wheat	geranium
germ oil	a few drops of red food
¼ tsp (1.25 ml) borax	colouring if desired

1 Melt the beeswax and lanolin together, stirring constantly.

2 Warm the oils gently and gradually beat them into the waxes. Dissolve the borax in the rosewater and slowly add to the oil and wax mixture, beating constantly until cool. Stir in the rose oil as the mixture begins to thicken.

3 Spoon into jars and label.

Ivy cellulite cream

Some doctors and scientists dispute the concept of cellulite; many people look at their skin and think otherwise. Whatever the outcome of this argument, the fatty "orange peel" deposits on the thighs and buttocks can benefit from extra attention.
Massage into areas of cellulite.

2 tsp (10 ml) beeswax	4 tbsp (60 ml) double
1 tsp (5 ml) emulsifying	strength ivy decoction
wax	8 drops each essential
3 tsp (15 ml) almond oil	oils of oregano,
1 tsp (5 ml) avocado oil	fennel, rosemary

1 Melt the waxes in a double boiler. Warm the oils and then stir them in well.

2 Beat in the ivy decoction and allow the mixture to cool before stirring in each of the essential oils.

3 Spoon into jars and label.

Avocado and nettle moisturizer

(for oily skins)

1 tsp (5 ml) beeswax	⅛ tsp (0.65 ml) borax
2 tsp (10 ml)	2 tbsp (30 ml) strong
emulsifying wax	nettle infusion, warm
8 tsp (40 ml) hazelnut	4 drops cedarwood
oil	essential oil
4 tsp (20 ml) avocado	
oil	

1 Melt the waxes together. Warm the oils and gradually beat them into the waxes.

2 Dissolve the borax in the warm infusion. Slowly beat this into the first mixture.

3 Allow to cool then mix in the essential oil. Spoon into jars and label.

Comfrey and calendula cream

(nourishing cream for all skin types)

Especially good for rough, dry skin as these herbs are nourishing and healing. This also makes an excellent hand cream for sore, chapped hands. Comfrey contains a substance that helps cell renewal.

1 tbsp (15 ml) beeswax	1 tsp (5 ml) glycerine
1 tbsp (15 ml) lanolin	¼ tsp (1.25 ml) borax
1 tbsp (15 ml) cocoa	2 tbsp (30 ml) comfrey
butter	leaf infusion, warm
1½ tbsp (22 ml)	6 drops essential oil of
calendula oil	petitgrain

1 Melt the beeswax. Melt the lanolin and cocoa butter and gradually stir them into the beeswax.

2 Warm the calendula oil and glycerine and slowly stir into the first mixture.

3 Dissolve the borax in the warm comfrey infusion and then add this to the main mixture, stirring well. Continue stirring until thick and cool, then mix in the essential oil.

4 Spoon into jars and label.

Herbal baths

Cleansing is the first and primary activity of external skin care, and an aromatic herbal bath is one of the most pleasurable and therapeutic ways of accomplishing this. You can add herbs to invigorate and stimulate circulation, or to relax and soothe muscles, unwinding the body for a peaceful night's rest. Select them for healing treatments to help a skin complaint, or simply for the pleasure of their aroma. Try to keep the water temperature around body heat. If it is too hot, the skin will perspire and not absorb any of the therapeutic herbal properties. To get most benefit, relax in the water for at least 10 minutes.

Herbal bath bags

The easiest way of adding herbs to a bath is to hang three or four herbal tea bags from the tap, or to place a small herb-filled tea infuser in the water. Alternatively, put a handful of herbs in the centre of a square piece of muslin or fine gauze, gather up the corners to make a pouch and tie securely, adding a long loop to hang over the hot tap so the water will run through the bag. Use a single herb or mix up to four in one bath. For a body scrub, add a little fine oatmeal or bran to the herb bag. Rub this over the body near the end of the bathing time.

Herbal bath infusions

Instead of adding the herb, you can extract its therapeutic properties by infusing 10 oz (275 g) dried herb or a handful of fresh herbs in a pint (570 ml) of boiled water. Leave for 10 minutes then strain and add to the bath.

Skin-soothing vinegar baths

A vinegar bath soothes itchiness and aching muscles and softens the skin. Add a cupful (225 ml) of the following mixture to your bath for its beneficial effects. Bring 1 pint (570 ml) cider vinegar and a handful of fresh bath herbs slowly to the boil then infuse overnight. Strain and bottle.

Skin-softening milk baths

Add 3 tbsp (45 ml) of powdered milk (not skimmed as it does not have the same healing qualities) to a fine gauze or muslin bag along with 2 oz (50 g) dried or 4 oz (110 g) fresh elderflowers, chamomile or fresh lime blossom. Put in bath water.

Therapeutic oil baths

The addition of 5–10 drops of essential oil to your bath allows you to lie in an envelope of fragrance and feel their beneficial power. Sprinkle the oil on hand-hot water after it has settled and gently swish around. Don't add oils under running hot water or they will evaporate. The temperature of the water will affect you as well. A relaxing sedative bath should be just under blood heat. For a stimulating bath, use a temperature below 85°F (29°C). If the temperature is too low, the oils will not evaporate readily.

- For dry skin, add the oils in a tablespoon (15 ml) of almond oil.
- For a more dispersible preparation, add the oils with a tablespoon (15 ml) of milk.
- For a bubble bath, add the oils with a tablespoon (15 ml) of mild liquid soap.

THERAPEUTIC BATH HERBS	
Relaxing bath herbs	
Chamomile	Lime flowers
Hops	Meadowsweet
Jasmine	Valerian
Stimulating bath herbs	
Basil	Mint
Bay	Pennyroyal
Eucalyptus	Pine
Fennel	Rosemary
Ivy	Sage
Lavender	Tansy
Lemon balm	Thyme
Lemon verbena	
Healing bath herbs	
Calendula	Lady's mantle
Comfrey	Spearmint
Houseleek	Yarrow
Spring tonic bath herbs	
Blackberry leaves	Lawn daisies
Dandelion	Nettle

Face packs

A face pack or mask draws impurities to the skin's surface, stimulates the circulation and tightens the skin. Apply the mixture to slightly moist skin and then rest with your feet higher than your head so gravity forces blood to the facial skin. Make cooling eye pads of cucumber or cotton wool soaked in a herbal infusion and place them against your eyelids to increase the absorption. Leave the mask on for 20 to 30 minutes before removing with warm water. Finish with a pore-closing infusion such as elderflower water, and then a moisturizer.

Do not apply a face mask just before preparing for a special occasion as the drawing power of the mask, particularly one with a cereal or clay base, can flush the skin.

HERBS FOR FACE PACKS

For normal skin fennel, juniper berries, lady's mantle, lime flowers, mint, nettle.

For dry and sensitive skin comfrey, houseleek, marsh mallow, pounded flax or quince seed (which contain a softening mucilage).

For oily skin sage, yarrow; 2 tbsp (30 ml) of pounded fennel or lupin seed to exfoliate dead skin and refine pores.

NON-HERBAL INGREDIENTS FOR FACE PACKS

• Milk products have softening and mild bleaching properties. Substitute 1 tbsp (15 ml) of creamy milk for 1 tbsp (15 ml) of the herbal infusion.
• Add 1 tsp (5 ml) honey for its healing properties.
• A few drops of lemon juice help to restore the skin's acid mantle.
• Add an egg yolk for dry skin or a beaten egg white for oily skin.
• Mashed cucumber, strawberries, tomatoes, lemon juice and grapefruit juice are all good astringents. Avocado and ripe peach are rich moisturizers.

Green herbal mask

Any of the herbs listed below can be used to create a green mask. Take 2 handfuls of fresh leaves or 3 tbsp (45 ml) of dried (softened by soaking in boiled water overnight). Add 2 tbsp (30 ml) of distilled or mineral water and liquidize at high speed for a few seconds.

This makes a rather wet mixture, but if you are in a bath or lying on a towel it can be applied as it is. If you wish to thicken the mixture add fuller's earth or ground almonds until it reaches the desired consistency.

Paste face packs

Ground oatmeal, ground almonds or fuller's earth used either singly or in combination form the basic carrier of a paste face pack. Each has the ability to draw impurities from the skin.

To 2 tbsp (30 ml) basic carrier, add 2–3 tbsp (30–45 ml) of a strong herbal infusion, or the juice of the herbs obtained by using a juice extractor.

A deep pore cleansing mask

This recipe is based on an expensive face pack offered by a famous salon – so treat yourself!

1 tsp (5 ml) beeswax	*optional additions*
1 tbsp (15 ml) lanolin	1 tsp (5 ml) Irish moss
2 fl oz (50 ml) rosewater	or pounded quince or flax seed.
1 tbsp (15 ml) fuller's earth	

1 Melt the wax and lanolin together over a gentle heat, stirring continuously.

2 Remove from the heat and add the rosewater, stirring until it has cooled.

3 Mix in the fuller's earth (and optional additions), stirring until you have achieved a smooth paste.

A selection of herbal bath products including herbal bath bag (p. 169); face mask (above) and aromatic bath oils (p. 169).

Hands

The skin of our hands is subject to adverse weather conditions, hot water, detergents, polishes and garden soil. The best defence is to wear either cotton or rubber gloves or gardening gloves, as appropriate, and to make lavish use of hand creams. Make up several bottles of your chosen recipe and leave them wherever you wash your hands. If you dislike wearing gloves or find that you keep removing them unconsciously, apply a barrier cream before doing any dirty work.

To make a particularly healing barrier cream, follow the recipe for Comfrey and calendula nourishing cream on p. 168, and add 1 tbsp (15 ml) warmed liquid paraffin to the wax mixture before adding the comfrey infusion. The recipe here is much stronger.

Regular herbal hand treatments

To soften and soothe hands, soak them in an infusion of lady's mantle, fennel, comfrey, yarrow, or marsh mallow; an infusion of calendula or chamomile flowers has the same softening effect.

To strengthen nails, soak them in an infusion of chopped horsetail and dill seed for ten minutes every other day. Make more than you need and bottle for future use.

Heavy-duty barrier cream

4 tbsp (60 ml) petroleum jelly	2 handfuls fresh elderflowers

1 Gently melt the petroleum jelly then add the elderflowers.

2 Leave to macerate for 45 minutes, reheating the jelly each time it solidifies.

3 Warm to a liquid and strain through a sieve into a screw-top jar. Cool and then seal.

Hand mask

Once a week treat your hands to this mask to whiten and soften the skin. Apply to the hands for 20 minutes, preferably just before going to bed. Wash off, then apply a rich moisturizing cream (and wear cotton gloves while you sleep). Wash off the cream the following morning.

2 tbsp (30 ml) finely ground oatmeal	1 tsp (5 ml) avocado oil
1 tbsp (15 ml) calendula petals	1 tsp (5 ml) lemon juice
	1 tsp (5 ml) glycerine

Mix the ingredients together to form a smooth paste. Use as instructed above.

Feet

The above treatments for hands can also be applied to feet. The enriching mask is particularly beneficial, but remember to wear cotton socks if you are going to put moisturizer on your feet overnight.

Herbal foot baths

The traditional foot bath is one of the most therapeutic treatments.

To refresh tired feet choose from the following: bay, lavender, sage, sweet marjoram, thyme. Place a large handful of fresh or ¼ cup of dried herb and 1 tbsp (15 ml) sea salt in a bowl of hot water. For convenience, these can be loose in the water.

● **To make a warming foot bath**, add 1 tbsp (15 ml) black mustard seed, bruised, to the water.

● **To soothe itchy feet**, add 4 tbsp (60 ml) cider vinegar to your foot bath.

● **To deodorize feet**, soak them in a strong decoction of sage or lovage.

Cold feet

Add 1 tsp (5 ml) cayenne pepper to talcum powder or fuller's earth and sprinkle on your feet to get a quick warming sensation.

Hair care

Although most aspects of hair, its colour, rate of growth, thickness and curliness are hereditary, a wide range of herbal ingredients has been used through the ages to improve and enhance what nature provided.

Advertising agents have decided we all fall into one of four hair types: dry, greasy, normal or "problem" hair, but herbal trichologists state that all hair is normal for that person and problems should first be dealt with by looking holistically at a person: that is, looking at his or her lifestyle. Too many spicy foods, fats and sugars can be responsible for greasy hair and synthetic shampoos can create dry hair. There is also concern about the effects that medicated shampoos can have on the hair and scalp if used routinely. Stress, hormonal changes, lack of sleep, too much sun, chemical hair treatments, rinses and dyes all cause hair problems too.

Hair treatments

Dry hair and any hair lacking lustre will benefit from a warm oil treatment before a shampoo.

Make a herbal oil using one of the herbs opposite and a polyunsaturated vegetable oil such as peach kernel, almond or sunflower. Alternatively, add 6 drops of essential oil to 2 tbsp (30 ml) of almond oil or any vegetable oil. Warm the oil, pour a small amount into your palm and rub your hands together. Massage well into the scalp and along the hair strands. Repeat as necessary. Cover the head with foil and a plastic shower cap and wrap in a hot towel (wrung out in hot water), replacing the towel when it cools. Leave on for 20 minutes, then wash off with a mild shampoo.

A quick herbal shampoo

Pour one application of a mild baby shampoo into a cup and add 2 tbsp (30 ml) of a strong decoction of your selected herb, or 4 drops of essential oil. Mix together and use in the normal manner.

Soapbark shampoo

Good for greasy hair. Simmer 2 tbsp (30 ml) soapbark chips (available from many health shops) in 1 pint (570 ml) water for 30 minutes.

Rosewater pick-up

This is an excellent way to clean and revive your hair between shampoos. Orange-flower water can be used instead, or lavender water for greasy hair.

You will need a number of 4 in (10 cm) squares of muslin or gauze dipped in rosewater. Force the muslin over a natural bristle brush and stroke through the hair in sections, removing dirt as you brush. Repeat with fresh muslin squares until the cloth picks up no more dirt. This treatment also gives a lovely fragrance to the hair.

Dry shampoo

This is a quick way of revitalizing hair. Mix together 2 tbsp (30 ml) powdered orris root and 2 tbsp (30 ml) powdered arrowroot. Part the hair in narrow, regular bands and sprinkle mixture along each row. Leave for 10 minutes to absorb any grease, then brush hair vigorously.

HERBS USED IN HAIR CARE

To condition dry hair Burdock root, comfrey, elderflowers, marsh mallow, parsley, sage, stinging nettle.

To condition greasy hair Calendula, horsetail, lemon juice, lemon balm, lavender, mint, rosemary, southernwood, witch hazel and yarrow.

To prevent dandruff Burdock root, chamomile, garlic and onion bulbs (powerful but unpleasantly scented), goosegrass, parsley, rosemary, southernwood, stinging nettle and thyme.

To soothe scalp irritation Catmint (leaves and flowering tops), chamomile, comfrey.

To provide a hair tonic (giving body and lustre) Calendula, goosegrass, horsetail, lime flowers, nasturtium, parsley, rosemary, sage, southernwood, stinging nettles and watercress.

To dispel lice An infusion of quassia chips, poke root, or juniper berries with a tablespoon of cider vinegar. Apply at two week intervals, three times.

Eye care

The best recipe for clear bright eyes is a good night's sleep. "Just enough regular and natural sleep is the great kindler of woman's most charming light", wrote a famous beauty of the nineteenth century. Failing that, eyes which are tired, irritated or bloodshot can often be soothed with a cooled herbal decoction. However, if you experience frequent or continuing eye irritation, it is advisable to consult a doctor.

When you are dealing with the delicate eye area, scrupulous cleanliness is vital. Sterilize all utensils and fabrics and use only absolutely fresh decoctions. Always boil herbs for an eye bath for 20 minutes to kill the greatest number of bacteria. Then filter the solution three times through a coffee filter paper to ensure no small bits remain to irritate the eye.

The most famous reputation for giving a brilliance and sparkle to the eyes goes to the modest little plant eyebright (*Euphrasia rostkoviana*). It can relieve tiredness and soreness, and halt running eyes from a cold or hay-fever.

Eyebright eye bath
Boil 2 tbsp (30 ml) fresh plant or 2 tsp (10 ml) of dried herb in 2 cups (450 ml) water for 20 minutes. Cool, strain and use immediately in an eye bath.

Agrimony eye bath
This herb is second to eyebright in its fame for adding lustre to eyes. Boil a handful of fresh tops in a pint (570 ml) of water for 20 minutes. Cool, strain and use immediately.

Eye compresses
Make 2 cups of chamomile or rosehip tea, using 2 tea bags, and brew for 3 minutes. Remove the bags and cool. Place the tea bags over your eyes for 15 minutes, put your feet up and rest. This can also be done with black tea bags and will refresh tired eyes.

Eye gels
Lotions or gels for the delicate, thin skin around the eye must be light so that the application does not drag or pull it. The ingredients should treat only the surface of the skin. Rich penetrating oils can contribute to a puffy appearance around the eyes.

Eyebright or elderflower gel
Dissolve a strong decoction of eyebright or elderflower water in gelatine (as manufacturer's instructions) for a soothing eye gel.

Soothing eye gel
Use equal quantities of chamomile, calendula and cornflower flowers and mallow leaves to make a strong decoction.

6 tbsp (90 ml) decoction
2 tbsp (30 ml) witch hazel
¼ tsp (1.25 ml) agar agar

pinch of sodium benzoate if required to improve keeping qualities

1 Heat the herbal decoction and witch hazel until just below boiling point. Stir in the agar (and benzoate) to dissolve. The agar agar must be thoroughly dissolved or it will feel grainy.

2 Leave to cool and thicken. If it forms a solid gel, put into a blender for a few seconds to thin. Store in screw-top jar in refrigerator.

HERBAL EYE REFRESHERS

Make a strong decoction of the herb. Strain, then soak sterilized squares of lint in the solution and apply over closed eyes.

Calendula Soothes sore or inflamed eyes.
Chamomile Reduces inflammation and removes a "tired look".
Cornflower Soothes and helps reduce puffiness.
Fennel seed Removes inflammation and gives sparkle.
Horsetail Reduces redness and swollen eyelids and can be effective for styes. (Must boil for 30 minutes.)
Mallow Softens skin around eyes.
Mint Minimizes dark circles under the eyes.
Rose Softens skin around the eyes.
Wormwood Reduces eye inflammation and redness; dab on a decoction with cotton wool.

Teeth

Most commercial toothpastes contain damaging abrasives, detergents and sweetening agents. Homemade products can achieve a better result without the use of harmful ingredients.

Instant tooth cleansers
• Rub a sage leaf over the teeth and gums to make them feel polished and clean.
• Peel a twig of flowering dogwood, chew the end to create a brush and rub on the teeth and gently on the gums.

Peppermint toothpaste
To make your own cleansing paste, take 1 tsp (5 ml) bicarbonate of soda, charcoal or powdered strawberry roots and 2 drops essential oil of peppermint. Add enough drops of water to create a paste. Mix and use as commercial products.

Stain removers
Strawberry: rub half a strawberry (alpine is best) over the teeth.
Lemon peel: rub the wet side on the teeth. The blanching property of lemon is good for removing tea and other brown stains.

Mouthwashes
Commercial mouthwashes are often so powerful that they damage the proper balance of digestive juices and can irritate the lining of the mouth. Seek further help for persistent bad breath as the digestive system may not be functioning properly.

To sweeten the breath, chew fresh parsley, liquidized nettle leaves or watercress, which are all high in chlorophyll, a green plant pigment used in many commercial breath sweeteners. For a quick mouthwash, gargle with a peppermint infusion, rosewater, lavender water, or diluted witch hazel (1 part witch hazel to 6 parts water). Alternatively, try the mint and rosemary mouthwash, right.

Toothache
As a short term measure to ease the pain, apply a drop of oil of cloves.

Apricot and lemon lip balm

A delicious, protective and healing gloss, especially good for chapped lips.

1 tsp (5 ml) beeswax	1 tsp (5 ml) calendula
1 tsp (5 ml) apricot	oil
kernel oil	a few drops essential oil
	of lemon or orange

1 Melt the beeswax. Add the apricot and calendula oils, stirring constantly.

2 Remove from the heat while stirring, and when partly cooled add the essential oil. Store in a small pot.

Mint and rosemary mouthwash

Both herbs sweeten the breath and rosemary has antiseptic properties. If you wish to make up larger quantities, add 1 tsp (5 ml) tincture of myrrh for its preservative properties.

1 pint (570 ml) distilled	1 tsp (5 ml) rosemary
or mineral water	leaves
1 tsp (5 ml) fresh mint	1 tsp (5 ml) aniseed
leaves	

1 Boil the water and infuse the mint, rosemary and aniseed for 20 minutes.

2 When cool, strain and use as a gargle.

HERBS FOR ORAL CARE

Dogwood Crushed twig stimulates gums.
Lavender water Sweet-smelling mouthwash.
Nettle leaves When liquidized, they sweeten the breath.
Cloves Oil of cloves gives relief to sudden toothache.
Parsley Sweetens the breath.
Peppermint An infusion makes a popular mouthwash.
Rosemary Use an infusion for a soothing gargle.
Rosewater Refreshing as a mouthwash.
Sage Polishes teeth, leaves a "clean" feeling.

· CHAPTER FIVE ·

HERBS FOR HEALTH

For thousands of years people have turned to plants for healing help, so it is rather ironic that this form of medicine should be considered "alternative" while the relatively new science of synthetic drugs should be viewed as "orthodox". What is important is that the best in every system should be valued and that proper attention is also paid to the dangers of any method.

Antibiotics, surgery and powerful drugs are often vital to save lives, but for minor or long-term ailments other forms of healing may have better results.

But it must be recognized that plants, too, are potent drugs, so accurate dosage is vital: herbs should never be taken in excessive amounts.

Whenever you are in doubt, or have a serious or recurring complaint, you should consult a trained herbalist. However, common ailments can be treated at home with a range of simple herbal remedies; follow the preparation instructions and advice in this chapter. General good health can be assisted by regularly including herbs in your daily diet.

Ancient herbal medicine
This section of a wallpainting of Queen Hatshepsut's journey to Punt shows men with herbs who accompanied her. Egyptian physicians worked with hundreds of different herbs.

A history of herbal healing

Throughout the world early tribes accumulated a useful body of herbal knowledge through a process of trial and error. Women, with the restricted mobility of the child-bearer, assumed the tasks of collecting and administering herbs, so that medicine was almost universally a female vocation in pre-scientific cultures. Early peoples also saw a link between health renewal and a woman's ability to create new life. The healing craft and plant knowledge were handed down from mother to daughter, and the efficiency of this system depended on both the accuracy of their observations and the nurturing qualities of the healer involved. To help their memories, nomadic tribes would select a visual attribute of each herb to remind them of its usage.

Difficulties in describing and remembering plants lessened with the advent of written language and, by 3000 BC, parallel cultures in China, Babylon, Egypt and India had begun to record their knowledge of medicinal plants.

Chinese herbalism

The country with the longest unbroken tradition in herbal medicine is China. By the time he died in 2698 BC, the legendary Emperor Shen Nung had "tasted one hundred herbs". His *Canon of Herbs* deals with 252 plants, describing how to preserve and administer them, and many are still in use.

A hundred years later the Yellow Emperor, Huang Ti, formalized medical theory in the *Nei Ching* and displayed a sophisticated understanding of human disease for the time: "In treating illness, it is necessary to examine the entire context, scrutinize the symptoms, observe the emotions and attitudes. If one insists on the presence of ghosts and spirits, one cannot speak of therapeutics." It was an optimistic book, stating that, with the growth of knowledge, all kinds of disease would eventually be curable.

The *Nei Ching* was frequently updated and in the seventh century, more than 800 years before the Western press was invented, the government of the Tang dynasty printed and distributed *A Revised Canon of Herbs*

throughout China. In 1578 Li Shizhen completed a world-famous *Compendium of Materia Medica*, which listed 1,800 healing substances and 11,000 recipes or compounds.

From the Far East to the Middle East

Clay tablets from 3000 BC record herbal imports into Babylon, and there is evidence of trade in ginseng between China and Babylon around 2000 BC. The Babylonians had an enormous pharmacopoeia with 1,400 plants; they used poppy as an anaesthetic and fennel as a digestive. The Greek historian Herodotus noted that every Babylonian was an amateur physician, since it was the custom to lay the sick in the street and solicit advice from anyone passing by.

The first known Egyptian physician was Imhotep (2980–2900 BC), a priest healer who also designed one of the earliest pyramids. He was greatly respected as a skilled healer and was eventually deified.

The Ebers papyri of 1550 BC list many herbal remedies and accompanying incantations, and around this time a form of astrology was incorporated into Egyptian medicine. Egyptian physicians worked with around 900 herbs, and, through their embalming skills, had a superior understanding of the human organism.

At about the same time, Indian physicians were developing advanced surgical and diagnostic skills and used hundreds of herbs in their treatments. Like the Chinese, they used all five senses when diagnosing, and developed a keen sensitivity to assessing breathing, pulse rate and skin odours.

Herbalism in the Ancient World

The Ancient Greeks acquired their knowledge of herbalism from India, Babylon, Egypt and even China. In the thirteenth century BC there lived in Greece a healer named Asclepius, skilled in the use of herbs. He designed a healing system, whereby people would live through a series of experiences intended to transform them by changing old thinking patterns. Many miracles of healing were attributed to Asclepius and his daughter

Hygieia. Eventually he was deified and healing temples sprang up across Greece. His system was practised in Greece for several hundred years, and some of his ideas are still relevant in today's health centres.

In the sixth century BC, the philosopher and mathematician Pythagoras set up a university to teach advanced knowledge. Herbs, particularly aromatic gardens, played an important part in the healing and restorative regime which preceded higher learning.

Hippocrates (460–377 BC) brought Western medicine into a scientific framework of diagnosis and treatment. He dismissed the idea of disease being punishment from the gods and considered food, occupation and climate important factors in disease. He believed that it was the individual's responsibility to aid self-healing through diet and plant medicines. He gave the medical profession a code of conduct that is still respected by doctors throughout the modern world.

The Dark Ages

During the Dark Ages, Persia became the centre of excellence. There the Nestorian Christians (an Eastern Church not affiliated with Rome) established a famous school and hospital where Greek medical manuscripts were translated into Arabic.

In contemporary Europe medical progress was hampered by the authorities of the Christian church: scientific learning was not highly regarded, experiment was discouraged and originality considered a dangerous asset. Most significantly, the Church viewed disease as punishment for sin. However, plant medicine continued to be practised by monks in the monasteries and by "herb women" in the remote villages.

The Renaissance

With the development in the fifteenth century of the Western printing press began a golden age of herbals. This was the beginning of the Renaissance, a time for re-examining old ideas, attempting to escape the limitations of old dogmas and giving rein to an eagerness for discovery. A new scientific attitude spread through medicine. The results of herbal remedies were observed more accurately, and the more bizarre drugs were dropped. Rather oddly, in this environment of growing reason, there occurred the cruellest witch-hunts in history. Women were forbidden to study, while non-professional healers were pronounced heretics. Because of this, even today some people equate herbalism with superstition, quackery and magic.

Herbalism today

With the ascendancy of science in the nineteenth century came the ability to synthesize plant parts and concentrate doses. Herb usage probably reached an all-time low in the mid-twentieth century. But now, because of a greater concern about the side-effects of drugs, an understanding of ecology and people's desire to take greater responsibility for their own health, herbal medicine is experiencing a remarkable revival.

Pharmaceutical companies on the one hand recognize the value of herbs and are busy investigating worldwide herbal lore with unprecedented zeal, while on the other hand they wish to maintain their lucrative near-monopoly over medicinal products. Some drug companies have tried to have herbs removed from the healing arena. One tactic has been to concentrate on finding and isolating a single, toxic constituent in a herb. This happened in the case of sage some years ago, but attempts to quash its usage failed after further research found that the other constituents in sage nullified any toxic element.

In order to use herbs safely, we need to find a sensible middle ground. One solution is a proposal on the statute books of Canada. This is to create a new class of "Folk Medicines". Each product would be labelled with botanical names, the plant parts used and the type of preparation. Ingredients would have to meet set standards of purity and concentration, and advertising would not make extravagant claims. Such a system would guarantee the safety of herbal medicines on the market and allow people to continue using these benevolent plants.

Herbal preparations

It is generally agreed that wild herbs or self-sown herbs, plants growing where Nature has decreed, have the most active ingredients, although with home-grown plants, you are more certain of having the species you want when you want them. There is also less risk of mistaking one plant for another. The dangers of inaccurate identification cannot be stressed strongly enough.

The quality of a herb is most important when it is to be used for healing. Pick perfect leaves, clean and unblemished, at their prime time, when most active constituents are present. Unless stated otherwise, leaves are at their prime just before the flowers open, flowers are at their prime just as they open, fruit as it comes to ripeness, roots in the autumn when goodness has passed from the leaves back into the roots, and bark after the spring when sap has risen.

Dried green herbs lose their medicinal potency after six or seven months; roots, seeds and bark after two or three years.

Remedy recipes and dosage

Generally a recipe can use either fresh or dried herb. Fresh herbs are likely to have the higher medicinal value but, because dried herbs are available all year round, recipes are given in amounts of dried herb. On average, for infusions, or teas, and decoctions, one teaspoon (5 ml) of dried herb equals three teaspoons or one tablespoon (15 ml) of fresh.

To make a single dose use 1 tsp (5 ml) of herb to a cup (225 ml) of water. For a day's dosage add 1 oz (25 g) to 1 pint (570 ml) of liquid. For young children, the weak and very elderly the amount of herb (if using potent plants) should be halved.

The usual dosage is 7 fl oz (200 ml) of infusion, or a third of the reduced quantity for a decoction. As a guide, take this three times a day before meals, reducing the amount until you no longer need the remedy.

It is important not to assume erroneously that, because herbs are "natural", any quantity or combination can be taken. Herbal guidelines must be followed.

PREPARATION METHODS

Infusion or tea

Follow the quantities given below left for dosage. For a hot infusion, boil water, wait 30 seconds and then sprinkle the herb onto the water to steep, stirring occasionally, for 10 minutes, or until cool, or leave overnight. This method is preferable for leaves and flowers that easily give up their medicinal properties (especially vitamins and volatile ingredients) to the liquid, but remember to keep the container covered. Use the purest water you can obtain or bottled mineral water. Water with a high lime content (very hard water) can prevent plants from fully releasing their active principles. Strain and sweeten with honey or raw brown sugar, if preferred.

Decoction

Follow the quantities given on this page for dosage. Place the dried herb in an enamel or glass lidded pan with cold water and slowly bring to the boil. Reduce the heat and simmer down to a quarter of its original volume (10 minutes or longer) and then steep with the lid on for 3 minutes or until cool. This method is used for hard materials such as roots, bark and seeds, which should first be bruised or crushed. Strain and take with honey or raw brown sugar if preferred. A decoction should keep refrigerated for up to 3 days.

Powder

Chop large dried plant parts, such as roots, bark or thick stems, into small pieces, then crush these or dried leaves and flowers with a pestle and mortar, or reduce them to powder in a coffee grinder. Powder can be added to drinks and soups or sprinkled on food.

Syrup

Syrups are used to mask unpleasantly flavoured herbs, especially for children, and to make cough medicine easier to take. Bring slowly to the boil 1 pint (570 ml) of selected infusion or decoction with 2–4 tbsp (30–60 ml) honey until the mixture turns syrupy. Store in the refrigerator.

To mix with a tincture, first heat 1 pint (570 ml) water with 4–6 tbsp (60–90 ml) honey and stir until the mixture begins to boil. Remove from the heat. Mix 1 part tincture with 3 parts syrup. Store in the refrigerator.

Tincture

Put 4 oz (110 g) powdered herb or 8 oz (225 g) fresh chopped herb in a container with a tightly fitting lid. Add 1 pint (570 ml) alcohol, which must be at least 60° proof (e.g. brandy or vodka). Neither treated ethyl alcohol nor surgical spirit is suitable. Stand the mixture in a warm place and shake it twice daily for 2 weeks. Strain through double muslin, squeezing out as much liquid as possible, and store in a well-stoppered dark glass jar. Alcohol preparations will keep for a long time. The dosage is usually 5–15 drops, which can be taken directly or added to a cup of hot water. Homeopaths use very dilute tinctures in many of their preparations.

Essential oils

These are the concentrated essences of plants usually extracted by steam distillation. It is possible to obtain minute amounts at home but more sensible to purchase them. It is important to find a source of pure unadulterated essential oils to ensure that an oil contains all of a plant's active principles. Essential oils are excellent for making tinctures, adding to massage oils, ointments and other external applications.

Ointments and creams

Prepare and strain a strong decoction or infusion of the herb and add this to a quantity of pure, cold-pressed vegetable oil, such as sunflower. Boil until the liquid has evaporated (bubbles cease to appear) leaving the herbal principles in the oil.

Alternatively use an infused oil (see p. 134). To stiffen as a cream, stir in melted beeswax – about 1 oz (25 g) should be enough for half a pint (275 ml). You can make a cream by melting and blending 1 oz (25 g) beeswax, lanolin or cocoa butter with 4 fl oz (110 ml) vegetable or herbal oil, following the method on p. 164. Add 1 oz (25 g) selected herb and simmer gently for 10 minutes, stirring frequently. Sift through

double muslin into a wide-necked container with a lid and label and date the container. A drop of tincture of benzoin or myrrh will extend its life. Do not use borax as it can damage broken skin.

Petroleum jelly acts as a non-penetrative base. Put 3½ oz (90 g) petroleum jelly in an enamel pan or bowl over boiling water and melt. Leave to cool, then stir in a few drops of essential oil (say, eucalyptus for nasal relief), pour into a container, label and date.

Hot and cold compresses

A compress is useful for applying a herbal remedy externally to the skin. For a hot compress, soak a clean linen or cotton cloth in a hot decoction or infusion and apply it to the affected part as hot as can be tolerated. Cover the compress with plastic and a folded towel or blanket to maintain the heat. When cooled, either replace with another hot compress or apply a hot water bottle over the plastic. Prepare a cold compress in the same way but allow it to cool before applying.

Poultice

A poultice is similar to a compress except that plant parts are used rather than liquid extraction. Mash or crush fresh plant parts and either heat in a pan over boiling water or mix with a small amount of boiling water. Apply the pulp directly to the skin, as hot as can be tolerated, holding it in place with a gauze bandage. If using a dried herb, first powder it and make a paste with a little boiling water. If the paste is liable to irritate the skin, apply it between two layers of cloth.

Poultices are generally more active than compresses. They are used to stimulate circulation, soothe aches and pains or draw impurities out through the skin, depending on the herb chosen. A poultice will introduce the active parts of the herb into the body without stressing or being affected by the digestive tract before reaching their target area.

A–Z of herbal treatments

Here is a list of some common ailments that often respond to treatment with herbs at home. Do not attempt to treat more serious problems yourself. Remember that many complaints are often caused by incorrect diet, stress and other external factors.

Botanical names are supplied for the less common plants and for those where there may be confusion between species. Consult the A–Z of Herbs for more detailed information. To be sure of getting the desired benefits, use the main species rather than varieties, cultivars or hybrids. You must be able to identify plants with complete confidence as some are highly poisonous.

It is always advisable to try a small quantity of any remedy before applying the full dosage. If you have an adverse reaction, or if a complaint seems to worsen or continue, seek professional advice from a qualified medical herbalist. For information on the recipes and dosages, see p. 180.

Abrasions *see* **FIRST AID**

Acne
After washing or thorough gentle cleansing, rinse the skin with an infusion of chamomile (*Chamaemelum nobile*), which is purifying, yarrow (*Achillea millefolium*), which helps eliminate toxins, catnip (*Nepeta cataria*), which is antiseptic, lavender (*Lavandula* spp.), which is calming and antiseptic, or thyme (*Thymus vulgaris*), which is a strong germ-killer.

Dab spots with neat lemon juice to kill germs, cool inflammation and improve blood circulation. Apply a calendula ointment to reduce inflammation and improve local healing. Acne can also be helped by changes in dietary habits, so consider what you eat and cut out sugars, fats and dairy products.

Appetite, lack of
Caraway (*Carum carvi*) and ginseng (*Panax ginseng*) are both powerful appetite stimulants, and a standard infusion of either can be drunk half an hour before a meal or whenever desired. Horehound (*Marrubium vulgare*) tea, 1 cup (225 ml) taken three times a day, will stimulate the appetite after flu, or any other appetite-suppressing ailment.

Asthma *see* **Coughs**

Bites, insect *see* **FIRST AID**

Boils and sores
To encourage boils to come to a head, apply neat lemon juice or secure over the boil half a warm baked onion (with the centre layer removed to create a small dome). For boils and sores, apply a poultice of antiseptic catnip leaves (*Nepeta cataria*), antiseptic plantain leaves (*Plantago lanceolata*) or pulverized fenugreek seed to reduce inflammation and improve local healing. If there is any inflammation or fungal infection, calendula petal ointment is a safe treatment.
NB: If boils recur, seek professional advice.

Bruises *see* **FIRST AID**

Burns, minor *see* **FIRST AID** *and* **Sunburn**

Chilblains and cold limbs
To warm hands and feet, massage gently with warmed macerated oil of honeysuckle flowers (*Lonicera caprifolium*). This will bring an increased flow of blood to the surface skin. For a foot bath to improve the circulation of cold feet and help chilblains, which are caused by poor circulation, use an infusion of 1 tbsp (15 ml) freshly ground mustard seed to 4 pints (2 litres) water. Cayenne seed powder is also a powerful stimulant to the circulatory system and helps blood flow to the extremities. In an ointment it can be used in moderation for unbroken chilblains.

Elder leaf (*Sambucus nigra*) ointment is useful for chilblains. Heat 1 part fresh leaves with 2 parts petroleum jelly until the leaves are crisp. Strain and label for storage.

To improve bad circulation, drink rosehip or horsetail (*Equisetum arvense*) or buckwheat (*Fagopyrum esculentum*) tea daily to strengthen small capillaries. Some spices and strongly flavoured herbs, such as black pepper, cloves, cinnamon, coriander, cumin, freshly grated root ginger, garlic, marjoram, rosemary and thyme, improve circulation. Include them frequently in your diet, especially in the winter months.

Colds and flu
• **To protect against colds**, eat or take the juice of a raw clove of garlic three times a day. Essential oils are very efficient at destroying harmful bacteria and viruses. They can also be used in steam inhalants or as a room freshener.

Rosehip tea, said to be high in vitamin C, can be used to build resistance to colds and other infections. Cayenne powder is also excellent at warding off colds as it strengthens and stimulates the circulatory and digestive systems. Infuse ½–1 tsp (3–5 ml) cayenne powder in 1 cup (225 ml) boiling water for 10 minutes. Strain and take 1 tbsp (15 ml) of this mixture topped up with hot water when needed or before each meal.

• **At the first sign of a cold**, take a mixture of elderflower (*Sambucus nigra*), peppermint (*Mentha × piperita*) and yarrow (*Achillea millefolium*). Infuse ½ tsp (3 ml) of each together in 1 cup (225 ml) boiling water for 20 minutes. Strain, add 1 tsp (5 ml) honey and ¼ tsp (2 ml) cayenne pepper. This should decrease the intensity and the discomfort of a cold or flu. If the mixture benefits you, the herbs are worth storing as a dried blend for winter use. Another remedy to take at the earliest possible moment is 9 small horehound leaves (*Marrubium vulgare*) chopped finely and eaten raw with 1 tbsp (15 ml) honey. Repeat as necessary.

• **To fight colds and flu**, take hot lemon and honey as often as desired as lemon has antibacterial properties. Take frequent hot drinks of elderflower (*Sambucus nigra*), peppermint (*Mentha × piperita*) or yarrow (*Achillea millefolium*) tea to promote perspiration and to reduce temperature. Elderflower is also useful for reducing any nasal inflammation from catarrh. If this is accompanied by a penetrating chill, add grated root ginger or cayenne. Black pepper sprinkled over food also has a restorative effect, or you could take an infusion of mustard seed, ¼ tsp (2 ml) powder infused for 5 minutes in 1 cup (225 ml) boiling water, three times a day, or add 4 pints (2 litres) of mustard infusion to bathwater.

• **For catarrh and flu**, golden rod (*Solidago virgaurea*) is good because it is antiseptic, clears catarrh and soothes inflammation. Infuse 2 tsp (10 ml) dried flowering stalks in 1 cup (225 ml)

boiling water for 10 minutes and drink a cup (225 ml) three times a day. Goldenseal root (*Hydrastis canadensis*) is also excellent for its healing and tonic powers on the mucous membranes. Drink an infusion of ½–1 tsp (3–5 ml) of powdered root in 1 cup (225 ml) boiling water three times a day. You can also try a hot infusion of borage (*Borago officinalis*), coltsfoot (*Tussilago farfara*), comfrey (*Symphytum officinale*) or ground ivy (*Glechoma hederacea*) to relieve catarrh.

NB: Do not take goldenseal root during pregnancy.

• **Relieve stuffiness** by inhaling the vapours from a steam bath of chamomile flowers (*Matricaria recutita*) or eucalyptus leaves (*Eucalyptus globulus*). A pinch of basil taken as snuff can bring back your sense of smell. When your temperature has returned to normal, drink a warm infusion of cleavers (*Galium aparine*) three times a day to continue a mild perspiration action, help prevent stomach upsets and promote restful sleep. Begin taking vegetable juices and progress to homemade vegetable soup, fresh fruit and salads. Reintroduce heavier foods slowly to avoid overloading the digestive system when it is still vulnerable.

Horehound tea restores an appetite that may need stimulating after flu. If lethargy or depression follow, take lemon balm (*Melissa officinalis*) or vervain (*Verbena officinalis*) tea. If this persists after a few days, seek professional advice.

Constipation

Roughage in the diet and regular exercise are important for healthy functioning bowels, while tension and emotional worries can contribute to constipation. Herbs can be used for short-term relief but the underlying causes should be addressed.

Syrup of figs is a valuable remedy, taken as required. An

infusion of crushed flax seed (*Linum usitatissimum*) has a purgative action which brings relief: drink 1 cup (225 ml) morning and evening.

Liquorice root (*Glycyrrhiza glabra*) is a mild and pleasant laxative. Chew root as desired or make a decoction of 1 tsp (5 ml) root in 1 cup (225 ml) water and take three times a day. Stewed rhubarb in moderate doses is a gentle laxative for children; large doses cause a more powerful reaction. Rosehip tea is also a mild laxative. Use a decoction or infusion with halved hips, but strain through filter paper to remove the seeds and tiny hairs, which are an irritant to the body. Drink whenever necessary.

NB: Long-term constipation, or any unusual changes in bowel habits, should be discussed with a medical herbalist or doctor.

Coughs

• **To fight bronchial infections**, eat raw garlic cloves for their strong antibiotic content. To help dispel fluid and mucus from the lungs and air passages, horehound (*Marrubium vulgare*) is the first choice. Drink a hot standard infusion three times a day. Another important herb in the treatment of coughs and colds, is coltsfoot (*Tussilago farfara*). An infusion of the leaves and flowers will soothe the air passages, encourage tissue healing and protect the delicate mucous membranes from further irritations.

• **To ease cough spasms** and help clear mucus, make cowslip flower (*Primula veris*) syrup or decoct cowslip root, simmering for 5 minutes, and drink 1 cup (225 ml) three times a day. It can be combined with coltsfoot and aniseed (*Pimpinella anisum*). Aniseed has an expectorant action and can help make cough mixture more palatable.

• **For an irritating cough** with a great deal of catarrh, the expectorant, antiseptic action of elecampane root (*Inula helenium*), along with the soothing effect of its mucilage, is an excellent remedy. Infuse 1 tsp (5 ml) shredded root in 1 cup (225 ml) cold water for 9 hours. Drink it hot three times a day. An irritating cough can also be soothed by an infusion of powdered marsh mallow root (*Althaea officinalis*). It combines well with horehound (*Marrubium vulgare*) and liquorice (*Glycyrrhiza glabra*).

For very dry coughs, combine coltsfoot with horehound and mullein (*Verbascum thapsus*).

• **To reduce catarrh**, apply a poultice of freshly-ground mustard seed to the chest. Mix 4 oz (110 g) seeds with warm water to make a thick paste. Apply the paste between two pieces of gauze with the bottom piece dampened so that it does not stick to the skin. Leave for one minute only. Flax seed can be used with mustard to help reduce catarrh. A tea of plantain leaves (*Plantago major*) is a gentle expectorant and the herb is widely cultivated by Russian pharmaceutical companies. A standard infusion of star anise (*Illicium verum*) has expectorant and antibacterial properties. In addition, it mixes well with other cough remedies.

Cuts *see* FIRST AID

Cystitis
Drink a standard infusion of silver birch leaves (*Betula pendula*) to help prevent cystitis and other urinary infections, and to remove excess water from the system. It can be combined with bearberry (*Arctostaphylos uva-ursi*).

A decoction of sweet Joe Pye root (*Eupatorium purpureum*), drunk three times a day, is helpful for urinary infections including cystitis. A standard infusion of yarrow (*Achillea millefolium*) is antiseptic and assists recovery from cystitis.

Depression
A lavender flower infusion, taken three times a day, can be an effective pick-me up, especially combined with rosemary (*Rosmarinus officinalis*) or skullcap (*Scutellaria lateriflora*). Rosemary is useful if your depression results from psychological tension or if you are feeling run-down after illness. Drink a standard infusion. It also combines well with skullcap.

Take a standard infusion of vervain (*Verbena officinalis*) to ease the melancholy which may follow flu. It also combines well with skullcap.

Digestion
Most flavouring and seasoning herbs stimulate the flow of digestive juices in the stomach and intestine, and this increases the efficiency with which fats are broken down into fatty acids and nutrients are absorbed by the body. Classic herb partnerships reflect this benevolent fact: rosemary helps the digestion of fatty lamb, fennel assists the digestion of oily fish and horseradish will aid in the digestion of beef.

Many of the aromatic seeds are useful digestives. Take 1 tbsp (15 ml) ground aniseed boiled in 1 cup (225 ml) milk and drink this twice a day to improve the digestive system. Cardamom increases the flow of saliva and adds a pleasing aroma to digestive mixtures. Take 1 cup (225 ml) of infusion half an hour before each meal. Hot peppermint tea can be taken after a meal. A dish of digestive herbs including aniseed, caraway, dill and fennel seed is sometimes offered at the end of an Indian meal and greatly assists the body to digest rich foods.

If there are regular difficulties with indigestion not caused by disease, then rushed eating, an unbalanced diet or tension may be the cause, and it is sensible to consider solutions to these at the

same time as taking herbs to alleviate the problem (*see also* **Stomach ache**).

NB: If there is persistent or severe pain with digestion, consult a medical herbalist or doctor.

Fevers *see* Colds and fevers

Flatulence
Seeds of aniseed, caraway or fennel are all effective at expelling wind but even more so in combination. Infuse crushed mixed seed and drink a cup (225 ml) slowly 30 minutes before each meal.

Many spice seeds help disperse wind; cloves or allspice can be chewed or infused as often as desired. Black pepper sprinkled on food removes wind. Infusions of root ginger, cardamom and coriander have pleasant aromas and relieve griping pains of wind. Star anise (*Illicium verum*) dispels wind. Take a standard infusion three times a day.

Lemon balm (*Melissa officinalis*) relieves flatulent spasms, and a dose of ¼–½ tsp (1–3 ml) powdered angelica root (*Angelica archangelica*) will quickly expel gas from the stomach and bowel.

Haemorrhoids
First choice for mild haemorrhoids is pilewort or lesser celandine (*Ranunculus ficaria*). It shrinks and soothes the swollen veins around the anus. Drink a standard infusion of the root or apply an ointment made with a strong infusion. For bleeding haemorrhoids, apply an ointment of self-heal (*Prunella vulgaris*).

An infusion of horse chestnut fruits (*Aesculus hippocastanum*) drunk three times a day or applied as a compress will tone and strengthen veins as well as helping heal haemorrhoids (*see also* **Varicose veins**).

Hangover
Lemon in water or in orange juice for extra vitamin C, hot

peppermint or wild thyme tea can alleviate the discomfort. A drink of yarrow (*Achillea millefolium*) and elderflower (*Sambucus nigra*) tea will help to eliminate all the toxins from the body.

Hay fever

Sufferers of hay fever and other allergies may benefit from an infusion of golden rod (*Solidago virgaurea*). Take half a cup (125 ml) four times a day. The irritated mucous membranes are relieved and soothed by drinking a warm infusion of hyssop (*Hyssopus officinalis*), lavender (*Lavandula* spp.), marjoram (*Origanum marjorana*) or thyme (*Thymus vulgaris*).

Apply cold compresses of witch hazel diluted in 4 parts boiled water to soothe the eyes. Hot mullein flower (*Verbascum thapsus*) tea and eyebright (*Euphrasia rostkoviana*) tea will help eliminate excess mucus, and eyebright will reduce redness around the eyes. Drink three times a day. Red and sore eyelids may result from other conditions. *NB: If symptoms persist, consult a qualified herbalist.*

Headaches and migraines

Herbs may bring relief though they will not remove the cause. Feverfew leaf (*Tanacetum parthenium*) has justifiably become

FIRST AID

Bruises and sprains

Apply distilled witch hazel (purchased from a chemist) with sterile cottonwool as soon as possible to small bumps and bruises. This will halt the swelling. Comfrey oil or ointment is good for messy scrapes, bruises and sprains. A poultice of comfrey leaves (*Symphytum officinale*) will reduce bruising and speed healing of sprains and fractures. It's best not used on deep wounds, as comfrey is such a powerful tissue healer that the surface skin may heal before the wound has healed deeper down.

Both a lotion of St John's wort (*Hypericum perforatum*) and arnica (*Arnica montana*) ointment are excellent for sprains and bruises, especially if there is any pain or inflammation of the skin.

An ointment of calendula petals, agrimony (*Agrimonia eupatoria*) or elder leaves (*Sambucus nigra*) is soothing and healing for bruises, sprains and other minor wounds. *NB: Do not use arnica where the skin is broken.*

Burns, minor

Immediately apply the cool inside surface of an aloe vera leaf to reduce pain, speed healing and leave a protective seal against infection. Later, apply calendula as a cool compress or ointment.

NB: Major burns are an emergency: summon professional help at once. Cool the burn with cool (not ice-cold) water while you are waiting, and give the patient 6 drops Bach Flower Rescue Remedy and reassure him.

Cuts and abrasions

First clean the cut by soaking in witch hazel diluted with 4 parts water, or an antiseptic herbal infusion; elder leaves (*Sambucus nigra*) are excellent. A speedy alternative is to add 3 drops thyme or rosemary oil or ½ tsp (3 ml) tincture of calendula to 1 cup (225 ml) hand-hot, boiled water. The antiseptic wash can also be gently swabbed on. A dose of 4 drops Bach Flower Rescue Remedy has a calming effect, while an infusion of lady's mantle (*Alchemilla vulgaris*) can be applied as a compress to arrest bleeding.

For slow-healing wounds, apply a compress or poultice of comfrey (*Symphytum officinale*), self-heal (*Prunella vulgaris*) or yarrow (*Achillea millefolium*). Add plantain leaves (*Plantago major*) for their antibiotic properties. If applying a poultice to an open wound, dip leaves briefly in boiling water to sterilize them. To continue treatment, a soft ointment of comfrey, calendula or agrimony (*Agrimonia eupatoria*) is soothing and healing.

Stings and insect bites

Wasp stings are alkaline: apply inside surface of a houseleek leaf (*Sempervivum tectorum*), onion slices, or dab on vinegar. Bee stings and ant bites are acid: apply sodium bicarbonate dissolved in ice-cold water. Remember to remove the bee sting.

● **Reduce painful swelling** with a drop of neat lavender or eucalyptus oil. To soothe any lingering irritation, apply a cold compress of tincture of calendula or calendula ointment.

● **To soothe nettle stings**, rub on crushed fresh dock leaves (*Rumex obtusifolius*).

Travel sickness

Recent research confirms that the best treatment to settle the stomach and help prevent nausea is an infusion of root ginger. Take a bottle of tincture of ginger when travelling, and give 10 drops in half a cup (125 ml) of water for adults or 2–3 drops mixed in a little warm water for children.

Pick large leaves of fresh angelica (*Angelica archangelica*) and crush them on the journey; the scent allays nausea and refreshes stale air.

the primary herbal remedy for migraine. A small to medium, fresh or frozen, leaf eaten between slices of bread (it can cause mouth ulcers in very sensitive people) three times a day has been found to reduce the intensity or frequency of 70 per cent of migraines (usually in sufferers who gain relief from warmth applied to the head). Its action is cumulative and can take up to six months to show results. Alternatively take half a cup (125 ml) of leaf tea twice a day to reduce the pain of migraine.

Lavender (*Lavandula* spp.) is useful for stress-related headaches and combines well with valerian (*Valeriana officinalis*). Drink an infusion of lavender flowers three times a day. A standard infusion of valerian is useful in tension headaches, when it combines well with skullcap (*Scutellaria lateriflora*). *NB: Do not take feverfew during pregnancy as it can stimulate the uterus.*

Insomnia
A cup (225 ml) of hop (*Humulus lupulus*) tea taken before retiring to bed is a useful sedative for insomnia except for anyone suffering from depression. It combines well with valerian (*Valeriana officinalis*), which reduces tension and anxiety, and passion flower leaves (*Passiflora incarnata*). Chamomile (*Chamaemelum nobile*) tea and catnip (*Nepeta cataria*) tea are traditional relaxing bedtime drinks that will reduce anxiety and promote restful sleep. Passion flower tea and orange blossom tea can also help insomniacs.

Menstrual cycle
The best remedy for the dull headache, irritability, mild depression, fluid retention or painful breasts experienced by many women just before their period is evening primrose oil. Tests at a London hospital

indicated that 85 per cent of those in the trial experienced improvement. The herb (*Oenothera biennis*) is easy to grow but extracting the oil from the seed is complex, so purchase capsules from a health shop. Those that also contain a marine oil are particularly recommended. Skullcap (*Scutellaria lateriflora*), chamomile (*Matricaria recutita*) and lime blossom (*Tilia cordata*) are safe teas to soothe and reduce discomfort of PMT (premenstrual tension). Take an infusion of any of these three times a day to relieve the symptoms.
• **For menstrual cramps** drink an infusion of chamomile or valerian (*Valeriana officinalis*) three times a day, of half a cup (125 ml) of feverfew (*Tanacetum parthenium*) tea taken twice a day.
• **For cramps with a feeling of heaviness**, a hot infusion of raspberry leaf (*Rubus idaeus*) tea is recommended.
• **To help reduce period pains** and heavy bleeding, try lady's mantle leaves (*Alchemilla vulgaris*), taken in a double-strength infusion three times a day. This also eases problems of the menopause.
• **To help relieve menopausal symptoms**, try dried berries of the chaste tree (*Vitex agnus-castus*), which regulate the activity of sex hormones. They are also of benefit in PMT and help to restore the body's natural balance after taking contraceptive pills. Infuse 1 tsp (5 ml) berries for 15 minutes; drink 1 cup (225 ml) three times a day. Motherwort (*Leonurus cardiaca*) reduces the discomfort of the menopause. When symptoms include irritability and anxiety, St John's wort (*Hypericum perforatum*) is recommended. Drink a standard infusion of flowering tops three times a day.

Nausea
Freshly grated ginger or powdered cinnamon bark infused

on their own or sprinkled in other teas can be taken whenever necessary to relieve nausea and vomiting. Cloves, as a flavouring in food or drunk as an infusion, will allay nausea and vomiting while stimulating the digestive system. Infuse about 10 cloves in 1 cup (225 ml) boiling water for 10 minutes and take as required.

Pregnancy and childbirth
Herbs with a strong action must be avoided during pregnancy, particularly those that stimulate the uterus, such as goldenseal (*Hydrastis canadensis*).

In the early stages of labour, a sponge wash with rosewater, lavender water or an infusion of rosemary has a pleasantly relaxing scent and mild antiseptic qualities.

Sores *see* Boils and sores

Spots *see* Acne

Sprains *see* FIRST AID

Stings *see* FIRST AID

Stomach ache
For those who already know what is causing their ailment, herbs can be helpful as long as the condition is monitored.
• **To soothe and heal** the delicate mucous membranes in the stomach, drink chamomile (*Matricaria recutita*) tea for its anti-inflammatory effect or marsh mallow (*Althaea officinalis*) as you feel necessary.
• **For digestive disorders**, slippery elm (*Ulmus rubra*) (purchased as a powder) is both a soothing remedy as well as a wholesome food for those unable to face solid food. Make a paste with ½–1 tbsp (8–15 ml) powdered bark and a little cold water. Stir in 1 cup (225 ml) of hot milk or water and sweeten with honey if desired. *NB: Sharp or prolonged pain in the stomach needs a professional medical diagnosis.*

• **For stomach cramps caused by indigestion,** drink an infusion of antiseptic catnip (*Nepeta cataria*).

Sunburn
Aloe vera leaf juice is cooling and healing for sunburn and minor burns. Apply directly to the area of sunburn. A compress of sorrel (*Rumex acetosa*) also has a cooling effect. Sorrel tea is said to help relieve the effects of sunstroke and exhaustion: take one cup (225 ml) three times a day.

A macerated oil of St John's wort (*Hypericum perforatum*) is excellent for minor burns once they have cooled.

Tension
In contrast to tranquillizers, herbs that work to relax nervous tension will in addition counter stress by reviving and toning the central nervous system.

The two finest treatments are skullcap flowering top (*Scutellaria lateriflora*), which is helpful for a wide range of nervous complaints, and valerian root (*Valeriana officinalis*), which is suitable for nervous spasms and tremors, phobias, insomnia and restlessness. Fortunately they work well together. Take an infusion individually or in combination. Take 1 cup (225 ml) infusion up to three times a day or half a cup (125 ml) every three hours in times of great stress, but not for long periods of time. A standard infusion of borage leaves (*Borago officinalis*) is a tonic to the adrenal glands, which react to stress. Borage flowers and leaves in wine have a traditional reputation for bolstering courage, and a wine-glassful (150 ml) will relieve nervous tension during times of stress.

After a hectic day, try drinking a tea of ginseng (*Panax ginseng*), lime blossom (*Tilia cordata*) or lavender (*Lavandula* spp.) to calm and tone the nervous system. Lime and lavender combine well to combat nervous exhaustion, while lemon balm (*Melissa officinalis*) relieves tension with a mild antidepressant action. It combines well with lavender flowers and lime blossom. Take a cup of mixed teas morning, evening and when required.

Wood betony (*Stachys officinalis*) strengthens the central nervous system and is mildly sedative, being especially good for headaches and neuralgia. Take 1 cup (225 ml) tea three times a day or combine it with skullcap.

• **For relaxants,** try chamomile (*Chamaemelum nobile*), which can be drunk as desired, and cowslip (*Primula veris*), which is a relaxing sedative for stress-related tension. Make an infusion of the petals and drink 1 cup (225 ml) three times a day. It can be combined with either lime blossom or skullcap.

• **To ease tension** a standard infusion of St John's wort (*Hypericum perforatum*) has pain-reducing and sedative properties, making it useful for anxiety-related conditions, unless there is also depression. Rosemary, on the other hand, is a stimulant to the nervous system and useful for tension that is causing depression.

Throat, sore
The anti-bacterial qualities of lemon are increased if you take it in an infusion with a natural antiseptic such as eucalyptus (*Eucalyptus globulus*) and honey. Thyme (*Thymus vulgaris*) is a powerful disinfectant and an excellent gargle for sore throats, laryngitis and tonsillitis.

Gargle with a standard tea of fenugreek seed, agrimony (*Agrimonia eupatorium*) or self-heal (*Prunella vulgaris*), or a decoction of bistort root (*Polygonum bistorta*) to relieve sore throats, inflammation of the mouth or tongue and laryngitis, or a cayenne infusion for laryngitis (see recipe, p. 183). The anti-inflammatory and antiseptic properties of chamomile (*Matricaria recutita*) make it a useful gargle for sore throats and the mouth infections that often accompany them, such as gingivitis. Use a double-strength infusion of the flowers to soothe symptoms. The menthol in peppermint (*Mentha* × *piperita*) makes it a pleasant infusion.

• **Soothe a sore throat** by wrapping round a hot compress of sage (*Salvia officinalis*) or thyme (*Thymus vulgaris*), kept warm and in place with a scarf. Chew liquorice root (*Glycyrrhiza glabra*) as desired.

Toothache
Cloves are a powerful local antiseptic and mild pain reliever. As a short-term measure, put a drop of oil of cloves (available from chemists and essential-oil suppliers) on the end of a cottonwool bud and dab on or near the tooth.

An alternative is to place a clove in the mouth near the tooth for as long as it is effective.

Travel sickness *see* FIRST AID

Varicose veins
Much can be done to prevent varicose veins. Tackle constipation, improve your diet, adding vitamins B, C and E, take more exercise, stop smoking, and avoid hot baths and standing for long periods.

Take spices that stimulate the circulation, such as ginger and cayenne, and an infusion of herbs that contain rutin, such as buckwheat (*Fagopyrum esculentum*), hawthorn berries (*Crataegus monogyna*) and horse chestnuts (*Aesculus hippocastanum*). Drink this no more than three times a day, or use as a compress or lotion.

If your veins are inflamed or they ache, a compress of calendula tincture or witch hazel will relieve the pain (*see also* **Haemorrhoids**).

· CHAPTER SIX ·

CULTIVATING AND HARVESTING HERBS

Herbs must be among the easiest plants to
cultivate, being amenable to most
conditions and rarely troubled by disease.
If you can give your herbs a good start by
choosing the right position in the garden
and the correct soil, then they should
grow into healthy specimens.
Overcrowding of any plot will produce
poor plants so take care to thin out your
herbs, where necessary, and pick them
when they are at the peak of perfection to
gain maximum benefit from them.
Because herbs are so adaptable, they can
be tucked into existing flower borders,
vegetable beds or decorative pots. Many
will grow happily on a balcony or patio, or
even indoors. Wherever you plant them,
as long as they have the soil and conditions
that suit them best, you will be rewarded
with decorative, aromatic plants that have
a multitude of uses. And care taken in the
harvesting and preserving of your herbs
will result in long-lasting perfume
and flavour.

Herbs in the garden
*A lush and colourful border with old roses and giant
angelica flowers amidst a range of traditional cottage
garden plants.*

A–Z of cultivation

This section gives notes on the conditions required by all the plants listed in the A–Z of Herbs, and some additional herbs and spices, in order for you to be able to cultivate them successfully. These include details of site or aspect (that is, whether they need sun, shade, or a mixture of both), and type of soil they prefer (acid, clay, loamy, well-drained, and so on), together with information on methods of propagating, and care needed while the plant is growing, what time of year to harvest, and appropriate preserving methods. In addition, for those herbs not included in the A–Z of Herbs, a brief description of its appearance and uses is given. For practical illustrated advice on methods of cultivating, growing, propagating, harvesting and storing herbs, consult pp. 216–31.

Achillea millefolium
Yarrow/Milfoil
Site Sunny. Tolerates light shade.
Soil Moderately rich and moist.
Propagating Sow or divide invasive roots in spring or autumn.
Growing Thin or transplant to 12 in (30 cm) apart. Plants will bloom a second time if they are deadheaded. Yarrow is not suitable for growing indoors.

Harvesting Gather leaves and flowers in late summer.
Preserving Dry both leaves and flowers.
See also p. 14.

Alchemilla vulgaris
Lady's mantle/Dewcup
Site Full sun or partial shade.
Soil Rich, moist, alkaline loam.
Propagating Sow or divide Lady's mantle either in spring or in autumn.
Growing Thin or transplant to 2 ft (60 cm) apart. Small plants can also be grown indoors with some success.

Harvesting Select large leaves as needed. They are best during flowering period.
Preserving Dry leaves.
See also p. 15.

Allium
Alliums
Site Sunny; or partial shade.
Soil Rich, moist and well drained; tolerates poorer soil.
Propagating Take offsets or divide in autumn or spring; plant garlic cloves 1½ in (4 cm) deep; sow seed in spring (not available for everlasting and tree onion).
Growing Transplant or thin to 9 in (23 cm) apart; garlic to 6 in (15 cm) apart. Water in dry spells and enrich soil annually (or monthly, when cutting chives).

Remove flowers for better flavour. Divide and replant clumps every 3–4 years. Pot up in autumn for indoor supply.
Harvesting (Chives) Cut leaves, leaving 2 in (5 cm) for regrowth. Pick flowers as they open. (Garlic) Dig bulbs in late summer.
Preserving Refrigerate chive leaves in a sealed plastic bag to retain crispness for 7 days, or dry them. Dry flowers and bulbs. Make garlic oil, and garlic and chive vinegars.
See also pp. 16–17.

Aloe vera
Aloe vera
Site Full sun or light shade in frost-free location.
Soil Gritty and well drained.
Propagating Sow in spring at 70°F (21°C). Remove offshoots in summer; then dry for 2 days before planting in 2 parts compost to 1 part sharp sand.
Growing Maintain 41°F (5°C)

minimum. Aloe vera is an excellent indoor plant.
Harvesting Cut leaves from plants as needed.
Preserving No method known at present, although a product called Aloe Vera gel is available. This contains 99.9 per cent aloe vera and is sold in a dark glass bottle which should be refrigerated.
See also p. 18.

Aloysia triphylla
Lemon verbena
Site Full sun. Needs shelter in almost frost-free position.
Soil Light, well drained and alkaline. Poor soil produces stronger plants able to survive cold winters.
Propagating Sow in spring. Take softwood cuttings in late spring.
Growing Thin or transplant to

3 ft (1 m) apart. Prune drooping branches to encourage new growth. Grow lemon verbena indoors in winter, though it may drop its leaves. Prune and spray with warm water in spring.
Harvesting Pick leaves anytime: best when flowers begin to bloom.
Preserving Dry leaves. Use fresh leaves in oil and vinegar.
See also p. 19.

Althaea officinalis
Marsh mallow
Site Full sun.
Soil Moist, moderate fertility.
Propagating Sow in spring. Divide base or try stem cuttings in spring.
Growing Thin or transplant to 1 ft (30 cm) apart; in second season, thin again to 2 ft (60 cm) apart. Grow outdoors only.

Harvesting Collect seeds when ripe. Pick leaves as required and dig up roots in autumn.
Preserving Dry seeds and leaves. Scrape and dry roots or make into syrup (see p. 136).
See also p. 20.

Anethum graveolens
Dill
Site Full sun. Protect from wind.
Soil Rich and well drained.
Propagating Sow in situ from spring until midsummer. Do not plant near fennel, as they cross-pollinate and flavours muddle. Self-seeds. Seeds remain viable for 3–10 years.
Growing Thin to 9–12 in (23–30 cm) apart. Can also be grown indoors.
Harvesting Gather leaves when young. Pick flowering tops just as

fruits begin to form. To collect seed, after flowering head turns brown, hang the whole plant over a cloth.
Preserving Dry or freeze leaves. Dry ripe seed. Make dill vinegar with flowering heads or seed.
See also p. 21.

Angelica archangelica
Angelica
Site Light shade. Benefits from a mulch when in full sun.
Soil Deep and moist.
Propagating Allow plants to self-seed or sow fresh in early autumn. Angelica seed loses most of its viability within three months.
Growing Seedlings should be transplanted in spring before the taproot becomes established. Leave a square yard/metre between plants.
Harvesting Cut stems before midsummer for crystallizing. Harvest leaves before flowering. Collect ripe seed in late summer. Dig up root in autumn of first year.
Preserving Dry leaves and root. Crystallize stems.
See also p. 22.

Anthriscus cerefolium
Chervil
Site Light shade in summer (ideally plant under a deciduous plant so autumn seedlings can enjoy full winter sun). In hot conditions, it quickly runs to seed.
Soil Light and well drained.
Propagating Ripe seed germinates quickly and can be used six to eight weeks after gathering. For a regular supply, sow monthly except in winter. Scatter on soil, press in lightly. Left to self-seed, chervil provides one early crop and a second one in late summer.
Growing Thin seedlings to 6–9 in (15–23 cm) apart; do not transplant. Although chervil is hardy, some cloche protection is needed to ensure leaves in winter. Chervil makes a good indoor plant, given light shade and humidity.
Harvesting Gather leaves before flowering, once the plant reaches a height of 4 in (10 cm).
Preserving Freeze or dry leaves. Chervil is also a good addition to vinegar.
See also p. 23.

Apium graveolens
Smallage/Wild celery
Site Sunny with midday shade. Shelter from strong winds.
Soil Rich, moist and well drained.
Propagating Sow under heat in early spring or outdoors in late spring. Germination is slow.
Growing Transplant or thin to 16 in (40 cm) apart. Smallage is not suitable for growing indoors.
Harvesting Pick leaves in late summer or as needed. Collect seeds when ripe.
Preserving Dry seed. Dry or freeze leaves or infuse in vinegar.
See also p. 24.

Armoracia rusticana
Horseradish
Site Open sunny position.
Soil Light, well-dug, rich and moist soil preferred.
Propagating Sow seed, divide roots or take root cuttings in spring. Choose roots ½ in (13 mm) thick. Cut into pieces 6 in (15 cm) long, and plant vertically, at a depth of 2 in (5 cm). Roots will spread if not restrained.
Growing Thin or transplant to 12 in (30 cm) apart. Not suitable for growing indoors.
Harvesting Dig up roots as needed or in autumn. Pick the young leaves.
Preserving Store roots in sand; or wash, grate or slice and dry; or immerse whole washed roots in white wine vinegar. Dry leaves.
See also p. 25.

Arnica montana
Arnica
Description Hardy perennial, growing 1–2 ft (20–60 cm) tall. Oval, hairy leaves form rosettes and large, scented, yellow flowers appear all summer.
Site Full sun.
Soil Sandy, acidic soil, rich in humus is necessary.
Propagating Divide creeping rhizomes in spring. Sow from seed in spring; slow to germinate.
Uses A good bee plant. Leaves and roots smoked in herbal tobaccos. Use a tincture of flowers for sprains, wounds and bruises, relief from rheumatic pain and on chilblains so long as the skin is not broken. Add to warm water to make a relaxing footbath.

Note: *Potentially toxic if taken internally.*

Artemisia
Artemisias
Site Full sun.
Soil Light, dry, well drained. *A. lactiflora* requires moist soil and will tolerate some shade.
Propagating Sow when available. Take semi-hardwood cuttings in late summer.
Growing Thin or transplant artemisias to 18 in–3 ft (45 cm–1 m) apart. Do not plant wormwood next to fennel, sage, caraway, anise and other culinary and medicinal herbs as rain washes a growth-inhibiting toxin out of the leaves that affects nearby plants.
Harvesting Pick flowering tops and leaves in mid- to late summer.
Preserving Dry leaves and flowering tops.
See also pp. 26–7.

Artemisia dracunculus
Tarragon
Site Sunny and sheltered.
Soil Rich, light and dry.
Propagating Divide roots in spring. Take stem cuttings in summer. (Russian tarragon) Sow in spring.
Growing Thin or transplant to 12–18 in (30–45 cm) apart. Cut back in autumn. Protect in winter with straw or similar mulch. Tarragon grows well indoors.
Harvesting Pick leaves anytime, but in late summer for main crop. If cutting branches, sever maximum of two-thirds of branch to allow for regrowth, unless it is the end of the growing season.
Preserving Freeze or dry leaves. Infuse leaves in oil or vinegar.
See also p. 28.

Borago officinalis
Borage
Site Open sunny position.
Soil Light and dry, well drained.
Propagating Seed on site or singly in pots in spring for summer flowers; autumn for spring flowers. Will self-sow freely on light soils.
Growing Set 12 in (30 cm) apart. Plant among roses or summer prune to keep tidy. Possible to grow small plants indoors.
Harvesting Pick both flowers and leaves.

Preserving Dry flowers; freeze in ice cubes; crystallize.
See also p. 29.

Brassica
Mustard
Site Sunny. Will benefit from light shade in summer to prevent bolting.
Soil Fertile and well drained.
Propagating Sow in spring for seed crop, or every 3 weeks throughout year for salad greens.
Growing Thin to 6 in (15 cm) for seed crop. It is not necessary to thin salad crops. Can also be grown indoors.
Harvesting Gather flowers as they open. Pick seed pods before they open in late summer. Cut salad leaves 8–10 days after sowing. Pick single leaves on older plants.
Preserving Dry seed in pods or infuse in vinegar. Dry leaves.
See also p. 30.

Calendula officinalis
Calendula/Marigold
Site Sunny position.
Soil Fine loam but tolerates most soils, except waterlogged.
Propagating Sow seed in spring in situ or singly in pots.
Growing Plant 12–18 in (30–45 cm) apart. Marigolds will flower continuously so long as they are deadheaded.
Harvesting Pick flowers when open, leaves when young.
Preserving Dry petals at low temperature to preserve colour, or macerate in oil.
See also p. 31.

Capsicum annuum
Sweet pepper/Chili pepper
Description Annual or biennial grown commercially in the tropics and subtropics. Grows 1–3 ft (30 cm–1 m) high with oval, pointed leaves and white flowers in summer. Fleshy, edible fruit with furrowed sides varies in colour (yellow, brown, purple, bright red) when mature. When unripe it is green but still edible.
Site Full sun. Grow under glass in temperate climates, avoid extremes of temperature.
Soil Rich.
Propagating Sow in spring.
Uses Eat fruit in salads, as a vegetable or add to casseroles and stews. Fresh or dried fruit is used as a stimulant and digestive. Sprinkle ½ tsp (2.5 ml), finely chopped, in ½ cup (125 ml) of boiling water or hot milk at the first sign of a chill. The dried fruit of *C. tetragonum* is crushed as paprika pepper. It has a sweet mild flavour, which is free of the hot pungency of chili. It should be brilliant red; if brown it is probably stale. Paprika is high in vitamin C and should be used generously in stews and meat dishes.

Carum carvi
Caraway
Site Full sun.
Soil Rich loam.
Propagating Sow outside in late spring or early autumn, in shallow drills in permanent position.
Growing Thin to 8 in (20 cm) apart, when large enough to handle. Caraway can be grown indoors so long as it is placed in a sunny position.
Harvesting Gather leaves when young. Pick seed heads in late summer or when seeds are brown. Dig up roots during the second autumn.
Preserving Hang seed heads upside down over an open container.
See also p. 32.

Cedronella canariensis
Balm of Gilead
Site Full sun.
Soil Well-drained, medium loam.
Propagating Sow in spring (and note that seedlings resemble nettles). Take stem cuttings in early autumn.
Growing Thin or transplant to 18 in (45 cm) apart. Balm of Gilead makes an excellent conservatory plant, but a 9–10 in (23–25 cm) pot is needed for it to reach its full size.
Harvesting Pick leaves just before flowers open or in autumn before pruning. (*Populus balsamifera*) Gather buds.
Preserving Dry leaves. (*Populus balsamifera*) Dry buds.
See also p. 33.

Chamaemelum nobile
Perennial chamomile
Site Full sun.
Soil Light and well drained.
Propagating (All except 'Treneague') Sow in spring. (Perennials) Divide in spring or autumn. Take 3 in (8 cm) cuttings from side shoots in summer.
Growing For a chamomile lawn or seat, plant 4–6 in (10–15 cm) apart. (*M. recutita*) Plant 9 in (23 cm) apart. (*A. tinctoria*) Plant 18 in (45 cm) apart.
Harvesting Gather leaves anytime. Pick flowers once they are fully open.
Preserving Dry both flowers and leaves.
See also p. 34.

Chenopodium bonus-henricus
Good King Henry
Site Prefers full sun but will tolerate light shade.
Soil Rich loam, deeply dug and well drained.
Propagating Sow in spring; cover seed with ¼ in (6 mm) of soil. Divide roots in autumn.
Growing Thin or transplant seedlings to 1 ft (30 cm) apart. Water in dry weather; fertilize during summer. Unsatisfactory when grown indoors.
Harvesting Allow plants 1 year to develop, then gather leaves as required and pick flowering spikes as they begin to open.
Preserving Freeze only when an ingredient in a cooked dish.
See also p. 35.

Chrysanthemum balsamita
Alecost/Costmary
Site Prefers full sun.
Soil Rich, dryish and well drained.
Propagating Divide roots in spring or autumn. Seed is not viable in cool climates.
Growing Transplant to 2 ft (60 cm) apart. Small alecost plants can be grown indoors.
Harvesting Pick leaves anytime or, for most aroma, as flowers start to open.
Preserving Dry leaves.
See also p. 36.

Chrysanthemum cinerariifolium
Pyrethrum
Site Sunny and open.
Soil Alkaline and well drained.
Propagating Sow in late spring to summer. Divide roots in spring.
Growing Thin or transplant to 6–12 in (15–30 cm) apart. Grow outdoors only – it is not a successful indoor plant.

Harvesting Gather open flowers.
Preserving Dry. Store away from light to preserve insecticide.
See also p. 37.

Cichorium intybus
Chicory/Succory
Site Sunny and open.
Soil Light, preferably alkaline soil. Dig deeply for good roots.
Propagating Sow in early summer: Witloof variety for chicons and Madgeburg or Brunswick for "coffee" roots.
Growing Thin or transplant to 18 in (45 cm) apart. To grow

chicons, dig up roots in autumn, cut leaves to 1 in (25 mm) and trim 1 in (25 mm) off root. Bury in sandy compost and water. Keep cool and dark. Chicons are ready to eat in 3–4 weeks.
Harvesting Gather leaves when young. Dig up roots in first autumn and chicons in winter.
Preserving Dry root and leaves.
See also p. 38.

Citrus limon
Lemon
Description Tender, subtropical, evergreen tree. Grows 10–20 ft (3–6 m) high with grey bark, elliptical leaves; clusters of white flowers, with pink outsides, appear at all seasons and are followed by sour-tasting, bright yellow fruits, which are indented with oil glands.

Site Full sun. Protect from wind.
Soil Light, well-drained, fertile soil is necessary.
Propagating By seed.
Uses Fruit, juice and peel, which are rich in vitamins and minerals, are widely used in cooking, sweets and drinks, and as an antioxidant. Add to potpourri, herb pillows, soaps and perfumes. Has many household uses: cleans brass,

silver, marble and rust stains. Use as an astringent and skin tonic. Bleaching properties may remove nicotine stains from nails and teeth, fade freckles and condition blonde hair. Juice soothes colds, coughs, sore throats, headaches, and fevers. Use as an antiseptic to neutralize bacteria.

Coriandrum sativum
Coriander
Site Full sun.
Soil Rich and light.
Propagating Sow in autumn, to over-winter in mild climates, or early spring in final position, away from fennel, which seems to suffer in its presence.
Growing Thin to 8 in (20 cm) apart. Coriander can be grown indoors but many people find its scent unpleasant in the home.
Harvesting Pick young leaves anytime. Collect seeds when

brown but before they drop. Dig up roots in autumn.
Preserving Dry seeds, store whole or infuse to make a coriander vinegar. Freeze leaves, or place their stems in water and cover with a plastic bag to retain their freshness.
See also p. 39.

Cuminum cyminum
Cumin
Description Tender annual. Grows 6–12 in (15–30 cm) tall. Leaves are slightly fragrant and thread-like; white or pinkish flowers appear in summer and are followed by aromatic seeds. These are similar in appearance to caraway seeds, with the exception that they are bristly.

Site Sunny and sheltered.
Soil Well-drained, rich soil.
Propagating Sow in late spring in warm situation.
Uses Powerfully flavoured seeds, whole or ground, are added to many Middle Eastern and Indian dishes, especially to lamb, curries and yogurt. Also used for pickling and flavouring liqueurs and cordials. The seed oil is employed in perfumery and in veterinary medicine. Cumin is thought to relieve flatulence, colic, indigestion and diarrhoea.

Cymbopogon citratus
Lemon-grass
Description Tender perennial grass from the tropics. Grows 6 ft (1.8 m) tall. Densely tufted with fragrant, very long, thin, pointed leaves with prominent mid-veins. Greenish flowers, with reddish tinge, appear in nodding clusters during the summer.

Site Full sun in the greenhouse, a minimum temperature of 55°F (13°C) is necessary.
Soil Moist.
Propagating Divide plants.
Uses Chop tender stalks into salads. Infuse leaves as a herbal tea. Use oil to clean oily skin and as a relaxant in bathwater. Add to perfumes and soaps.

Dianthus caryophyllus
Clove pink
Site Open sunny position.
Soil Well drained and alkaline soil is necessary.
Propagating Sow seed or take stem cuttings during spring. Divide roots or layer plants in late summer.
Growing Thin or transplant to 1 ft (30 cm) apart. Clove pinks can also be grown successfully indoors in a sunny position.
Harvesting Pick flowers once they have opened.

Preserving Air dry flowers or put in silica gel. Infuse in almond oil for sweet oil or in wine vinegar for floral vinegar. Petals can be crystallized.
See also p. 40.

Elettaria cardamomum
Cardamom
Description Tender perennial from the tropics. Reaches 6–10 ft (1.8–3 m) high. Leaves are lance-shaped and dark green, with paler, silky undersides; creeping roots are large and fleshy. Small yellow flowers spread along the ground during mid- to late spring, followed by green, three-celled pods containing dark red-brown seeds.

Site Needs a tropical climate with high humidity and shade.
Soil Rich, moist.
Propagating Sow seed. Divide the rhizomes.
Uses Whole seeds used to flavour marinades, liqueurs, punches, mulled wines and pickling liquids. Add ground seeds as a spice to fruit salads, curries, cakes, breads, biscuits and coffee. Chew seeds to freshen breath. Use in potpourri and in perfumes. Helps to relieve flatulence, indigestion and headaches.

Eucalyptus globulus
Eucalyptus
Description Evergreen tree whose young leaves are susceptible to frosts. Grows to 300 ft (90 m) or more. Bark is peeling and papery; leaves, when mature, are leathery, lance-shaped, bluish-green and covered with oil-bearing glands. Has small, petal-less, white flowers.

Site Sunny position, protected from cold winds.
Soil Any well-drained soil.
Propagating Sow fresh seed in spring.
Growing Plant pot-grown plants in spring, cut back weak growth in spring.
Uses Leaves provide an effective flea repellent. Timber is used as an exterior building material.

Leaves are included in dry potpourris. Volatile, greenish-yellow oil from mature leaves useful for catarrh, sore throats, bronchitis, indigestion, fevers and as an inhalant, antiseptic, deodorant and stimulant. Apply diluted externally for burns, wounds and ulcers.
Note: *If taken in large doses, eucalyptus is toxic.*

Eupatorium purpurea
Sweet Joe Pye
Site Partial shade or sun.
Soil Any rich, alkaline soil. (*E. cannabinum*) Prefers marshy soil.
Propagating Sow fresh seed in autumn. Divide either in spring or autumn.
Growing Thin or transplant to 3 ft (1 m) apart. Sweet Joe Pye is not suitable for indoor cultivation.
Harvesting Pick leaves anytime. Dig up roots in autumn; remove small side roots. Collect seed heads when petals have dropped.

Preserving Dry leaves, roots and seed heads.
See also p. 41.

Euphrasia officinalis
Eyebright
Description Annual. Grows 2–8 in (5–20 cm) high with deeply cut, hairy, toothed, oval leaves and square, branched stems. Numerous small, white flowers with purple and yellow spots or stripes appear from midsummer to late autumn.
Site Any.

Soil Chalky soil.
Propagating Sow seeds in spring. Semi-parasitic on certain grass species, so difficult to grow.
Uses Infuse whole plant or crush fresh stem and use strained juice to relieve eye inflammations, eye strain and other eye ailments; also for hay fever, colds, coughs and sore throats. *E. rostkoviana* is the most useful species for eye

treatments. Apply externally as an eye compress and in a poultice to aid wound healing.

Note: *Seek medical advice before treating eyes.*

Filipendula ulmaria
Meadowsweet
Site Sun or partial shade.
Soil Moist, fertile and alkaline soil necessary.
Propagating Sow in spring; divide meadowsweet in autumn.
Growing Thin or transplant to 12 in (30 cm) apart. Meadowsweet is not a suitable herb for growing indoors.

Harvesting Gather young leaves before flowers appear, and pick flowers when new.
Preserving Dry both leaves and flowers.
See also p. 42.

Foeniculum vulgare
Fennel
Site Full sun is needed in order to ripen seed.
Soil Well-drained loam. Clay soils should be avoided.
Propagating Sow in late spring to early summer. (Self-seeds when established.) Divide plants in autumn.
Growing Thin or transplant to 20 in (50 cm) apart. Do not grow near dill, as seeds will cross-pollinate, or coriander, as it reduces fennel's seed production.

Remove seed heads if not required to give better leaf production. Fennel is not a suitable herb for growing indoors.
Harvesting Pick young stems and leaves and use as required. Collect the ripe seed. Dig up "bulbs" in autumn.
Preserving Freeze leaves or infuse in oil or vinegar. Dry seed. *See also p. 43.*

Fragaria vesca
Wild strawberry
Site Cool, sun or shade, sheltered.
Soil Alkaline, moist, well drained.
Propagating Sow in spring at a temperature of 65°F (18°C). In spring, sever the daughter plants produced on runners and transplant to 12 in (30 cm) apart.
Growing Apply a potash fertilizer

as fruits begin to form. Can also be grown indoors.
Harvesting Pick fruit as ripe. Collect leaves as required. Dig up roots in autumn.
Preserving Freeze or bottle fruit. Dry leaves.
See also p. 44.

Galium odoratum
Sweet woodruff
Site Semi-shade, particularly good under trees. Leaf colour fades in bright sun.
Soil Prefers moist, porous loam but will survive on less rich soil.
Propagating Sow seeds when ripe in late summer in moist shaded soil. Propagation, however, is easiest by dividing the

creeping rootstock after flowering is finished.
Growing Transplant in spring, 6–9 in (15–23 cm) apart. Sweet woodruff is not suitable for growing indoors.
Harvesting Pick leaves and flowering stems.
Preserving Store leaves whole to preserve scent.
See also p. 45.

Glycyrrhiza glabra
Liquorice
Description Hardy herbaceous perennial. Grows 2–5 ft (60 cm– 1.5 m) tall with long, narrow, dark green leaflets. Its taproot has several long branches, which are wrinkled and brown, with yellow flesh. Yellow or purplish flowers appear in summer, followed by reddish-brown pods.

Site Full sun.
Soil Requires deep, moist, rich, sandy loam.
Propagating Divide roots in autumn or spring.
Uses Root flavours beers, confectionery, tobaccos and snuffs. Root pulp is incorporated in mushroom compost. Root contains glycyrrhizin, a substance many times sweeter than sugar.

Infuse as a refreshing tea and as a remedy for coughs and chest complaints. Strong decoction makes a laxative for children and may reduce fever.

Hamamelis virginiana
Witch hazel
Description Hardy tree. Grows 8–10 ft (2.4–3 m) high with brown bark and toothed, elliptical leaves with hairy undersides. Scented, yellow flowers, with strap-like petals, appear during late autumn.
Site Sun or partial shade.
Soil Moist, lime-free soil.

Propagating By air layering during autumn.
Uses Forked branches formerly used as water divining rods. Apply distilled extract from young flower-bearing twigs (available commercially as witch hazel) externally for bruises, sprains, varicose veins, haemorrhoids, insect bites and to stop bleeding. Used as an astringent cosmetic.

Note: *A tincture from the bark or leaves may disfigure skin.*

Helianthus annuus
Sunflower
Site Full sun.
Soil Any well-drained loam.
Propagating Sow seeds in their shells in spring. Avoid planting near a potato plot as growth becomes stunted.
Growing Thin or transplant to 12–18 in (30–45 cm) apart. Not suitable for growing indoors.

Harvesting Pick leaves and flower buds as required. Cut flower heads when they droop. Hang until seeds fall. Gather stems in autumn.
Preserving Dry leaves and seed. *See also p. 46.*

Helichrysum angustifolium
Curry-plant
Site Full sun.
Soil Rich and well drained.
Propagating Take stem cuttings in spring or autumn.
Growing Plant 12 in (30 cm) apart. Prune lightly in early autumn or spring. In areas with light frost, curry plants may die back temporarily. Protect leaves with 5 in (12 cm) sleeve of straw set between chicken wire. In areas where temperature drops below 22°F (−5°C), bring curry plants indoors for winter protection.
Harvesting Pick leaves anytime.
Preserving Dry both leaves and flowers. *See also p. 47.*

Hesperis matronalis
Sweet rocket
Site Full sun or light shade.
Soil Prefers rich loam in beds or light woodland.
Propagating Sow outdoors in late spring.
Growing Thin seedlings or transplant in autumn to 18 in (45 cm) apart. Sweet rocket is too tall to grow indoors.
Harvesting Gather leaves when young for eating but at flowering time for medicinal properties. Collect flowers as they open.
Preserving Dry both leaves and flowers. *See also p. 48.*

Humulus lupulus
Hops
Site Sunny open position.
Soil Fertile and deeply dug.
Propagating Reproduce female plants only. Divide roots and separate rooted stems and suckers in spring. Take cuttings in early summer. Avoid sowing, as plant gender cannot be discerned for 2–3 years.
Growing Grow 3 ft (1 m) apart against support. Hops can be grown indoors but they seldom flower indoors.

Harvesting Pick young side-shoots in spring. Gather young leaves as required. Pick ripe flowers in early autumn. Collect stems in late autumn.
Preserving Dry leaves and stems. Dry and use female flowers within a few months, or the flavour becomes unpleasant.
See also p. 49.

Hydrastis canadensis
Goldenseal
Description Hardy herbaceous perennial. Grows 6–12 in (15–30 cm) tall with hairy stems, toothed, lobed leaves and thick, knotted, yellow rootstalk. Greenish-white flowers (without petals) appear in late spring and early summer, followed by raspberry-like, inedible fruits.

Site Partial shade.
Soil Well-drained, moist, rich soil.
Propagating Divide rootstock in early autumn.
Uses Root yields a yellow-orange dye. Take a few drops of tincture to relieve constipation or add them to distilled water to make a lotion for skin ulcers. Use as a weak infusion for conjunctivitis and as an antiseptic mouthwash.

Hyssopus officinalis
Hyssop
Site Full sun.
Soil Light, well drained, alkaline.
Propagating Divide roots in spring. Take stem cuttings from spring to autumn. (Species) Sow in spring.
Growing Transplant or thin to 2 ft (60 cm) apart, or to 1 ft (30 cm) apart, for hedging. Cut back to 8 in (20 cm) in mild-winter areas after flowering; otherwise in spring. Hyssop can also be grown indoors.
Harvesting Pick flowers and young flowering tops as flowering begins. Gather leaves anytime.
Preserving Dry young leaves and flowering tops.
See also p. 50.

Illicium verum
Star anise
Description Tender evergreen tree. Grows 15–30 ft (4.5–9 m) high with aromatic, white bark, aromatic, glossy, elliptical leaves and whitish, yellow or purple flowers surrounded by many narrow petals. These are then followed by star-shaped, grey-brown fruits.

Site Sunny and sheltered.
Soil Well-drained.
Propagating By seed or by taking stem cuttings.
Uses Seed oil provides important substitute for aniseed as a flavouring agent. Seed employed as a spice. Add to drinks. Seed promotes digestion and appetite, and relieves flatulence, coughs, bronchitis and rheumatism.

Inula helenium
Elecampane
Site Prefers a sunny position out of doors.
Soil Moist and fertile.
Propagating Sow in spring or divide plant in spring or autumn.
Growing Thin or transplant to 3–4 ft (1–1.2 m) apart. Elecampane may require staking; it can become untidy. Prune in late summer. It is not suitable for indoor cultivation.
Harvesting Dig up second- or third-year roots in autumn.

Preserving Slice and dry root. May also be crystallized.
See also p. 51.

Iris 'Florentina'
Orris root
Description Hardy perennial. Reaches 2–3 ft (60 cm–1 m) high. Its stout rhizomatous roots are scented of violets and its leaves are sword-shaped. Large white flowers tinged with pale lavender and with a yellow beard appear in early to midsummer.
Site Full sun.

Soil Deep, rich, well drained.
Propagating Divide roots in late spring or early autumn.
Uses Roots provide bitter flavouring for certain liqueurs. Powdered root imparts a refreshing scent to linen; also used as a base for dry shampoos, tooth powders and face packs as well as perfumery. Powdered root used as a fixative in potpourri. The root

is a powerful purgative and now considered too strong to use medicinally. Dried root used to be used for coughs, hoarseness, bronchitis, colic and congestion in the liver. It also used to be chewed for disagreeable breath.

Laurus nobilis
Bay/Sweet bay/Laurel
Site Full sun. Protect from wind.
Soil Rich, moist and well drained.
Propagating Take 4 in (10 cm) stem cuttings or layer in late summer. Plant cuttings in heated propagator with high humidity.
Growing Transplant to 4 ft (1.2 m) apart, in frost-free area for first 2 years. Bay can be

container-grown but bring indoors should the temperature drop below 5°F (−15°C).
Harvesting Pick leaves anytime.
Preserving Dry leaves. Use to flavour vinegar.
See also p. 54.

Lavandula angustifolia
Lavender
Site Sunny and open, to discourage fungus disease.
Soil Well drained, sandy soil with lime content.
Propagating Take 4–8 in (10–20 cm) stem cuttings in autumn or spring, or divide or layer plant. (Species only) Sow from fresh seed in late summer and autumn.

Growing Thin or transplant to 18 in–2 ft (45–60 cm) apart. Remove faded flower stems; prune hedges and straggly plants in spring. Clip hard as soon as flowers begin to fade. (*L.a.* 'Grappenhall') Plant 4 ft (1.2 m) apart.
Harvesting Gather flowering stems just as flowers open. Pick leaves anytime.

Preserving Dry flowering stems by laying on open trays or hanging in small bunches.
See also pp. 52–3.

Lawsonia inermis
Henna
Description Perennial tropical shrub. Can grow up to 10 ft (3 m) high. Bushy with narrow, grey-green leaves and small, sweet-scented pink or cream flowers, which give way to clusters of blue-black berries.
Site Requires artificial heat in temperate climates.
Soil Dry, well-drained soil.
Uses Dried leaves produce a strong red dye and have been used for centuries in the East to colour hair, skin and nails. Dried leaves also have astringent properties. Apply in a cold compress to soothe fevers, headaches, stings, aching joints and skin irritations.

Levisticum officinale
Lovage
Site Full sun or partial shade.
Soil Rich, moist and well drained.
Propagating Sow fresh ripe seed in late summer. Take root cuttings in spring or autumn.
Growing Thin or transplant to 2 ft (60 cm) apart. Tie straw around stems 2–3 weeks before harvesting for blanched tender vegetable. Not suitable for growing indoors.
Harvesting Pick leaves as needed, but retain young central leaves. Gather young blanched stems in spring. Dig second- and third-season roots before flowers open each year. Gather ripe seed.
Preserving Freeze or dry leaves. Dry seeds and roots.
See also p. 55.

Marrubium vulgare
Horehound
Site Full sun. Needs protection from cold winds.
Soil Dryish and alkaline soil is necessary for cultivation.
Propagating Divide horehound in mid-spring. Sow in late spring. Take stem cuttings at the end of the summer.
Growing Thin or transplant to 1 ft (30 cm) apart. Protect from excessive winter wet. Prune in spring. Horehound can be cultivated indoors.
Harvesting Pick leaves and flowering tops at flowering time or as needed.
Preserving Dry leaves and flowering tops or make into syrup.
See also p. 56.

Melilotus officinalis
Melilot/Sweet clover
Site Sun preferred, but will also tolerate light shade.
Soil Well drained.
Propagating Sow in spring or late summer. Will self-seed in light soils.
Growing Thin or transplant to 18 in (45 cm) apart. Not suitable for growing indoors.
Harvesting Gather leaves and flowers anytime.
Preserving Dry both leaves and flowers.
See also p. 57.

Melissa officinalis
Lemon balm

Site Full sun with midday shade.
Soil Grows in any moist soil.
Propagating Sow in spring, slow to germinate. Divide plant or take stem cuttings in spring or autumn.
Growing Thin or transplant to 2 ft (60 cm) apart. It is also possible to grow small specimens in pots indoors.

Harvesting Pick leaves anytime, but handle gently to avoid bruising. Their flavour is best when flowers begin to open.
Preserving Dry leaves. Add fresh leaves to vinegar.
See also p. 60.

Mentha
Mints

Site Partial shade or sun.
Soil Moist, well-drained, alkaline soil, rich in nutrients.
Propagating Take root or stem cuttings, or divide mint, in spring and autumn. In summer, root stem cuttings in water. (Pennyroyal) Sow in spring.
Growing Thin or transplant, to 12 in (30 cm) apart, into large pots or polythene bags to restrain invasive roots. All flowering stems should be removed to avoid cross-pollination between species. If rust appears, dig up plant immediately and burn. Mints can also be grown indoors.
Harvesting Pick leaves just before flowering.
Preserving Dry, freeze or infuse leaves in oil or vinegar.
See also pp. 58–9.

Monarda didyma
Bergamot/Bee balm

Site Sun, or part shade in hot climate. Add a mulch in spring.
Soil Rich, light and moist.
Propagating Divide or take root cuttings in spring, stem cuttings in summer. (Species) Sow in spring.
Growing Thin or transplant to 18 in (45 cm) apart. Divide every 3 years, discarding dead centre.

Bergamot is not suitable for growing indoors.
Harvesting Collect leaves in spring or in summer when flowers form. Pick flowers when open.
Preserving Dry both leaves and flowers.
See also p. 61.

Morus nigra
Black mulberry

Description Hardy tree. Grows to 30 ft (9 m). Bushy, with thick, toothed, heart-shaped leaves and unisexual green catkins, which appear in late spring and early summer. They are followed by oblong, purplish-red fruits.
Site Warm position. Protect from cold winds and frosts.

Soil Well-drained, loamy soil.
Propagating Sow seed in spring. Take stem cuttings in early spring, layer in autumn.
Uses Fruit is rich in vitamin C and grape sugar; eat raw or cooked and make into wines and jams. Leaves used for silkworm rearing (until replaced by white mulberry) and diabetes. Fruit provides a laxative, a convalescent syrup,

and colouring and flavouring for other medications. White mulberry (*M. alba*) has similar properties.

Myrrhis odorata
Sweet cicely/Myrrh
Site Light shade. Tolerates sun.
Soil Rich in humus.
Propagating Sow outdoors in autumn; seed requires several months of cold winter temperatures before it begins to germinate.
Growing Transplant 2 ft (60 cm) apart in spring.

Harvesting Pick young leaves any time. Collect unripe seed when green; ripe seed when dark brown. Dig up roots in autumn.
Preserving Dry or pickle unripe seed. Clean and peel root, then infuse in wine or brandy.
See also p. 62.

Myrtus communis
Myrtle
Site Full sun. Protect from wind.
Soil Any well-drained soil or potting compost.
Propagating Take stem cuttings in mid- or late summer.
Growing Transplant to large pots. Grow indoors or outside.
Harvesting Pick buds, flowers and ripe berries as available. Pick leaves when myrtle is in flower for sweetest scent, or as needed.
Preserving Dry buds, flowers and berries. Dry leaves or infuse in oil (for cosmetic use) or in vinegar (for the kitchen).
See also p. 63.

Nepeta cataria
Catnip/Catmint
Site Sun or light shade.
Soil Well drained.
Propagating Sow or divide whole plant in spring. Take softwood cuttings in late spring.
Growing Thin or transplant to 12 in (30 cm) apart. Cut back in autumn. The scent released by any bruised leaf or root will attract cats, who then molest the plant, so plants grown from seed in situ are less likely to be damaged than transplanted plants, which may need protection. *N. mussinii* grows indoors.
Harvesting Gather leaves when young and flowering tops.
Preserving Dry whole plant.
See also p. 64.

Ocimum basilicum
Basil
Site Warm sun. Protect from wind, frost and from scorching, midday sun.
Soil Well drained and moist.
Propagating Sow thinly in heated location. After all danger of frost has passed, sow in pots or in position out of doors.
Growing Avoid overwatering seedlings as they are prone to "damping off". Thin to 8 in (20 cm); avoid transplanting. Always water at midday, not in the evening. Syringe leaves in hot weather. Basil is excellent pot-grown indoors.
Harvesting Pick leaves when young. Gather tops as flowers start to open.
Preserving Freeze leaves (first paint both sides with olive oil) or dry them. Store whole leaves in olive oil with salt or dry-pack them with salt. Infuse leaves in either oil or vinegar.
See also p. 65.

Oenothera biennis
Evening primrose
Site Sunny and open.
Soil Well drained.
Propagating Sow spring to early summer. Self-seeds in light soil.
Growing Transplant to 12 in (30 cm) apart by autumn. Evening primrose is not a suitable herb for growing indoors.
Harvesting Collect seed when ripe. Gather leaves and stem "bark" when flowering stems have grown. Dig up roots in the second year.
Preserving Both seeds and leaves may be dried.
See also p. 66.

Onopordum acanthium
Cotton thistle
Site Full sun or light shade.
Soil Tolerates any soil, but requires rich loam to reach maximum height.
Propagating Sow in late spring in situ or in pots to be transplanted in autumn. May self-seed in warm climates. It is also possible to start cotton thistle in early spring in a cloche or conservatory.
Growing Thin or transplant to 2½ ft (75 cm) apart. Not suitable for indoor growth.
Harvesting Pick flowers, leaves and stems as required. Collect seed and dig up roots in autumn of the plant's second season.
Preserving Dry leaves.
See also p. 67.

Origanum
Marjorams & Oregano
Site Full sun. (Gold leaf forms) Need midday shade.
Soil Well drained, dryish, alkaline, nutrient rich. Unlike most other herbs from the same family, marjorams have a stronger flavour when grown in rich soil.
Propagating Sow in spring (germination can be slow). (Hardy perennials) Divide in spring or autumn. Take root or stem cuttings from late spring to midsummer.
Growing Thin or transplant to 12–18 in (30–45 cm) apart. Cut back marjorams by two-thirds before they die down for winter. If site is not too windy, leave seed heads for bird food. Marjorams can be grown indoors.
Harvesting Pick young leaves anytime. If leaves are to be used for preserving, gather just before flowers open.
Preserving Freeze or dry leaves. Macerate in oil or vinegar. Dry flowering tops.
See also pp. 68–9.

Panax quinquefolius
American ginseng
Description Hardy perennial. Grows 1–1½ ft (30–45 cm) tall with finely toothed, oval leaflets and aromatic, fleshy, spindle-shaped, pale yellow to brown root. Small yellow or pink flowers appear in late summer and are followed by bright red berries.
Site Shade.
Soil Cool, humus-rich soil.
Propagating Sow seed in early spring in a heated greenhouse. Transplant outside. Harvest after 3–9 years.
Uses Infuse dried root as a tonic drink for increased mental and physical vigour, against depression caused by exhaustion or stress, as an appetite and digestive stimulant, and for relief from nausea. It is helpful for coughs and chest disorders. Oriental ginseng (*P. pseudoginseng*) has similar uses.

Papaver
Poppies
Site Full sun.
Soil Well drained and cultivated.
Propagating Sow in spring or autumn in flowering site, just pressing seed into soil. Field poppy requires a cold spell to trigger germination. Will self-seed freely.
Growing Thin to 12 in (30 cm). Poppies are not suitable for indoor cultivation.
Harvesting Collect seed when capsule is ripe.

Preserving Dry seed heads; then shake to extract seeds.
See also p. 70.

Pelargonium
Scented geraniums
Site Needs a sunny, well-ventilated position.
Soil Plant in well-drained potting compost.
Propagating Sow in early spring. Take tip cuttings in spring or in late summer. Root in potting compost, allowing one cutting for each 3 in (7.5 cm) pot.

Growing Grow pelargoniums in pots so they can be moved indoors in winter. Thin or transplant to individual pots. Pinch out growing tips when plants reach 6 in (15 cm). Cut back one-third of growth before bringing indoors.
Harvesting Pick leaves just before flowers open.
Preserving Dry leaves.
See also p. 71.

Petroselinum crispum
Parsley
Site Full sun or light shade.
Soil Rich, moist and deeply dug.
Propagating Sow from spring to late summer. For fast germination: soak seed overnight in warm water, pour boiling water in drill before sowing or grow in seed tray and maintain 70°F (21°C). Self-seeds.

Growing Thin or transplant to 9 in (23 cm) apart. Protect in cold weather. Grows well indoors.
Harvesting Pick leaves during first year. Collect seeds when ripe. Dig up roots in autumn of second year.
Preserving Dry or freeze leaves. Dry or blanch and freeze roots.
See also p. 72.

Pimpinella anisum
Anise/Aniseed
Site Sunny and sheltered.
Soil Well drained and alkaline.
Propagating Sow in situ in late spring. Seed loses viability after second year.
Growing Thin to 8 in (20 cm) apart; do not transplant, so keep well weeded. Anise can also be grown indoors.

Harvesting Pick lower leaves as required. Collect flowers as they open. For seed, cut plant at ground level when fruit begins to turn grey-green at the tips. Gather stems and dig up roots in autumn.
Preserving Dry seed by suspending plant until ripe (see p. 231).
See also p. 73.

Piper nigrum
Black pepper
Description Tender perennial climbing shrub from the tropics. Grows to 20 ft (6 m) or more. Strong, woody, twining stems bear broad, oval, glossy dark green leaves with prominent veins. White flower clusters appear in summer, followed by aromatic, wrinkled, red fruits.

Site Needs tropical climate, with high humidity and shade.
Soil Well-drained, humus-rich soil.
Propagating By taking softwood cuttings.
Uses Dried unripe fruit used as a spice and a condiment; add freshly ground to all savoury foods. It kills bacteria so employ as a food preservative. Use as a diuretic, stimulant, digestive and anti-flatulence remedy. In addition, good for constipation, nausea, vertigo and arthritis.

Poterium sanguisorba
Salad burnet
Site Sun or light shade.
Soil Prefers limy soil.
Propagating Sow seeds in spring or autumn. Once it has been allowed to flower, salad burnet will continue to self-seed.
Growing Plant seedlings 12 in (30 cm) apart, when large enough to handle. Cut flowering stems and old leaves regularly to produce plenty of tender young leaves.
Harvesting Pick young tender leaves whenever required.

Preserving Dry leaves.
See also p. 74.

Primula veris; Primula vulgaris
Cowslip & Primrose
Site Semi-shade or sun.
Soil Cowslip favours limy soil; primrose prefers moist soil.
Propagating Divide large plants in autumn. Seed picked in early autumn will germinate quickly; ripe, dry seed needs cold then warm temperatures to break its dormancy. Sow in autumn and cover with glass.
Growing Plant out in the following autumn, 6 in (15 cm) apart. Primrose, unlike cowslip, is not suitable for indoor cultivation.
Harvesting Pick leaves and flowers as they open.
Preserving Crystallize flowers. Dry leaves and roots.
See also p. 75.

Prunus dulcis
Almond
Description A somewhat frost-sensitive tree. Grows 30 ft (9 m) tall with finely-toothed pointed oval leaves. Pink or white flowers in late spring precede ovoid light-green fruits containing two nuts.
Site Full sun, must be protected from cold winds.
Soil Well drained.

Propagating Bud onto rootstock in spring.
Uses Nuts used in cakes, sweets, savoury dishes, confectionery and liqueurs. Use ground nuts to make marzipan. Hard pale red timber provides tool handles, veneers and ornaments. Oil is valued for perfumes, skin creams, facial masks and is the most popular carrier oil in aromatherapy massage. It is a soothing oil for sunburn, cough medicine and a laxative.

Rosa
Roses
Site Sunny, or light shade, and open; not too windy.
Soil Well-drained loam.
Propagating Take cuttings in autumn. Plant seed for species.
Growing Thin or transplant from autumn to spring. Deadhead in summer. Prune lightly in spring. Do not grow indoors.

Harvesting Pick buds when formed, petals when first open, hips when ripe or, for wine, after the first frost when softened.
Preserving Dry petals and buds. Crystallized petals. Dry hips.
See also p. 78.

Rosmarinus officinalis
Rosemary
Site Sunny. Protect from cold winds. In cold or exposed gardens, grow in a large pot; sink it in outdoor soil in summer, but return it to the greenhouse or a sunny interior in winter.
Soil Needs excellent drainage. On limy soil, rosemary is a smaller but more fragrant plant. To provide additional lime, apply eggshells or wood ash.
Propagating Sow under heat in spring or outdoors in summer. Germination is erratic; needs at least 70°F (21°C). It is best to propagate by cuttings or layering.
Growing Transplant when large enough to handle, leaving 2–3 ft (60–90 cm) between plants. Can be container-grown indoors.

Harvesting Pick small amounts all year round. Gather main leaf crop before flowering.
Preserving Dry sprigs and branches. Strip off leaves before storing. To release the aroma, crush leaves only just before use.
See also pp. 76–7.

Rubus fruticosus
Bramble
Description Perennial shrub. Reaches 10 ft (3 m) tall with thorny biennial stems and toothed leaves. Pink or white flowers appear from summer and are followed by blackberries in late summer and early autumn.
Site Any.
Soil Any.

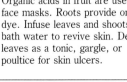

Propagating Tip layer in summer. Sow seed in autumn.
Uses Fruits are high in vitamin C; eat raw or cooked in puddings, jams, jellies, wine and vinegar. Organic acids in fruit are useful in face masks. Roots provide orange dye. Infuse leaves and shoots in bath water to revive skin. Decoct leaves as a tonic, gargle, or poultice for skin ulcers.

Rumex acetosa
Sorrel
Site (*R. acetosa*) Sun or light shade; (*R. scutatus*) Full sun; sheltered spot.
Soil (*R. acetosa*) Moist, rich with iron; (*R. scutatus*) Well drained.
Propagating Sow seed in spring; germination takes 7–10 days. Divide roots in autumn.
Growing Thin seedlings or transplant to 12 in (30 cm) apart. Water to keep leaves juicy; protect from snails. Divide and replant every 5 years.

Harvesting Gather leaves when young for culinary use. For a supply during the winter, cover sorrel with cloches.
Preserving Dried sorrel has little flavour. Best frozen and used in cooked dishes.
See also p. 79.

Ruta graveolens
Garden rue
Site Full sun. Will also tolerate light shade.
Soil Well drained and alkaline; poor to moderate fertility for hardiest plants.
Propagating Divide in spring. Take stem cuttings in late summer. (Species only) Sow in spring, slow to germinate.
Growing Thin or transplant to 18 in (45 cm) apart. Prune in late spring. In severe winters, give protection. Rue can also be grown indoors in a sunny position.
Harvesting Pick young leaves just before flowers start to open. Collect seeds.
Preserving Dry leaves and seed.
See also p. 80.

Salvia officinalis
Sage
Site Full sun.
Soil Light, dry, alkaline and well-drained soil.
Propagating Grow common sage from seed. All forms take easily from cuttings; rooting time is about four weeks in summer.
Growing Cut back after flowering, replace woody plants every four to five years. Plant 18–24 in (45–60 cm) apart. Prune frequently to keep bushy. Yellowing leaves can mean roots need more space. Small green caterpillar eats leaves; remove by hand, or prune and burn leaves.
Harvesting Pick leaves just before flowers appear.
Preserving Dry leaves slowly.
See also pp. 82–3.

Santolina chamaecyparissus
Santolina
Site Full sun.
Soil Well drained, sandy.
Propagating Take 2–3 in (5–8 cm) stem cuttings in spring or autumn (protect from frost).
Growing Transplant to 18 in–2 ft (45–60 cm) apart. Clip in spring or summer. Deadhead in autumn. If temperatures drop below 5°F (−15°C), protect with a sleeve of two layers of chicken wire filled with straw, or bracken. Santolina can be grown indoors.
Harvesting Pick stems in late summer. Gather leaves anytime.
Preserving Dry flowering stems and leaves.
See also p. 81.

Saponaria officinalis
Soapwort
Site Full sun or light shade.
Soil Fertile and moist.
Propagating Sow in spring. Divide plants or take pieces of underground runners between autumn and spring. Self-seeds.
Growing Thin or transplant to 2 ft (60 cm) apart. Use twiggy sticks to support stems. Cut back after flowering to induce second blooms. Scent strength varies according to where soapwort is planted. Do not grow near fish ponds as its root excretions can poison fish. Not suitable for indoor cultivation.
Harvesting Pick flowers, leaves, stems and roots as required.
Preserving Dry flowers and leaves. Slice roots and dry in sun.
See also p. 84.

Satureja montana
Winter savory
Site Full sun.
Soil Well drained and alkaline. (Summer savory) Rich loam.
Propagating Sow in autumn or spring. Divide plant in spring or autumn. Take stem cuttings during summer.
Growing Thin or transplant to 18 in (45 cm) apart. Prune in late

spring. Protect winter savory in winter. Can be grown indoors. (Summer savory) Thin or transplant to 9 in (23 cm) apart. Prune to prevent woody growth.
Harvesting Pick leaves just as flower buds are formed. Collect flowering tops in late summer.
Preserving Dry leaves. Infuse to make savory vinegar and oil.
See also p. 85.

Sempervivum tectorum
Houseleek
Site Sunny; traditionally positioned on porches or roofs.
Soil Dry, well drained and thin; houseleek is also suitable for rock gardens.
Propagating In spring, take offsets and leaf cuttings (cut a leaf at the base with an eye from the stem); sow seed in spring.

Growing Thin or transplant to 9 in (23 cm) apart. Will also grow indoors.
Harvesting Gather the thickest leaves for use.
Preserving Extract and freeze juice (no tests appear to have measured its properties after being frozen).
See also p. 86.

Sium sisarum
Skirret
Site Full sun or light shade.
Soil Rich, well-drained, alkaline loam; but tolerates most soils.
Propagating In spring, sow seed or divide crown (stem base), leaving about three tubers to each piece. Plant each piece 3 in (8 cm) deep, 12 in (30 cm) apart.
Growing Thin or transplant

seedlings to 12 in (30 cm) apart. Keep moist in summer, and feed with diluted liquid manure.
Harvesting Gather young shoots in spring. Dig roots as required; sever from base of stem.
Preserving Store tuberous roots in sand until required, or lightly scrub, blanch for 1 minute, cool and freeze.
See also p. 87.

Smyrnium olusatrum
Alexanders
Site Sun or part shade.
Soil Grows readily in any soil.
Propagating In late summer or the following spring, sow ripe seed outdoors where it is to flower. Alexanders will self-seed readily.
Growing Thin out seedlings until 2–2½ ft (60–75 cm) apart. In spring of second year, cover over with soil or straw for three or four weeks to blanch for a sweeter flavour. Alexanders is not suitable for indoor growth.

Harvesting Gather leaves in summer, and stems when young or blanched. Dig up roots in late summer of second year.
Preserving Dry only leaves gathered before flowering time.
See also p. 88.

Stellaria media
Chickweed
Description Vigorous creeping annual, 4–12 in (10–30 cm) long. Succulent, oval leaves grow on very straggly, brittle, much branched stems that are hairy on only one side. Small, star-like, white flowers appear almost all year round, from early spring until midwinter.

Site Any position.
Soil Prefers moist soil.
Propagating Sow in spring. Self-seeds readily.
Uses Leaves contain vitamin C and phosphorus and are delicious eaten raw in salads or boiled as a vegetable. Fresh leaves in a poultice relieve inflammation and ulcers. Decoct whole plant to treat constipation, piles and sores.

Apply in an ointment to heal eczema, psoriasis and other irritating skin diseases.

Symphytum officinale
Comfrey
Site Fun sun. Position carefully as comfrey is difficult to eradicate.
Soil Rich in nitrogen; neutral pH.
Propagating Take root offsets (root section with growing tip) any time except midwinter.
Growing Transplant 2ft (60 cm) part. For a higher nutritious yield, give each plant a bucketful of

crude manure in spring and again in late summer.
Harvesting Pick leaves in midsummer. Dig up roots in late autumn or winter.
Preserving Clean roots. Chop finely and dry. Dry leaves or make into a skin-healing "oil".
See also p. 89.

Syzgium aromaticum
Clove
Description Tender evergreen tree from the tropics. Reaches 30 ft (9 m) or higher with large, leathery, oval, glossy leaves in pairs. Bell-shaped, red flowers appear for two separate periods during growing season. Pink flower buds turn reddish-brown after drying.

Site Shade, with wind protection.
Soil Well-drained acid soil.
Uses For a spicy flavour, add whole, dried, unopened flower buds, known as cloves, to curries, stewed fruit, marinades, pickling liquids, mulled wine; grind cloves for breads, biscuits, cakes. Use in pomanders and potpourri. Chew as a breath freshener. Infuse as a tea to relieve nausea. Drop clove

oil into a tooth cavity to stop toothache. Apply externally to ease neuralgia and rheumatism.

Tagetes patula
French marigold
Site Sunny and open.
Soil Well cultivated; prefers moderately rich loam but tolerates dry and poor soil.
Propagating Sow under glass in early spring.
Growing (*T. patula*) Transplant to 12 in (30 cm) apart in late spring. Deadheading improves growth. Can be grown indoors. (*T. minuta*) Start under glass, when 6 in (15 cm) tall, transplant 12 in (30 cm) apart.

Harvesting Gather open flowers.
Preserving Petals should be separated and dried.
See also p. 90.

Tanacetum parthenium
Feverfew
Site Prefers sunny position.
Soil Dry and well drained.
Propagating Sow in spring or autumn. (Feverfew self-seeds profusely.) Take stem cuttings in summer. Divide roots in autumn.
Growing Thin or transplant to 12 in (30 cm) apart. Feverfew can be grown indoors in cool air.

Harvesting Pick leaves and flowers anytime.
Preserving Dry both leaves and flowers.
See also p. 91.

Tanacetum vulgare
Tansy
Site Full sun or light shade.
Soil Any that is not too wet.
Propagating Sow in spring. Divide roots in spring or autumn.
Growing Thin or transplant to 2–3 ft (60 cm–1 m) apart; it is a very vigorous spreader. Tansy is not a suitable herb for indoor cultivation.

Harvesting Pick leaves as required. Gather flowers when they start to open.
Preserving Dry leaves and flowers. Store separately.
See also p. 92.

Taraxacum officinale
Dandelion
Description Very common hardy perennial weed. Grows 2–12 in (5–30 cm) high. Long, milky taproot and stem bear oblong, toothed leaves in flat rosettes. Golden flowers appear from spring through to mid-autumn when they are followed by globular clusters of tufted seeds.

Site Sunny and open.
Soil Most soils.
Propagating Sow seeds in spring to early autumn. Dandelion will self-seed profusely.
Uses Leaves, which are high in vitamins A and C, niacin and various minerals, and roots can be eaten raw in salads. Grind dried and roasted root as a coffee substitute. Root yields a magenta

woollen dye. Latex in the leaves is a rich emollient for facial steams, cleansing milks and moisturizers for all skins. Add to bathwater as a tonic. Decoct flowers as a cosmetic wash. Root increases bile production and is an effective diuretic; also good for rheumatism, gout, eczema, constipation and insomnia.

Thymus
Thymes
Site Full sun.
Soil Light and well drained, preferably alkaline.
Propagating Take 2–3 in (5–8 cm) stem cuttings with a "heel" anytime except winter. Divide roots or layer stems in spring or autumn. (Species only) Sow in spring.
Growing Thin or transplant to 9–15 in (23–38 cm) apart. In summer, prune frequently. In very cold areas, protect thyme in

winter. Thyme can also be grown indoors in a sunny position.
Harvesting Pick leaves in summer. They are best while thyme is in bloom.
Preserving Dry leaves. Make thyme vinegar and oil.
See also pp. 94–5.

Trigonella foenum-graecum
Fenugreek
Site Full sun.
Soil Needs fertile, well drained, alkaline soil.
Propagating Sow thickly in rows 9 in (23 cm) apart in spring for main crop; continue to sow throughout summer for young salad leaves.
Growing Thin to 4 in (10 cm) apart; difficult to transplant. Small plants can be grown indoors.
Harvesting Pick young leaves as needed. Cut whole plant in autumn. Pick seed when ripe.
Preserving Dry leaves and seed.
See also p. 93.

Tussilago farfara
Coltsfoot
Description Hardy perennial. Reaches 3–12 in (8–30 cm) high with small, white, spreading roots and toothed, dark green leaves with grey undersides; small yellow flowers appear in spring.
Site Any soil is suitable; coltsfoot can be invasive.
Soil Moist.
Propagating Sow in spring. Take root cuttings in spring and autumn. Divide plant in autumn.
Uses Eat fresh leaves in a salad; dried ones are included in herbal tobaccos. All parts of coltsfoot contain a mucilage, which is good for coughs and bronchitis. Decoct leaves for colds, flu and asthma.

Urtica dioica
Nettle
Description Perennial with separate male and female plants. Grows up to 4 ft (1.2 m) high. Leaves are toothed, pointed and oval; they sting when touched. Bristly, square stems also bear minute, greenish flowers from early summer to early autumn.
Site Any.
Soil Any.
Propagating Sow seed in spring. Divide roots in spring.
Uses Young nettles are rich in vitamins and minerals; eat in a salad, boil as a vegetable, or drink as a herbal tea. Use to make nettle beer. Whole plant yields a greenish-yellow woollen dye. Nettle fibres spun into rope and made into cloth and paper.
Astringent young leaves used in facial steams, bath mixtures and hair preparations. Infuse or decoct herb as a digestive, diuretic, and an astringent.

Valeriana officinalis
Valerian
Site Full sun or light shade. Ideally prefers cool roots and warm foliage.
Soil Prefers rich, moist loam.
Propagating Sow in spring, pressing seed into soil but do not cover for germination. Divide roots in spring or autumn.
Growing Transplant or thin to 2 ft (60 cm) apart. Can be grown as an indoor plant.
Harvesting Dig complete root in second season in late autumn.
Remove pale, fibrous roots, leaving edible rhizome.
Preserving Slice rhizomatous root to dry.
See also p. 96.

Verbascum thapsus
Mullein
Site Sunny and sheltered.
Soil Well drained; chalky or poor.
Propagating Sow in spring or summer. Self-seeds in light soils.
Growing Thin or transplant to 2 ft (60 cm) apart. Stake verbascum in exposed sites or on rich moist soil. Not suitable for indoor cultivation.

Harvesting Collect flowers as they open and leaves during their first season.
Preserving Remove green parts from flowers; then dry gently, without artificial heat, as its healing power is connected with the yellow colouring matter. Leaves can be dried.
See also p. 97.

Verbena officinalis
Vervain
Site Sun or light shade.
Soil Prefers fertile, well-drained loam soil.
Propagating Sow in spring at 65–70°F (18–21°C). Germination is erratic and may take as long as 3–4 weeks.
Growing Thin or transplant to 12 in (30 cm) apart. Can also be grown indoors.
Harvesting Pick leaves as and when required. Cut the whole plant when in bloom.

Preserving Dry leaves or whole plant if required.
See also p. 98.

Viola odorata
Sweet violet
Site Semi-shade. Benefits from sun either early or late in the day.
Soil Rich and moist.
Propagating Easy to propagate from runners. Seed germination is erratic as many flowers miss pollination.
Growing Transplant in early spring, leaving 4–5 in (10–13 cm) between plants. Sweet violets are not suitable as indoor plants.
Harvesting Pick leaves in early spring. Gather flowers when they are newly opened, and roots in autumn.
Preserving Dry leaves, flowers and roots. Crystallize flowers.
See also p. 99.

Zingiber officinale
Ginger
Description Tender creeping perennial from the tropics. Grows 3–4 ft (1–1.2 m) high. Thick, aromatic, fibrous, knotty, buff-coloured, tuberous roots produce erect, annual stems bearing long, narrow to lance-shaped leaves. Sterile, fragrant, white flowers with purple streaks appear rarely.

Site Ginger requires a tropical climate, with high humidity and partial shade.
Soil Rich, well-drained loam.
Propagating Take root cuttings.
Uses Fresh ginger root peeled and sliced, or grated, can be added to stews, sauces and oriental dishes. Use ground root in gingerbread, cakes, biscuits, mulled wine, liqueurs and cordials.

Preserve young green roots in syrup. Apply fresh root externally as a "rouge" as it stimulates circulation. Infuse root as a tea to cleanse the body's systems, ease a cold and to bring warmth on cold days. Chew root to soothe a sore throat. Recent research confirms that an infusion is excellent to settle the stomach and prevent nausea when travelling.

Soil preparation

Many herbs can survive on poor, stony ground, but few can cope with water-logged soil. Ideally, they prefer a light, open soil which is well aerated yet able to retain moisture and nutrients. To help them thrive, prepare the soil in early spring before sowing or planting. Dig deeply and create a fine tilth, then rake to a smooth, level surface. Allow the soil to settle at least one week before planting seed.

Improving drainage
To increase air spaces and drainage in heavy soils, first dig over in early winter, as the presence of frost helps to break down solid clods of earth. In early spring, mix coarse grit, horticultural sand or vermiculite into the top 18 in (45 cm). Add compost to supply a more fibrous texture and nutrients.

Aromatic Mediterranean herbs such as rosemary, sage, thyme, lavender, or savory tend to like dry, sunny conditions and limy soil with good drainage. When planting these herbs add a child's bucket of grit to each cubic foot (30 cm) of planting space to help the drainage.

If soil is very waterlogged, you can improve it for a few years by building a rubble drain. Dig an 18 in–2 ft (45–60 cm) deep ditch angled toward an existing ditch or drainage facility. Half fill with coarse rubble and cover with a 3 in (8 cm) layer of gravel, clinker or ash, replacing the top soil. For a more permanent solution, make the ditch 2 ft 6 in–3 ft (75 cm–1 m) deep with plastic drainage pipes along the bottom leading to a soakaway and proceed as before. Alternatively, if soil is prone to being waterlogged, consider making raised beds.

Eliminating weeds
While preparing the soil for planting, it is important to get rid of persistent weeds such as bindweed (*Convolvulus arvensis*), couch grass (*Agropyron repens*) and ground elder (*Aegopodium podagraria*), which can quickly take over a herb bed. Dig up weeds with taproots, taking care not to break off any of the root or it will sprout. Fork out longer straggling roots over a period of about a month. Dig through the soil at weekly intervals. Don't throw uprooted weeds on the compost heap; you'll transplant them.

Enriching soil
A light, free-draining sandy soil does not hold moisture and is usually low in nutrients. Although the Mediterranean herbs can thrive on such a soil and respond badly to excess compost, manure or fertilizers, others, such as mint and chives, may benefit from such additions. These are best worked in after winter rains so most of the nutrients will be available to aid spring growth. Peat helps to retain moisture but it does not contribute any nutrients and may make the soil too acid if used in large quantities.

Most herbs are like vegetables in their preference for a slightly alkaline soil. If your soil is acidic, add a sprinkling of lime, not as a plant food but as a catalyst to help the plants take up the nutrients present. Use the lowest amount recommended. Ashes from wood fires contribute lime and potash to the soil.

Avoid using artificial fertilizers as these can make growth too lush, which will result in a plant with poor flavour. Use only if growth is poor or mineral deficiencies are apparent.

Mulching
Once herbs are established they will benefit from a mulch, a covering of organic matter spread over the soil. The mulch helps to stop the soil drying out and provides nutrients. Applied during the growing season, it boosts lush growth in salad herbs such as sorrel and purslane, and in shade- and moisture-loving herbs such as mint, angelica and sweet cicely. It can also protect plant roots from frosts.

Mulching is usually most beneficial after heavy rain. Spread light, organic matter over the soil and around plants in a layer up to 3 in (8 cm) deep. The Mediterranean herbs such as rosemary, thyme, sage and lavender may benefit more from a layer of gravel or clinker if the soil is very moist. Mulching also helps to control weed growth by blocking out light.

Propagation

Many herbs will grow from seed and readily self-seed once established. A large proportion can also be grown from cuttings and division.

Sowing seed on site

Annual plants of the Umbelliferae family (anise, chervil, dill, coriander and cumin, and the biennial parsley) are best sown on site, where you wish them to grow, as any root disturbance in transplanting can make them run to seed before they have produced a useful crop of leaves. Parsley seed is exceptionally slow to germinate so do be patient.

As a rule, sow seed in mid- to late spring after the soil has been prepared and warmed up. Sow seeds thinly in shallow drills.

If the soil feels heavy and lumpy, spread a layer of fine sand along the drill to give seeds a better start. Barely cover seeds with a fine sprinkling of soil and tap down gently. Water with a fine spray. Mark each row with the name of the herb and date of sowing.

Covering with cloches gives seeds a head start and provides protection from late frosts and wildlife. Lay the cloches in position a few weeks before you sow so the soil warms up.

Thin out seedlings when they have reached a height of 2–4 in (5–10 cm). Water the soil the day before you remove them. Use a trowel or your fingers to lift them from the soil and handle very carefully when replanting.

Growing seed indoors

It is better to grow expensive, rare or unfamiliar seeds in seed trays indoors, where all conditions can be controlled.

Buy a proprietary loamless seed-growing mixture or mix your own with two parts sterilized loam, one part fine peat, one part coarse sand and a dash of fertilizer. Blend well and pass through a ⅜ in (8 mm) sieve.

A shallow seed tray 2 in (5 cm) deep is the best size for sowing small seeds. Small pots can also be used and are better if you only wish to sow a few seeds. If using deeper containers, fill the lower section with clean drainage material – a layer of gravel, perlite or broken crocks. Add growing mixture to within ¼ in (6 mm) of the top. Give the tray or pot a sharp downward tap then press the soil surface gently with a flat board. If the mixture is very dry, water and leave it to drain. Sow seeds thinly, mixing fine seeds with sand so they spread out evenly. Sprinkle over a fine layer of potting mixture to hold the seeds in place. Cover larger seeds with a layer of potting mixture as deep as the seed.

Water with a fine rose, beginning and ending the flow off the tray. Label, date and cover with a layer of glass and a layer of newspaper.

Sowing seeds outdoors
Draw a shallow drill ¼–½ in (6–13 mm) deep. Sow seeds thinly 2 or 3 per inch (2.5 cm). If they are crowded together, there is less chance of them sprouting.

Seeds

Growing mixture

Drainage material

Preparing pots and trays
A shallow tray is best for small seeds, but use small pots for a few seeds only.

HERBS WORTH GROWING FROM SEED

An enormous number of herbs, common and rare, can be grown from seed, but the group listed below is generally the easiest. If you require only one plant, it is often cheaper to buy it.

All the annuals

anise	chamomile, annual	dill	purslane
basil	chervil	mustard	salad rocket
borage	coriander	nasturtium	summery savory
calendula	cumin	orach	sweet marjoram

Biennials

angelica	parsley, curled and	wild celery (smallage)
caraway	broad leaf	woad

Perennials

catnip	good King Henry	oregano	thyme, common
chamomile, flowering	hyssop	rue	winter savory
chives	lovage	sage	wormwood
fennel, green and	marjoram, French	salad burnet	
bronze	marsh mallow	sorrel	
feverfew	onion, Welsh	sweet cicely	

Germination
Seeds germinate faster in the warmth of a greenhouse or indoors (preferably in a warm place such as the airing cupboard) and need to be watched daily. If further watering proves necessary, set the pots in water until the top appears damp.

When sprouting begins, move the trays into the light. Lift the covering at one edge for two days. Then take off the cover but shade the seedlings from bright sun for several days.

Transplanting seedlings
As soon as plants are large enough to handle, thin them out or transplant them to a larger box or a pot to prevent overcrowding. Wait, though, until the first pair of true leaves has formed, after the cotyledons – two seed leaves which are a completely different shape.

Handle young seedlings by a leaf rather than by their stems and take them carefully out of the soil to avoid breaking or bruising their tiny new roots and stems. Make a hole in the soil then insert the seedling. Firm the compost, water it and site the plants in a light location out of direct sunlight.

Once seedlings are growing well, remove any feebler ones and leave the strongest to grow on. Transfer to larger pots with a potting grade compost or plant out.

Planting out
Plants propagated indoors should move outdoors gradually. Set them out in a sheltered position during the day, and take them in at night. After several days, leave them out at night as well. Plant out after about a week. Make sure the soil is moist then make a hole the size of the root. Carefully insert the plant, fill the hole with soil and firm down.

Transplanting a seedling
Firm in a seedling after careful transplanting.

OTHER FORMS OF PROPAGATION
Herbs can also be grown easily using vegetative means of propagation: cuttings, dividing and layering. With these methods, you can be more certain of the resulting flower and leaf shapes and colours on the new plant, whereas plants grown from seeds are often more variable.

Propagating from cuttings

There are three main types of stem cuttings which are suitable for herbs: softwood, from new shoots which have not yet hardened; semi-hardwood from new growth when it has started to firm up at the base; and hardwood, from woody shrubs and trees.

Softwood cuttings are taken in late spring from strong new growth, or in late summer after flowering. Semi-hardwood cuttings are taken from midsummer to mid-autumn, from herbs such as rosemary and myrtle. Hardwood cuttings are taken in mid- to late autumn.

Planting cuttings

To plant cuttings in open ground, choose a warm, sheltered spot. Spray leaves lightly, and frequently during dry weather.

When planting in containers, follow the directions below. Open the bag every few days to change the air and prevent mould building up. As soon as cuttings show signs of growth, place them in a sheltered, sunny position and add plant nutrients.

PLANTS FOR CUTTINGS

The following grow well from cuttings taken from a healthy parent plant.

curry plant	rue varieties
hyssop varieties	sage varieties
lavender varieties	santolinas
lemon verbena	tarragon, French
marjorams	thyme varieties
myrtle	winter savory
pelargoniums	wormwood varieties
rosemary varieties	

Planting a stem cutting
1 Plant cuttings to one third of their depth in potting compost.

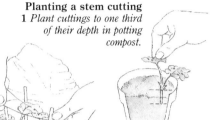

2 Plant several cuttings from one species in a pot and cover with a plastic bag, raised so it doesn't contact the leaves.

HOW TO TAKE A CUTTING

Follow the same method for all three types of cutting. For softwood cuttings, take sturdy pieces 2–4 in (5–10 cm) long with plenty of leaves; for semi-hardwood cuttings, take pieces 4–6 in (10–15 cm) long; for hardwood cuttings, take pieces 6–15 in (15–38 cm) long.

Take cuttings from just below a leaf node; use a sharp knife or secateurs to make a clean cut without ragged edges. If the cutting is torn from the main stem, trim the heel, leaving a neat sliver of the main stem wood.

Strip the lower third of leaves away, taking care not to tear the stem, before planting.

Taking a hardwood cutting
Cut off any soft growth from the top of hardwood cuttings.

Taking a softwood cutting

1 Cut shoot below a leaf node, leaving a short length of stem.

3 Gently remove leaves from the lower third.

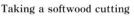

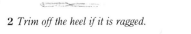

2 Trim off the heel if it is ragged.

Plant division

Several herbs benefit from being divided. This method checks their spread and keeps them hardier. Dig up the plant preferably in autumn or early spring when it is dormant. Remove old flower stems and carefully separate the plant into individual sections, each having a growing point and some roots. Replant, nurture and water these sections until the roots have re-established themselves and there are signs of new growth.

Dividing a plant
Divide young plants by hand, ensuring that roots have new growth.

Taking a root cutting
Cut the root into short pieces and insert in potting compost, just below the surface.

HERBS SUITABLE FOR PLANT DIVISION

alecost	meadowsweet
bistort	primrose
chives	skirret
cowslip	sorrel
elecampane	sweet Joe Pye
good King Henry	sweet violet
lawn chamomile	tansy
lemon balm	tarragon
lovage	thymes
lungwort	wall germander
marjorams	wormwood

Root sections

This is the easiest form of propagation. Dig up the plant in spring or autumn and take 2–4 in (5–10 cm) pieces of roots, each with growing buds; plant these approximately 1 in (2.5 cm) deep in a pot of compost. Use longer pieces if planting straight into the ground. This method is most suitable for spreading plants with creeping roots: bergamot, dwarf comfrey, mints, soapwort and sweet woodruff.

Root cuttings

Herbs such as horseradish, comfrey and skirret can be propagated from thick pieces of root cut 2–3 in (5–8 cm) long (see above right).

Layering

If cuttings are difficult to root, you can try layering. With this method, you encourage new sections of a plant to root while still attached to the parent plant. This is how many shrubby plants like thyme spread in the wild.

Peg a stem to the ground so its underside is in contact with the soil. Once the new roots seem well developed, separate the new shoot from its parent. If the soil is heavy, add some sand or peat before you start.

Another similar method is mound layering. In spring, pile soil over the centre until only the young shoots show. By late summer, roots will have formed on many of the shoots, and these shoots can be taken from the parent plant and transplanted.

Layering
1 *Layer by pegging down a stem against the soil.*

2 *Mound layer by covering a plant's woody centre with soil.*

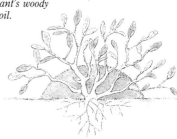

Winter protection for herbs

Many herbs will not survive a cold winter if left outdoors, but by being brought indoors in pots, annuals can have their lives extended by some months, and less hardy perennials often benefit too (see p. 222 for potting up and pp. 226–7 for growing herbs indoors). At the first sign of crisp autumn air, basil should be brought indoors. Pale, mottled or otherwise unhappy leaves may be signalling the plant's displeasure at cold evenings. Before a heavy frost, pineapple sage (*Salvia rutilans*), fringed lavender (*L. dentata*), pelargoniums, balm of Gilead (*Cedronella triphylla*) and Crete dittany (*Origanum dictamnus*) need to be brought indoors. All will reward your effort with aromatic leaves and occasionally with winter blossoms too.

In colder climates with longer periods of frost and snow, rosemary, sage, winter savory, curry plant, lavender and the more delicate thymes should be brought indoors to survive the winter. Protect mature plants that winter outside by layering soil, straw or compost around their roots.

If you grow herbs in pots all year (see pp. 222–3), plunged in soil in summer, it's easier to bring them indoors. Trim any roots which may have grown through the base, or pot on if the maximum pot size has not been reached. Try to make the transfer while outdoor and indoor temperatures are similar. If that is not possible, go through an intermediate stage using an unheated greenhouse for a few days, or a cool garage for a few nights, in order to ease the transition.

Some herbs, such as chives, have an intimate relationship with the seasons and feel

Winter protection
Cover the roots of mature shrubs in winter for extra protection.

strongly that autumn onwards is rest time. Practise a little deception: pot them on in early autumn, water and cut back the growth as necessary. Put them in a warm, humid place, out of direct sun, for a week or two to encourage root growth into the new soil. Then put them into a cooler location for a few weeks, while you still have other chives growing outside. When the other chives die back, bring the potted ones indoors so that they can start their "spring" growth, with additional artificial light if possible.

Much less trouble to bring in is the Welsh onion, which has a larger onion leaf than chives and maintains some green throughout the winter, even outdoors. Chervil and winter purslane do well indoors as they prefer growing at this time of the year, while summer-sown parsley and tarragon will tolerate being moved indoors. Don't bother transplanting whole mint stems; pot 3–4 in (8–10 cm) healthy cuttings with plump leaf buds. Within six weeks you should have fresh new mint leaves available for harvesting.

ENCLOSURES

An important aspect of a traditional herb garden, an enclosure reduces wind damage, raises the overall average temperatures, creates privacy and retains the perfume of aromatic herbs. It can be as permanent or temporary as you require. Upkeep and expenditure vary from type to type.

Hedging, once established, is the easiest form of tall, long-term enclosure, and gives further opportunities for using herbal and aromatic plants around the garden, as many shrubby herbs are evergreen and clip well. Hedging can be neat and formal or soft and wild in effect, depending on the plants you select and how you trim them. However, it cannot be an immediate solution. All plants suitable for hedging take some years to reach a good height.

Growing herbs in containers

Most herbs are willing to grow in pots, so town-dwellers with a balcony, roof garden or outdoor windowsill can enjoy them.

Before planting out containers on a balcony or roof garden, check the strength of the structure, as the combination of soil and water can be very heavy. Wind factor and drainage must also be taken into consideration.

Potting up

All containers need drainage holes and all, except for hanging baskets, need a layer of gravel, perlite or broken crocks in the bottom to prevent waterlogging. Fill containers with a good potting mixture.

A traditional potting compound can be made using seven parts loam, three parts peat and two parts grit or sharp sand, with some well-rotted compost or comfrey leaves (mixed with the peat the previous season so they have had time to decompose and have their nutrients absorbed). Sun-loving Mediterranean herbs benefit from a larger proportion of grit or horticultural sand in the mixture, say six parts loam and three parts sand. Do not use builder's sand as it has a rounded surface and makes drainage worse.

To provide the alkalinity herbs prefer, mix agricultural lime with the potting compost each year – a teaspoon (5 ml) of lime for a 4½ in (11.5 cm) pot. A layer of charcoal granules near the bottom of the soil, about a tablespoon (15 ml) to a 4½ in (11.5 cm) pot, will be helpful in keeping the soil sweet by absorbing any waste products.

General care

Pots can be moved outdoors or plunged into soil in spring or early summer. Introduce plants to sunlight gradually. Clip or pick leaves often to encourage bushy new growth. For specific information on watering and feeding, follow the advice on p. 226.

Potting on

When the roots of a herb are protruding through the base of a pot, it is time to transplant it into a bigger pot.

The best time to do this is in the spring. Avoid transferring when the plant is dormant as no new roots will grow to anchor the plant into the new soil.

Carefully remove the plant from the original pot, then clear any weeds or moss from the soil's surface, line the new pot with drainage material and a large spoonful of granulated charcoal. Add a little of the soil and check to see the plant will sit at the same level. Then loosen the roots, put in the herb, fill with soil, firm gently and water well.

Newly potted herbs will not require fertilizing for at least a month or six weeks because of the nutrients present in the soil.

Perennial herbs should be potted on in stages until they are in 4½–6 in (11.5–15 cm) pots for good bushy specimens of smaller varieties and 8–10 in (20–25 cm) pots for larger herbs. In general, the larger the pot, the better the crop. All the smaller herbs can be grown in pots (see p. 217), but annuals grown for their seed may bolt because of the confined root space.

Taprooted herbs such as borage, parsley and dill do better in deep pots. For lovage and fennel, it is best to put three seedlings in a 6 in (15 cm) pot and use the leaves when the plants are young. After one restricted season they often make a desperate attempt to set seed and neglect to produce further succulent leaves. Alternatively, put three seedlings into a 12 in (30 cm) pot for two years of growth.

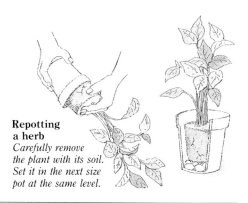

Repotting a herb
Carefully remove the plant with its soil. Set it in the next size pot at the same level.

Planting a large container
Insert long, open-ended tubes to help water reach the lower depths of tall containers.

PLANTING UP A LARGE CONTAINER

Always set a large container in position before filling it with soil and planting. Once filled, you will not be able to move it. Alternatively, keep it on a base with castors, so you can reposition it with ease. Fill some of the centre depth with lightweight rubble or perlite to save compost and weight, and fill with a soil-based potting mixture to within 1 in (2.5 cm) of the rim. Plant up with herbs which enjoy the same growing conditions, say parsley, chives and buckler leaf sorrel for a culinary collection set near the kitchen door.

Contained planting schemes

Grow more of the plants you use most often. Use a 12 in (30 cm) pot for sun-loving seedlings of sweet basil, lemon basil and sweet marjoram. Chervil, coriander and parsley could share a pot as they all prefer a bright position without constant direct sun, and like the environment to be a little cooler and wetter than the first group.

Several varieties of mint can be grown in one pot as they enjoy moderately wet soil and all tend to spread their roots. Angelica does not take kindly to being in a small pot, but planted in a cool location in a large container, a splendid tropical-looking specimen can be grown. Angelica and mint make excellent bed-fellows. When the angelica has reached the conclusion of its three-year life cycle, it would also be time to replant the mint.

Bay, rosemary, santolina, sweet myrtle, box, lemon verbena, sage and lavender make fine single specimens in 9½–12 in (24–30 cm) pots, and the first five also lend themselves to topiary. These herbs might benefit from a carpet of aromatic herbs to keep the soil shaded and restrict evaporation – scented thymes in sunny spots; perennial apple-scented chamomile prefers dappled light while the tiny peppermint, *Mentha requienii*, is better suited to a cool location.

Unusual containers
An old chimney pot or stone sink makes a very attractive miniature herb bed.

Chimney pot

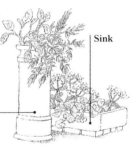

Sink

CHOOSING CONTAINERS

Containers come in all shapes and sizes and in a wide range of materials. For individual herbs, pots are probably the most practical and useful. Plastic pots are reasonably priced, easy to clean and store, and lightweight.

Clay pots

Unglazed clay pots have greater aesthetic appeal and allow excess water to evaporate through their fabric. Check the moisture content of the soil by sharply rapping the pot with your knuckles: a dull thud means the soil is too wet, a hollow ring means it is too dry. New clay pots should be soaked in water for 24 hours before use.

Understanding pot sizes

Traditional round pots are listed by a number, which is their diameter and roughly their height. So the 3 in (8 cm) pot in which many herbs are sold is 3 in (8 cm) across the rim and 3½ in (9 cm) from the top of the rim to the base. Vigorous herbs quickly outgrow this size so check when you buy a herb in such a pot as it may already need transplanting. If roots appear through the bottom, or the herb seems overcrowded, move it on to the next size up.

New square pots are stamped as 6 k, 8 k, 10 k, etc. This refers to the volume of the pot and the width across the top in centimetres.

HANGING BASKETS

A hanging basket is an ideal way to bring height into a patio or balcony, though it also demands some careful attention: herbs are vigorous plants to grow in a confined space. If they are too cramped or watered irregularly, they will soon drop their lower leaves and give a sad, spiky appearance.

Hang the basket on a well-secured, strong bracket. Ensure that it is set clear of the wall and that there is no danger of it falling. A planted-up basket can be heavy. Take care not to position hanging baskets between tall buildings where powerful wind tunnels often exist, causing damage to delicate herbs. Baskets can be hung indoors, too. Fill one with prostrate sage and creeping pennyroyal and position it over a stairwell.

Baskets may need watering two or three times a day in high summer so you need to consider ways of watering conveniently. Small long-necked watering cans are ideal, or use a hose pipe to avoid lifting a heavy can.

HERBS FOR A HANGING BASKET

Select plants sympathetic to the shape of the container: plants whose leaves appear to grow in layers or horizontal mounds, or herbs with graceful arching or trailing branches. Avoid upright plants for a hanging basket unless they are surrounded by several others to soften the outline. The following all make attractive hanging-basket herbs.

When hanging in a sunny location:

different creeping thymes such as lemon-scented, caraway-scented thyme, pine-scented creeping thyme	catmint (*Nepeta mussinii*) ivies lady's mantle prostrate rosemary prostrate sage prostrate winter savory

For the shady side of a hanging basket:

variegated mints with ginger mint	pennyroyal periwinkle

With so many trailing and horizontal herbs to choose from, it's easy to tuck in a parsley out of direct sunlight, or a clump of chives, to provide a complete mini herb garden in a basket to hang near the kitchen door.

MAKING A HANGING BASKET

To plant a hanging basket follow the procedure below. Make a rough plan before you start to ensure that you have enough room for all the plants you intend to use.

1 *To plant up a hanging basket, balance it on a bucket. If it is a wire basket, line with sphagnum moss, then black plastic punctured with drainage holes.*

2 *Half fill with a moisture-retentive compost. Loosen the soil of any pot-grown plants you wish to add and blend it into the new compost mixture.*

3 *Place trailing herbs around the outer rim and plant two or three in the outside of the basket through the moss and the holes in the plastic lining. Put taller herbs in the centre.*

4 *Top up with compost and water well. Drain before hanging the basket in position.*

WINDOW BOXES

Given a sunny aspect and proper attention to watering and pruning, a useful selection of herbs can be grown in a window box. Particularly appropriate for such a location are many of the culinary and aromatic herbs, arranged for convenience and so their fragrance will waft indoors.

Before you plant up a window box, check local byelaws and tenancy contracts in case window boxes are prohibited, and make sure the windowsill is sound and strong enough to take the weight. Whatever fixing you use, it must remain secure, as a falling window box could prove fatal to a pedestrian below. For extra security and peace of mind, attach the box to the wall with a chain or strap. When positioning the window box, consider where water will drain: use a removable drip tray, if possible, to prevent excess water running down outside walls.

Choosing a window box

Plastic troughs are light and easy to maintain but wood is visually more pleasing. For timber, choose treated hardwood such as oak or elm, or marine plywood. Raise the base slightly on wedges to allow the bottom to dry out occasionally and give space for a drip tray. Clay window boxes are available at many garden centres and complement the foliage of many herbs. They are often supplied with raised supports. However, they may crack or flake in a cold winter.

If you have wide sills on the insides of your windows, consider fixing boxes there. Fill them with herbs to enhance different rooms: a clipped bay or sweet myrtle in a sunny porch; peppermint in the moist air of a bathroom; scented geraniums or lemon verbena in a living room and lavender in the bedroom.

HERBS FOR A WINDOW BOX

With a small space you will want to make every herb count. For culinary usefulness, grow parsley, chives, a small rosemary and a golden creeping lemon thyme, and basil if the position is sheltered. A marigold (calendula) adds cheerful colour and flower petals for salads and rice dishes. A nasturtium provides trailing leaves and colourful flowers which you can add to summer salads. If your position is hot and dry, try the saffron crocus (*Crocus sativus*) for its valuable crop for the kitchen.

FILLING A WINDOW BOX

Position the box and cover the first 1 in (2.5 cm) with broken crocks or other drainage material. A sheet of heavy plastic punctured with drainage slits will help retain moisture.

In colder climates a layer of polystyrene will give the roots of the plants some protection from rapid freezing and thawing. Another solution is to keep perennial herbs in individual clay pots, which allow moisture to permeate through, and then plant these in a trough of moist peat compost. Plant any annuals in the peat.

When filling a plastic box, add a thin layer of charcoal granules to keep the soil sweet. Then add a soil- or peat-based compost.

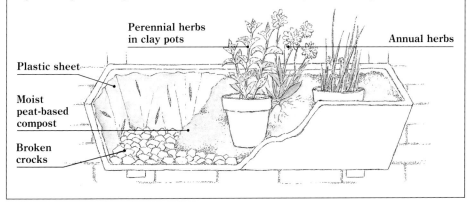

Perennial herbs in clay pots

Annual herbs

Plastic sheet

Moist peat-based compost

Broken crocks

Growing herbs indoors

Sun-loving herbs need at least six hours of sun a day to thrive, which is why many do not do well indoors. With inadequate light, plants become thin and elongated, producing smaller leaves and a poorer aroma. When selecting a location for herbs indoors, keep in mind that the reflective properties of glass can reduce light by 30 to 50 per cent. Turn herbs a little each day so all parts receive the same amount of sun, or consider artificial lighting as a supplementary source.

Basil requires the sunniest position and tolerates dry air. Thyme, sage, marjoram, pelargoniums and dwarf lavender also enjoy direct sun. Dill, savory and chives like full sun but a cooler temperature. Rosemary likes a bright situation (this can be reflected light) but prefers a cooler atmosphere of 60°F (15°C) to produce its flowers. Coriander, salad burnet and parsley also prefer this combination.

Tarragon and lemon balm take full sun but tolerate light shade. Mint and chervil enjoy some sun but not the hot midday sun, and both like a moist, cool soil. Lemon verbena and bay prefer filtered sun with rich soil in a cool spot.

TEMPERATURE

Most herbs prefer a pleasantly warm temperature of 60–70°F (15–21°C) with a 10°F (5°C) drop at night. Herbs will tolerate from 45–75°F (7–24°C) but do not thrive at the lower temperatures.

Draughts affect growth and survival. Every sharp temperature drop is a stressful shock to a herb and weakens its constitution, so attempt to position herbs where there will be a minimum of temperature changes.

Although herbs do not like draughts, they do like some fresh air each day. This removes stale air, hinders airborne diseases and helps to disperse possible oil or gas fumes from central heating systems.

WATERING

Potted herbs are more vulnerable than plants in the open ground and more dependent on your care. Pots can dry out very quickly. During hot weather check the soil each day. In

Watering herb plants
Spray plants to keep them moist and stand them on a gravel tray to drain.

autumn water only when the soil is dry. Seedlings usually need daily watering. Herbs with large leaves, in active growth or in small pots also need frequent watering.

Plants prefer a substantial watering when dry to a little water more frequently, as sometimes the bottom area of soil does not receive moisture. It is best to use tepid water and apply it in the morning, so that excess moisture evaporates during the day.

Do not over water. Air is an important requirement for root hairs, and if vital air pockets in the soil are eliminated by waterlogging, a perfect environment is created for rootrot fungus to thrive.

If a pot with a peat-based mixture has dried out and become very light, this will create a gap between the pot and soil. Plunge the pot in water for 15 minutes or more to just below the rim of the pot. This allows the water to permeate the peat. Peat particles have a natural waterproof coating which helps retain moisture when it is wet but actually prevents water being absorbed if it has dried out. Many modern mixtures have a wetting agent added to counteract this.

Moisture in the atmosphere is also important to most herbs. Grouping plants together helps create a humid environment, as does a layer of sphagnum moss on the soil's surface; you can also place the pots on trays of moist pebbles, vermiculite or perlite. A quick spray of tepid water with a mist atomizer all around the plants is useful in hot weather.

Ensure that all containers are adequately drained. Indoors they require a drip tray or outer container where excess water can collect. A large tray containing clean gravel is best as this holds the herbs above excess water, and can double as a humidifier.

FEEDING
Herbs that are regularly harvested need feeding with a weak liquid fertilizer every two weeks in spring and summer, reduced to a monthly feed as the growth-rate slows. Do not feed plants during the winter and never use more fertilizer than the manufacturer's instructions recommend.

Leaf blemishes
Pale yellow leaves or yellow spotting, as frequently seen on the outside leaves of parsley, fennel and overcrowded seedlings, are an indication that fertilizer is needed. Other signs are lower leaves dropping early and weak growth with susceptibility to disease.

Signs of over-fertilization are brown patches or scorched edges to leaves and possibly malformed leaves. A blanket of green moss, liverworts or slime means an excess of nitrogen. This usually occurs in winter when plants are dormant and it is less likely to develop in dry interiors.

Types of fertilizer
Liquid fertilizers dissolved in water are reliable; apply from above or below.

If you buy larger evergreen herbs in pots, you may notice little white globules, smaller than peas, mixed with the soil. These are slow-release fertilizer pellets, which provide feed for a whole growing season.

Herbal fertilizers
You can grow and make your own herbal fertilizers from a surprising number of herbs.

To make up a standard fertilizer: pour 2 pints (1 litre) of boiling water over a good handful of fresh herb or 2 tablespoons (30 ml) dried herb, cover and allow to infuse for at least 10 minutes. Strain before using. Select from the following:
Coltsfoot (*Tussilago farfara*) provides sulphur and potassium.

Couch grass (*Agropyron repens*), although a weed, is rich in minerals, potassium and silica.
Dandelion (*Taraxacum officinale*) is a good source of copper.
Dill (*Anethum graveolens*) is rich in minerals, potassium, sulphur and sodium.
Fat hen (*Chenopodium album*) contains iron and other minerals.
Fenugreek (*Trigonella foenum-graecum*) The sprouted seed heads are rich in both nitrates and calcium.
Horsetail (*Equisetum hyemale*) has high concentrations of silica.
Nettle (*Urtica dioica*) is a treasure house of iron and nitrogen, in addition to several minerals and trace elements.
Sunflower (*Helianthus annuus*) The ash of sunflower stalks is high in potash.
Tansy (*Tanacetum vulgare*) is rich in potassium and other minerals.
Tea leaves contain nitrogen, phosphoric acid, manganese and potash. These are locked in the tannin but released by brewing.
Yarrow (*Achillea millefolium*) provides copper and is a good general fertilizer.

CARE AND CLEANING
If your water has a high lime content which manifests itself as a white deposit on the soil's surface, scrape it off periodically and top up with fresh compost.

A mist spray of water on the leaves of all indoor herbs helps to keep any dust from clogging their pores.

Cleaning herb plants
Use a small, soft paintbrush to clean woolly-leaved plants such as clary sage.

Keeping herbs healthy

Routine plant care, common sense and observation are the main requirements for maintaining healthy plants. Herbs are mainly disease-free but over-crowding or too much water can weaken plants so look for physical conditions which might require attention.

PESTS: PREVENTION AND CURE

When you buy or are given a plant, check to make sure it has no small creatures lurking under leaves or in the leaf axils. A good prevention is to plunge each plant into a bucket of mild solution of washing-up liquid.

Removing pests
Dip new plants in a mild solution of washing-up liquid to remove insects.

Organic insecticides
If you do have problems with insects, try to combat them with an organic or herbal insecticide. Derris is a vegetable insecticide taken from the roots of *Derris elliptica*, a tropical legume. It is available ready to mix from organic suppliers and comes with full instructions.

Several herbs have insecticide properties which can be sprayed onto troubled leaves. Use the formula for chamomile flowers below unless indicated otherwise, adding a teaspoon (5 ml) of washing-up liquid or soft soap flakes to help the mixture stick to the leaves.

For scale insects on sweet bay or citrus plants, scrub the leaves with a solution of washing-up liquid and a soft nail brush, dislodging persistent scales with your fingernail.

Removing scale insects
Remove scale insects from bay by scrubbing the leaves with a strong detergent solution.

Diseases: Prevention and Cure
Avoid using harmful chemicals on edible herbs. To help fight ailments, spray plants with one of these brews.
Chamomile flowers help prevent damping off mould in seedlings. Pour 2 pints (1 litre) of boiling water over a handful of fresh or 2 tbsp (30 ml) of dried herbs. Cover with a lid and steep for 10 minutes, then strain, cool and use at once.
Couch grass rhizome tea sprayed onto leaves helps to prevent mildew and fungus diseases. Prepare and use as described for chamomile flowers.
Horsetail (*Equisetum hyemale*) is useful against mildew, rust and other fungus diseases. Use only half a handful of fresh horsetail or ½ tbsp (8 ml) dried to 2 pints (1 litre) water. Boil for 20 minutes, covered, and stand for 24 hours before straining and using.

Companion planting
Many gardeners have observed how certain herbs benefit the growth of nearby plants: garlic and chives under roses deter greenfly, nasturtium repels woolly aphids from apple trees and some tagetes secrete chemicals which kill ground elder and bindweed.

Companion planting
Plant dill and tagetes among cabbages to divert pests.

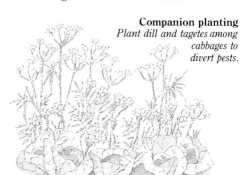

Harvesting herbs

Fresh leaves can be picked for immediate use at any time during the growing season (see below). Evergreen herbs such as thyme can be picked throughout the year, although new growth should be given the chance to harden before winter sets in.

Place cut plants, leaves and flowers gently in a flat-bottomed basket, trug or wooden box. Do not put them in a sack or bag or they'll be crushed, bruised and start to sweat. In this condition, they are not worth preserving.

If collecting from the wild, be certain of identification: it is easy to confuse plants, and some are highly poisonous. Also check the legality as most countries have some protected species, and do not collect too much from any one plant. Do not pick any parts that grow where car fumes or chemical sprays may have affected the plant.

Leaves

Collect in the morning after the dew has evaporated from the leaves.

Leaves are most tender and sweet when the plant is young, up to flowering time. From this point on the plant's priorities change and the energy goes into reproduction.

Pick the succulent leaves of sorrel, bistort, good King Henry, angelica, and all the salad herbs, when young. This type of leaf is not generally suited to drying and should either be frozen in a cooked dish or preserved in oil or vinegar (see p. 134).

Treat all leaves gently, taking care not to bruise or crush them. Pick only healthy whole leaves without blemish or insect damage.

Leaves of aromatic evergreens (rosemary, sage, thyme, savory) can be picked throughout the year, but for maximum flavour collect them just before flowering.

With tall plants like marsh mallow, collect only the top growth.

Whole plant

Harvest a whole plant just before the flowers open. If you want the green parts only, cut back annuals 3 in (8 cm) above the ground, but take no more than a third from perennials.

Flowers

Flowers are best collected at midday in dry weather. Pick them just as they open fully, their moment of greatest beauty. Treat all flowers with great care. Avoid damaged and wilted flowers, particularly if you wish to crystallize them. Once picked, keep flowers loose in open containers as they bruise easily and soon begin to sweat.

Seeds and fruit

Pick seed on a warm dry day when it is fully ripe but before it has been dispersed. It should be buff, brown or black, with no green remaining, and it should be hard with paper dry pods. Shake small seed into a paper bag or cut the flower head on its stalk and hang it over a tray to catch the seed. Keep all seed separate, label and date.

Roots and rhizomes

Harvest roots in autumn when plant parts above ground are beginning to wither and die. This is also the time when the greatest concentration of therapeutic compounds is stored in the roots. Dig up annuals when their growing cycle has been completed at the end of the year. Gather up perennial roots in their second or third year of growth, when the active components should have developed.

Dig up the whole root, taking care not to damage or cut the sections. Separate off the amount required and replant the remainder.

Most roots such as horseradish and comfrey can be scrubbed clean and have their fibrous hairs removed, but others, such as valerian, should not be scrubbed as their precious constituents are contained in the epidermal (surface) cells.

In Britain it is illegal to dig up roots from any land other than one's own without permission.

Bark

Bark peels off readily in damp weather and should be collected from young branches or trunks, preferably on trees already cut down. Trees can be killed if too much bark is taken, especially in a circle round the trunk.

Preserving and storing herbs

Most herbs wilt soon after cutting, so to keep picked herbs fresh for a few days, or to revive wilted cut herbs, place them in a plastic bag filled with air and tightly secured. Store in the refrigerator and they should remain in good condition for several days.

Many herbs keep their flavour well when dried, and some even seem to improve with drying. However, successful preserving requires care and specific conditions. For information, refer to entries in the A–Z of Herbs (pp. 12–99).

DRYING HERBS

As soon as a leaf or flower is separated from the plant, metabolic changes begin. Individual cells start to die as their supply of moisture and nutrients ceases. Enzymes which previously helped to create active constituents now begin to break down these substances. With this decomposition, the medicinal values and flavour are reduced on a sliding scale. The sooner drying begins and the quicker the system, the better the quality and colour of the dried herb will be. The speed is limited however as moisture must be removed gradually from a plant. Drying leaves in the oven is not satisfactory as the water evaporates too quickly and essential oils are lost. Microwave ovens do speed up the process considerably without affecting the flavour of herbs but they may destroy some of the therapeutic properties in the process.

Drying leaves

Wipe off any soil or grit and avoid washing leaves unless absolutely necessary. Keep the leaves out of sunlight as this extracts and evaporates essential oils.

Choose a warm, dry, dark situation with adequate ventilation – an airing cupboard, warm loft or outhouse, for example. A drying temperature of 90°F (32°C) is ideal for the first 24 hours with a reduced temperature of 75–80°F (24–26°C) thereafter. Leaves which are not unduly thick will take about four days at these temperatures. Allow one to two weeks in cooler temperatures.

Hang stems of leaves such as sage, rosemary, savory and thyme in small bunches, tied with string. Do not pack stems too tightly together as air needs to circulate through and around the bunch. About 10 stems at a time should be the maximum. Hang bunches stems upwards. If you are hanging them in a room that tends to be dusty, secure large paper bags loosely over the flower heads, leaving the bottom ends of the bags open.

When drying small quantities, spread the leaves thinly on muslin, cheesecloth, or brown paper punctured with fine holes. Stretch the material over a frame or wire cooling rack so air can circulate freely.

When drying is completed, the leaves should be paper dry and fragile, but not so dry that they powder on contact. Avoid drying strongly flavoured herbs such as lovage close to others as their flavour may spread.

Storing dried leaves

Once dried, remove leaves from stems. Keep them whole so they retain their scent and goodness for as long as possible; break them up only if you have to fit them into jars. Crush them just before using.

Leaves should be stored in airtight bottles made from dark glass, away from sunlight, moisture and dust. Plastic and metal containers are not suitable for dried herbs as they may affect the chemistry of a herb.

Label bottles with the name and the date. If you notice any condensation on the glass, the leaves were not dried enough before you stored them. Remove them immediately and dry them further.

Some herbs are hygroscopic when dried – they absorb moisture from the air. This can reactivate their enzymes enough to cause chemical deterioration so they should not be stored for too long. Marsh mallow and lady's mantle leaves behave this way.

Check dried leaves periodically for moisture, moulds and insects and discard them promptly if you discover anything. Most herbs deteriorate after a year, by which time you can replace them with a new harvest.

Drying flowers

Dry flowers in the same way as leaves. When dried correctly they should retain their colour. Delicate flowers such as borage and sweet violets must be spread out carefully so they maintain their shape. Allow one to three weeks' drying time depending on the thickness of the petals. Store flat if possible. For marigolds (calendula), remove the dried petals to store. Keep chamomile, lavender and smaller-headed flowers intact.

Drying seed and fruit

After removing the seed-heads of annual and culinary herbs such as fennel and dill, hang them to dry over a box or sheet of paper, or with a paper bag tied lightly over the head to collect seeds as they fall. Dry sunflower heads whole and separate the seeds for storage when they become loose.

Seeds dry very quickly in an airy, dry, warm environment, usually within two weeks, and should be labelled and stored in dark airtight jars. Seed required for sowing should be kept in a cool, dark place, free of frost.

Berries and fruits such as rosehips take longer to dry and can be placed in an airing cupboard to speed up the process. Fleshy fruits need frequent turning until they have dried out thoroughly.

Drying roots

All roots should be clean with fibrous parts removed before drying. Cut large thick roots in half lengthways and then into small pieces to facilitate drying. Roots require higher temperatures – 120°F (50°C), even up to 140°F (60°C). You can dry them in the oven, turning them regularly, until they break easily. Peel the roots of marsh mallow and the rhizomes of liquorice before drying.

Once dried, store roots in dark, airtight containers. Roots of parsley and angelica re-absorb moisture from the air. Discard if they become soft.

Drying bark

Bark may need washing to remove insects and moss, then dry out in a dry, warm, airy, dark place as flat as possible. When completely dry, store in airtight jars and label.

FREEZING HERBS

Freezing retains colour and flavour as well as most of the nutritive value of fresh young leaves. This is now the most popular way to preserve culinary herbs because it is convenient and fast. It is also a far more satisfactory method of preserving the more delicate culinary herb leaves such as fennel, salad burnet, chervil, parsley, basil, tarragon, sweet cicely and chives. Rinse when necessary and shake dry beforehand.

The easiest way to freeze herbs is simply to pack them into plastic bags and label, either singly or in mixtures such as bouquet garni. Store small packets in larger rigid containers in the freezer to avoid the possibility of them being lost or damaged. Alternatively, put finely chopped leaves into ice-cube trays and top up with water. One average cube holds one tablespoon (15 ml) of chopped herb and one tablespoon (15 ml) of water – a convenient quantity for cooking.

OTHER METHODS OF PRESERVING

The flavour of herbs can be preserved in herb vinegars and oils, as described on p. 134. This is an excellent method for well-flavoured culinary herbs, and the resulting liquid makes an interesting addition to salad dressings, pickles and marinades.

There are numerous alternative techniques for preserving culinary herbs: in pickles, jellies, syrups and alcohol, as described on pp. 134–7.

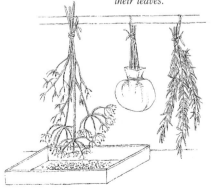

Drying herbs
A selection of herbs being dried for their seeds and their leaves.

Glossary

Acid A term applied to soil with a pH content of less than 6.5 and which contains no free lime.

Alkaline A term applied to soil with a pH content of more than 7.3. Some herbs actively prefer an acid soil, but most will thrive in alkaline soil.

Annual A plant that is grown from seed, flowers then dies all in one growing season.

Astringent A substance that contracts living tissue.

Axil The angle between the upper side of a leaf stalk and its stem.

Biennial Taking two growing seasons to complete a life-cycle.

Bract A small, modified leaf at the base of a flower.

Compress A piece of linen or cloth soaked in a herbal infusion or decoction and applied externally.

Cordial A warming, reviving drink.

Coumarin A compound present in certain plants which, in large amounts, can cause haemorrhage.

Crown The base of a herbaceous perennial plant from which the roots and shoots grow.

Cultivar A cultivated variety of plant.

Cutting A leaf, bud or part of the stem or root removed from a plant to form the basis of a new plant.

Deadhead To remove withered flowers, often to prevent seeding.

Deciduous A plant, especially a tree or shrub, that sheds its leaves at the end of the growing season.

Decoction A herbal dose obtained by boiling or simmering.

Distillation Extraction of component parts of a liquid by evaporation and condensation.

Diuretic A substance that promotes the flow of urine.

Emetic A substance that causes vomiting.

Emollient A softening substance.

Evergreen A plant that bears living foliage all year round.

Expectorant A substance that encourages phlegm to be coughed up from the lungs.

Genus The botanical name for a group of closely related plants.

Half hardy May not survive severe frosts.

Hardy Capable of surviving outdoors without protection.

Herbaceous Usually refers to perennial plants whose stems are not woody and which die down at the end of each growing season.

Infusion A herbal dose obtained by steeping a herb in a liquid.

Maceration The extraction of a drug from a herb by steeping it in a solvent.

Mucilage A gelatinous substance occurring naturally in some herbs.

Mulch A soil covering laid down to protect plant roots.

Narcotic A substance which in small doses deadens pain but in large doses can damage the nervous system.

Nervine A substance or remedy used to treat nervous disorders.

Perennial Living year to year.

pH scale A system devised for measuring the acid-alkaline content of soils.

Poultice Crushed herb or plant extracts heated and applied to bruised or inflamed skin.

Propagate To increase and reproduce plants.

Prostrate Growing flat over the surface of the soil.

Purgative A strong laxative.

Rhizome A horizontally creeping, underground stem storing food.

Rootstock The crown and root system of herbaceous perennials and suckering shrubs. Also, a plant onto which another is grafted.

Runner A stem that spreads along the soil surface, rooting when it comes in contact with moist soil.

Salve A soothing ointment.

Self-seed A term applied to plants that drop their seed around them, from which new plants grow.

Shrub A perennial whose branched stems are woody.

Species A classification applied to a plant or plants within a genus.

Stamen The pollen-bearing part of a flower.

Subshrub A low-growing shrub with woody base, but soft stems.

Sucker A shoot which grows up from below ground level.

Tincture A solution of extracts of medicinal plants obtained by steeping the plants in alcohol or in a solution of alcohol and water.

Topiary The clipped shaping of evergreen trees and shrubs.

Tuber A swollen root or underground stem storing food.

Umbel A flat-topped mass of small flowers on stalks that radiate out from a central point.

Variegated A term used to describe leaves that have markings in a secondary colour.

Variety Originally a naturally occurring variation of species, now also a cultivar.

INDEX

Page numbers in italic refer to illustrations and captions.
Page numbers in **bold** refer to entries in the A–Z of Herbs

ACKNOWLEDGMENTS

Designers: Nick Maddren, Hilary Krag
Editor: Maureen Maddren
Illustrator: Lorraine Harrison
Studio: Del and Co
Typesetter: Opus, Oxford
Reproduction: Colourscan, Singapore

Dorling Kindersley
Managing editor: Jemima Dunne
Managing art editor: Derek Coombes
Editorial assistance: Candida Ross-Macdonald, Julia Harris-Voss
Design assistance: Mark Regardsoe
Production: Jeanette Graham

Photographic credits
All photography by Dave King, except: pp 8/9, 10/11 Heather Angel; pp12/13
Clive Boursnell; pp 108/109 Linda Burgess/Insight; pp 100/101, 160/161
Robert Harding; pp 176/177 Michael Holford; pp 6/7 Michael Warren